I0884401

Using Servant Leadership

Using Servant Leadership

How to Reframe the Core Functions of Higher Education

ANGELO J. LETIZIA

Rutgers University Press
New Brunswick, Camden, and Newark, New Jersey, and London

Library of Congress Cataloging-in-Publication Data

Names: Letizia, Angelo, author.
Title: Using servant leadership : how to reframe the core functions of higher education / Angelo J. Letizia.
Description: New Brunswick, New Jersey : Rutgers University Press, [2017] | Includes bibliographical references and index.
Identifiers: LCCN 2017033862| ISBN 9780813587356 (cloth : alk. paper) | ISBN 9780813587349 (pbk. : alk. paper) | ISBN 9780813587363 | ISBN 9780813587370 | ISBN 9780813598048
Subjects: LCSH: Educational leadership. | Servant leadership. | Education, Higher—Aims and objectives. | Educational accountability. | Universities and colleges—Planning. | Universities and colleges—Administration. | College teachers—Professional relationships. | College teaching—Social aspects.
Classification: LCC LB2322.2 .L47 2017 | DDC 371.2—dc23 LC record available at https://lccn.loc.gov/2017033862

A British Cataloging-in-Publication record for this book is available from the British Library.

Copyright © 2018 by Angelo J. Letizia
All rights reserved
No part of this book may be reproduced or utilized in any form or by any means, electronic or mechanical, or by any information storage and retrieval system, without written permission from the publisher. Please contact Rutgers University Press, 106 Somerset Street, New Brunswick, NJ 08901. The only exception to this prohibition is "fair use" as defined by U.S. copyright law.

∞ The paper used in this publication meets the requirements of the American National Standard for Information Sciences—Permanence of Paper for Printed Library Materials, ANSI Z39.48–1992.

www.rutgersuniversitypress.org

Manufactured in the United States of America

I dedicate this book to my maternal grandfather, Ubaldo Sorrentino, and to my paternal grandfather, Lawrence Angelo Letizia, both of whom had a tremendous impact on my life. As always, I dedicate this book to my wife, Janet, and my children, Troy, Rosalie, and Cecelia. Without you, I could accomplish nothing.

Contents

Preface

The election of Donald Trump as president of the United States will most likely turn out to be a pivotal point in American and world history. Many across the globe are wondering, what impact will the election have? Some are also trying to gauge what the election represents about the United States as a country and a people. Some view the election of Trump as a wonderful event, as way to fight against an entrenched and out-of-touch establishment, as a way to give voice to a forgotten segment of America and make America's borders secure. In contrast, many others view the rise of Donald Trump as a triumph of bigotry, anti-intellectualism, and, in the widest sense, fascism. As will most likely become obvious throughout the book, I am of the latter camp. I should mention, however, that I also did not think Hillary Clinton was a viable option either; her presidency grieved me almost as much as a Trump presidency. Nevertheless, the election of Donald Trump represents something entirely different. Even if the election is not as bad as we thought, even if Trump turns out to be a pragmatic deal-maker and not a zealot, what still is so troublesome is the fact that a person running a campaign on blatant bigotry and vacuous policy proposals could be elected (even if he lost the popular vote). This fact in itself helps to demonstrate the rampant anti-intellectualism in this country. Donald Trump also represents a brutal vision of the future, a future devoid of love, a future where human beings are viewed as objects, where all communal bonds are eviscerated. Of course, as Giroux (2011) has argued, we have been living in such a state for over three decades. The election of Trump and Republican control of government, however, will most likely exacerbate this situation.

Of course, right now, it is simply too early to prognosticate what the future holds. Progressives, myself included, may be exaggerating, or our fears may not materialize in such a dire manner. Another likely scenario is that the election is a beginning; it will help to facilitate far-reaching changes. The full impact of these changes will most likely not be known for generations to come. I am reminded of the last line of T. S. Eliot's (1964:80) poem "The Hollow Men," which reads: "This is the way the world ends/Not with a bang but a whimper." The world does not end all at once in a catastrophic bang; no, it simply degenerates and devolves until it is unrecognizable. The election will most likely not usher in some apocalypse, but it will bring about important and frightening changes in American society.

If this is the case, then I believe a work such as mine is vital. Following Zizek (2009), I do not believe there is anyone waiting to save humanity. As such, I do not believe the election signals an irresistible or predetermined line of events. I think that progressives have the opportunity, and following Thomas Jefferson's exhortation in the Declaration of Independence, the duty, to resist in a number of ways. (In addition, it is not only progressives who oppose Trump; many true conservatives do as well, and they need to be engaged.) The world does not end with a giant bang; rather, the election may set in motion of variety of changes, each change that further eviscerates society. And it is at the outset of these changes that we must act. If the future we are heading toward is one of brutality and increased anti-intellectualism, then servant leadership is even more necessary. Larry Spears (1995), a longtime promoter of servant leadership, argued that change can be revolutionary or it can be evolutionary. Revolutionary change is usually short term and political, while evolutionary change occurs over a much longer duration of time and "involves personal growth and change by individuals" (Spears 1995:1). Spears (1995) argues that servant leadership is evolutionary. Following this distinction, this book is grounded in the notion of evolutionary change, of a long-term, deep-seeded transformation that shakes the roots of higher education. The changes occurring now because of the election must not only be met with short-term political resistance, but, just as important, with actions meant to spur long-term evolutionary change. This will ensure that change is long lasting. The ideas presented in the following chapters are an attempt to promote this evolutionary change within the walls of higher education during this volatile time.

This book examines how servant leadership can help to reframe the main functions of higher education institutions in America. The first chapter serves as an introduction to the variability of servant leadership research and acts as a guide for the rest of the book. The core functions of higher education examined are pedagogy, discussed in chapter 2; research, discussed in chapter 3; strategic planning, discussed in chapter 4; accountability, discussed in chapter 5; and assessment, discussed in chapter 6. Chapter 7 discusses the synergy between servant leadership and other leadership theories, while chapter 8 discusses some further opportunities and barriers to implementing and practicing servant leadership. Finally, the last chapter is the conclusion. Chapters 2–6 each tackle a different function of higher education. Of course, this list is not exhaustive.

Why pedagogy, research, planning, accountability, and assessment? Why did I choose these functions? Pedagogy, research, and service to the university are traditionally three main responsibilities of faculty (Mamiseishvili, Miller, and Lee 2016; Toews and Yazedjian 2007). Thus, pedagogy and research are each given a chapter. While service to the university is not an entire chapter, I have examined how servant leadership can help to reframe certain aspects of service (mainly, service to the university, specifically committee work) in the case study in chapter 7 and in a section in chapter 8. Strategic planning was given its own chapter because planning is now vital for many public institutions (Bryson 2011). Assessment of student learning is now performed on most colleges campuses (Fuller et al. 2016), and thus was given its own chapter as well. Finally, accountability may seem like an odd choice. It is not really a function of the university; rather, institutions are supposed to be accountable to various parties, and this is usually dictated by policy (Burke 2005). Nevertheless, I argue that accountability, if framed with the ideas of servant leadership, can be become something a university does; universities and individuals in those universities can show how they are accountable to society in variety of novel ways. There are many other functions of higher education that I have not examined that may lend themselves to further examination and integration with servant leadership.

Each chapter concludes with relevant case studies to illustrate how the ideas in the chapter may look in actual practice and a set of reflection questions to help the reader further contemplate the ideas in the chapter.

Using Servant Leadership

1

What Is Servant Leadership?

What does it mean to serve another human being? How does one human being help another human being grow and develop? What exactly is growth, and how do we measure it? These questions all point to the phenomenon of servant leadership, which has emerged over the last forty years due chiefly to the writings of Robert Greenleaf. Greenleaf argued leadership could be conceived of as service to followers. For Greenleaf (2002), the most important test of servant leadership is "Do those served grow as persons? Do they, *while being served*, become heathier, wiser, freer, more autonomous, more likely themselves to become servants?" Greenleaf (2002) did not just view servant leadership as an individual phenomenon, however; he also called for the ideas of servant leadership to transform institutions.

The terms "servant" and "leader" are opposed in some sense; thus the idea of servant leadership is paradoxical (SanFacon and Spears 2011; Spears 2004). Yet as SanFacon and Spears (2011) note, when opposites join, paradoxes ensue and can open our eyes to new, previously unknown ideas. The new possibility is a leader who serves (Spears 2004). As Greenleaf noted, servant leaders want to serve before they want to lead. In contrast, leaders who lead first may simply have a desire for power (Greenleaf 2002). Greenleaf called these leaders "leader-first," and for them, leading comes before serving. Of course, as Greenleaf (2002) notes, in real life leaders usually fall into a number of complex gradations between these two concepts of leadership. Greenleaf's voluminous work set in motion the ideas and research for servant leadership that spans until the present day.

Servant leadership may sound too good to be true. However, many other philosophers and thinkers throughout the ages have postulated ideas that, while largely unattainable, were nonetheless important because they pushed others' thinking forward and in new directions. In his study of the Frankfurt school in midcentury Germany, Jay (1996) notes how many of the members of the school understood that their utopian ideas, which centered on building the perfect society, were largely unattainable. Nevertheless, this did not deter them; in fact, they realized that even though unattainable, they had to pursue these utopian ideas to give hope in volatile times. This sentiment animates this entire book. The point is that while the ideas of servant leadership may be unattainable, this is even more reason to pursue them. Servant leadership can provide hope in our own volatile time.

The Research on Servant Leadership

Servant leadership is a complex idea, incorporating a variety of different facets (Parris and Peachey 2013; van Dierendonck 2011; Winston and Fields 2015). As Parris and Peachey (2013), van Dierendonck (2011), and Winston and Fields (2015) argue, there is not much agreement upon a definition of servant leadership. Of course, as Hernandez and colleagues (2011) note, there is much variation in the definitions of leadership in general. Van Dierendonck (2011) surveyed a number of prominent measurement instruments over the last two decades. Pousa (2014) surveyed a variety of instruments to measure various aspects of servant leadership spanning from 1999 until 2011. In short, over the last fifteen years or so, scholars have theorized and tested a number of facets of servant leadership, some of which I review below. These varied studies point in a number of directions and offer potential for the study of servant leadership, but many questions remain.

After Greenleaf, Larry Spears is probably the most impactful scholar of servant leadership (Parris and Peachey 2013; Pousa 2014; van Dierendonck 2011). Spears (1995:4–7) furthered the work of Robert Greenleaf by elaborating ten attributes that servant leaders should possess: listening, empathy, healing (helping to mend people's brokenness and pain), awareness (includes awareness of the situation and self-awareness), persuasion (as opposed to coercion), conceptualization (being able to "dream great dreams"), foresight (drawing on experience, understanding the likelihood of future events), stewardship, commitment to the growth of people, and building community (Barbuto and Wheeler 2006; Pousa 2014). Spears's early work in the 1990s represented one of the first coherent frameworks for servant leadership (Barbuto and Wheeler 2006; Pousa 2014). Spears's ten attributes, which were created not by a literature review but by drawing on his experience, helped to lay the groundwork for most of the later studies of servant leadership (Pousa 2014).

Parris and Peachey (2013) note that in 1999, Farling, Stone, and Winston (1999) urged scholars to undertake empirical studies on servant leadership, which until that time had largely been non-empirical (Winston 2010). A number of scholars heeded this call (Parris and Peachey 2013). Following Spears, other scholars began to put forth operational definitions of servant leadership (Pousa 2014). Later, Pousa (2014) noted that scholars began to create measurement instruments. Parris and Peachey (2013) also note that a measurement strand developed, as well as a strand of model development. Not surprisingly, Pousa (2014) observed that a progression of servant leadership research has occurred; essentially, models have grown more complex and sophisticated. In addition, there is variability in the definition and understanding of servant leadership, and there is a high degree of overlap (Pousa 2014; van Dierendonck 2011). (Due to this overlap and to avoid redundancy, I have not defined every dimension of servant leadership articulated in every study.) Pousa (2014) and van Dierendonck (2011) have provided some excellent summaries and classifications of the more prominent studies of servant leadership, which helped to guide my thinking.

Definitions of Servant Leadership

As noted above, Spears was the first to pin down a list of attributes for servant leaders and overlapping definitions followed (Pousa 2014). Pousa (2014) notes that Laub also articulated a definition as well as a measurement instrument; I focus on the instrument to avoid redundancy.

Russell and Stone (2002) sought to create a model for servant leadership from existing studies (Pousa 2014). Beginning with Spears's ten attributes, Russell and Stone (2002:147) articulated twenty attributes of servant leaders, which they further delineated into what they labeled as nine functional attributes (vision, honesty, integrity, trust, service, modeling, pioneering, appreciation of others, and empowerment) and eleven accompanying attributes (communication, credibility, competence, stewardship, visibility, influence, persuasion, listening, encouragement, teaching, and delegation). The functional attributes are the core attributes, and the accompanying attributes help to complete the core attributes (Pousa 2014; Russell and Stone 2002). Russell and Stone (2002) note that the idea of servant leadership can promote individual and organizational change. Some later scholars examined servant leadership in both individual and organizational contexts (Hunter et al. 2013).

Patterson (2003, 2010) calls attention to the notion of love and its role in servant leadership. Patterson calls this agapao love. Patterson (2010:68) stresses that agapao love is moral in nature, and she calls it "the cornerstone of the servant-follower relationship." Dennis and Bocarnea, (2005:602), following Winston (2002), argue that agapao love is "love in a social or moral sense." Again, following Winston, Dennis and Bocarnea (2005) note that in this type of love, leaders always treat people as ends in themselves, never as a means to the leaders' own ends. Patterson (2010) stresses that leading with love allows subordinates to develop and grow and engage in risk-taking. Patterson presented a unique model of servant leadership that consists of seven "constructs" (Dennis and Bocarnea 2005; Patterson 2003; Pousa 2014): agapao love, humility, altruism, vision, trust, empowerment, and service (Dennis and Bocarnea 2005:601–602). Further, these are not dimensions in the normal sense. Rather, each construct builds off each other (Pousa 2014).

Instruments of Measurement

Jim Laub created the Organizational Leadership Assessment (OLA) in the late 1990s, which derived from his dissertation (Parris and Peachey 2013; Pousa, 2014). Laub's tool gauges organizational health in six areas: values people, develops people, builds community, displays authenticity, provides leadership, and shares leadership (Laub 2017; Parris and Peachey 2013:383). Drawing from the OLA Group (Laub 2017), Parris and Peachey (2013) note that Laub's research focused on servant leadership as an organizational quality, as opposed to an individual attribute. Parris and Peachey (2013) note that behind Greenleaf and Spears, Laub is the most highly cited author for servant leadership studies.

Wong and Page first created the Servant Leadership Profile in 2000 (van Dierendonck 2011), then revised it and developed the Revised Servant Leadership Profile (Pousa 2014; Wong and Page 2003). This instrument measures servant leadership attributes such as team-building, visioning, empowering others, and integrity, to name a few (Wong and Page 2003:4). Their study also calls attention to phenomena in organizations that can act as barriers to servant leadership: egotism and hierarchy. Wong and Page (2003:8) call egotism and hierarchy "the evil twins, which have consistently hindered and undermined the implementation of SL [servant leadership]." This attention to the barriers of servant leadership is important, and unfortunately these barriers are all too prevalent in contemporary society (Wong and Page 2003).

Drawing on the ideas of leadership scholar Max DePree (2002), Dennis and Bocarnea (2005) argue that leaders need ideas to help frame and ground their understanding in moral terms. Patterson's constructs can be this type of moral guide for leaders (Dennis and Bocarnea 2005). Dennis and Bocarnea (2005) expanded on Patterson's work by creating an instrument that measured Patterson's constructs and which ultimately allows servant leaders to gauge their own effectiveness. Dennis and Bocarnea (2005:601) argue that

Patterson's constructs help to "define servant leaders, shaping their attitudes, characteristics and behavior."

Barbuto and Wheeler (2006:300) found support for five factors of servant leadership: altruistic calling, emotional healing, persuasive mapping, wisdom, and organizational stewardship. Altruistic calling entails leaders wanting to influence others' lives in beneficial ways. Emotional healing is described as being able to help people recover from despair and difficulties they experience. Wisdom entails an anticipation of possible future actions and an understanding of one's current environment and situation (Barbuto and Wheeler 2006). Persuasive mapping is "mapping issues and conceptualizing greater possibilities" for organizational members (Barbuto and Wheeler 2006:319). Finally, organizational stewardship calls for leaders to help their organizations leave a beneficial legacy (Barbuto and Wheeler 2006).

Liden and colleagues (2008), following a number of earlier scholars, elaborated and found support for seven dimensions to the construct of servant leadership: emotional healing, creating value for the community, conceptual skills (understanding what needs to be done and assisting others to do it), empowering (facilitating followers), helping subordinates grow and succeed, putting subordinates first, and behaving ethically (Liden et al. 2008:162, 173). Liden and colleagues (2008) developed the SL-28, a twenty-eight-item scale that measures dimensions of servant leadership. Liden and colleagues (2015) reduced the original twenty-eight-item scale to a seven-item scale (the SL-7). Liden and colleagues' (2008) instrument also examines servant leadership on the individual and group levels for a variety of phenomena (Hunter et al. 2013).

Sendjaya, Sarros, and Santora (2008) created the Servant Leader Behavior Scale. As Sendjaya (2010) notes, this instrument is unique in the servant leadership literature because it adds a spiritual dimension to servant leadership (Pousa 2014). This book draws on the spiritual (but not fundamentalist or dogmatic) aspect of servant leadership, and thus Sendjaya and colleagues' instrument is especially important to the present work. As such, I delve a little more deeply into this instrument.

The Servant Leader Behavior Scale consists of six dimensions: voluntary subordination, authentic self, covenantal relationship, responsible morality, transcendental spirituality, and transforming influence (Sendjaya, Sarros, and Santora 2008:409). Sendjaya and colleagues (2008), following Foster (1989), argue that an element of voluntary subordination entails a leader serving others out of need, not simply when it suits the leader. Following McGee-Cooper and Looper (2001) and Swindoll (1981), Sendjaya and colleagues (2008) argue that the next dimension, authentic self, entails leading with humility. The third dimension, covenantal relationship, is rooted in positive relationships between followers and leaders. Following Marshall (1991),

Sendjaya and colleagues (2008:407) argue that an important consideration of covenantal relationship is the notion of "radical equality," which entails equal relationships between leaders and followers. Further, following Daft and Lengel (2000), Sendjaya and colleagues (2008) note that relationships between leader and followers should allow followers to thrive and create new ideas. The next dimension is that of responsible morality, which is centered on ethical behaviors of leaders.

Transcendental spirituality is the next dimension. This dimension calls attention to the role of a servant leader in increasingly meaning-starved organizations (Sendjaya, Sarros, and Santora 2008). Sendjaya and colleagues (2008:408), following Fairholm (1997) and Mitroff and Denton (1999), argue that "servant leadership responds to the needs of individuals whose lives in today's modern workplace are often characterized by disconnectedness, compartmentalization and disorientation." The notion of meaningful work is especially important for this book. Too many times students seek the credential, or professors seek the publication, without paying attention to the work that is actually done. The work that students, professors, administrators, staff, coaches, and all in higher education achieve should be meaningful and a record of achievement, and not achievement in a competitive manner, but as a record of contribution. The notion of meaningful work, and, more important, of conceiving of helping people (students, professors, and so forth) to produce meaningful work as an act of service is foundational to this book. Transforming influence in the final dimension in Sendjaya and colleagues' (2008) model. Following Greenleaf, this dimension focuses on how servant leaders positively transform people and create more servant leaders (Sendjaya, Sarros, and Santora 2008).

Dierendonck and Nuijten (2011) developed the servant leadership survey (SLS). This instrument included eight dimensions of servant leadership: empowerment, accountability, standing back, humility, authenticity, courage, interpersonal acceptance, and stewardship (Pousa 2014). One important aspect of the Dierendonck and Nuijten (2011) scale is that of accountability, which they argue has been neglected in many other measurement scales. Following Conger (1989), Dierendonck and Nuijten (2011) describe accountability as fostering a sense of responsibility for one's actions over which one has control.

Other Relevant Works

A central question of servant leadership is perhaps the basic question of what is it? Another question is how do you do it? This is a question of implementation. A notable work of implementation is Sipe and Frick's (2015) work: *Seven Pillars of Servant Leadership: Practicing the Wisdom of Leading by Serving.*

This work mainly focuses on business and the for-profit sector. Sipe and Frick (2015:7) took Spears's ten characteristics and used them to create a framework, which in their words "will enable you to acquire, master and measure the knowledge, skills and abilities of a Servant-Leader." This contention, the idea of implementation and practical usage of servant leadership, is also at the heart of this book as well. The fundamental question is how does one actually practice servant leadership?

Sipe and Frick (2015:5–6) categorized Spears's ideas into a seven-part framework: person of character, puts people first, skilled communicator, compassionate collaborator, has foresight, systems thinker, and leads with moral authority. The seven principles are then further broken down into seven subpoints. The subpoints, following Sipe and Frick (2015:5–6), are: person of character is broken down into maintains integrity, demonstrates humility, and serves a higher purpose. Puts people first is broken down into displays a servant's heart, is mentor minded, and shows care and concern. Skilled communicator is broken down into demonstrates empathy, invites feedback, and communicates persuasively. Compassionate collaborator is broken down into expresses appreciation, builds teams and communities, and negotiates conflict. Has foresight is broken down into visionary, displays creativity, and takes courageous and decisive action. Systems thinker is broken down into comfortable with complexity, demonstrates adaptability, and considers the greater good. Leads with moral authority is broken down into accepts and delegates responsibility, shares power and control, and creates a culture of accountability.

While the above characteristics share many similarities with characteristics in other studies, the notion of systems thinker is important for this book. This pillar of servant leadership moves the servant leader out of the realm of individual action and toward organizational and systemic understandings. As Sipe and Frick (2015) point out, servant leaders who are systems thinkers can situate the actions of individuals in a much wider organizational context. This sentiment is crucial for servant leadership. Contemporary organizations are complex, and servant leaders must be cognizant of this complexity and situate individual action, others' and their own, within it (Sipe and Frick 2015).

Each chapter in their book examines the seven principles and its subpoints in detail. Sipe and Frick's (2015) work is a work of implementation. However, they note, "Servant Leadership cannot be implemented with a few memos and pep talks" (Sipe and Frick 2015:13). Rather, effective implementation "requires a dedicated effort of study, skill practice, feedback, and reflection about your deepest values" (Sipe and Frick 2015:13). Following this sentiment, my book can only act as a rough guideline. Sipe and Frick (2015) also note that most servant leaders will not be able to embody all of these traits at all times. This admission speaks to something larger; no one, not even servant leaders, is perfect. Servant leaders have faults and make bad decisions. This is also an important point to keep in mind when practicing and implementing servant leadership.

Van Dierendonck (2011) put forth a conceptual model that synthesized a number of recent research studies. As van Dierendonck (2011:1232) explains, this model is important because it distinguishes "between antecedents, behaviors, mediating processes and outcomes" that have been unclear in earlier studies. Van Dierendonck (2011:1243) argues that at the root of his proposed servant leadership model is the "need to serve combined with a motivation to lead." Further, the servant leader embodies certain individual characteristics, such as self-determination and moral development. Van Dierendonck (2011) also explores the roles of national cultures. He notes that certain cultures may be more conducive to servant leadership, such as more caring cultures. Next, he (2011:1232–1234) observes that servant leaders perform certain actions such as empowering people, showing humility, being authentic, accepting people, providing direction, and being stewards. Through mediating factors of relationships and a positive organizational climate, individual outcomes aligned with servant leadership, such as positive job satisfaction and engagement; performance outcomes, such as positive organizational citizenship; and organizational outcomes, such as sustainability can emerge (van Dierendonck 2011:1233).

A note on terminology. Throughout this book, I refer to organizational culture as opposed to organizational climate. As Bess and Dee (2012) note, organizational culture is much more entrenched and evidenced by observation, whereas organizational climate is less entrenched and evidenced by people's perceptions (obtained in interviews and surveys). Many studies show that servant leadership can promote positive organizational climate (Walumbwa, Hartnell, and Oke 2010; Black 2010). Obviously, culture and climate are related. Nevertheless, for consistency, I focus on studies that reference organizational culture.

The distinction between behaviors and outcomes is especially useful for servant leaders to help bring about change and conceptualize their actions. Following van Dierendonck (2011), certain activities in this book can be conceived of as a behavior or behaviors to bring about certain outcomes. As I explain in each chapter, each aspect of servant leadership can be framed with findings of previous servant leadership definitions, models, and measurement instruments. I incorporate many of the studies that van Dierendonck (2011) used to build his model. The desired outcomes could align with some of the ones that van Dierendonck (2011) postulated, but other outcomes may be more abstract, esoteric, and harder to measure, such as the creation of meaning in society and democracy.

Winston and Fields (2015) performed one of the more recent studies of servant leadership. They (2015:424) identified ten essential servant leadership behaviors: practice what he or she preaches; serves people without regards to nationality, race, or gender; sees serving as a mission of responsibility to others; is genuinely interested in employees as people; understands that serving others is most important; is willing to make sacrifices to help others; seeks to instill trust rather than fear; is always honest; is driven by a sense of higher calling; and transcends self-interest. More than simply creating another scale, Winston and Fields (2015) correlated their scale with Liden and colleagues' (2008) scale. Their study also examines how servant leadership behaviors are spread to institutional members.

As pointed out in the beginning of this section, there are still many questions to the study of servant leadership that have not been resolved. The ideas in this book must always be considered against the backdrop of this uncertainty. Further, van Dierendonck (2011) noted that much of the early literature on servant leadership was prescriptive, and, as such, he has called for more empirical studies on servant leadership. While I agree this is crucial (the ideas in this book have drawn heavily on the empirical work on servant leadership over the last twenty years), I would also issue a caution. In our zeal to define what servant leadership is empirically, we should not neglect what it *can* be. And this may require newer and more creative undertakings in the research process. This uncertainty may also provide potential and may allow for creativity and novel directions. While dimensions vary, many scholars have postulated similar or identical dimensions; in addition, many dimensions overlap (Pousa 2014; van Dierendonck 2011). Some similar dimensions and overlapping ideas are empowerment, stewardship, ideas of equality, and humility, as well as the notion of meaningful work and intrinsic motivation, to name a few. These ideas can form of a constellation of sorts, which I examine shortly.

It should be noted that servant leadership shares many characteristics with other leadership theories, most notably "transformational leadership, authentic leadership, ethical leadership, Level 5 leadership, empowering leadership, spiritual leadership, and self-sacrificing leadership" (van Dierendonck 2011:1235). One of the crucial differences between servant leadership and these other theories is that servant leaders desire to serve others; this motivation is entwined with their leadership. Servant leadership places the growth and development of followers before institutional progress (Lynch 2012; van Dierendonck 2011). While it is similar to other leadership theories, servant leadership is unique.

Servant Leadership in Higher Education

Greenleaf wrote at a volatile time in American history. The 1960s brought tremendous social and political changes. Higher education was situated directly in this volatility. Greenleaf (2002) stated that his notion of servant leadership developed due to his involvement with higher education institutions during the campus upheavals of the 1960s and 1970s. Greenleaf was critical of universities in many respects, but he did believe that higher education institutions had great potential to help foster the ideas of servant leadership. As such, Greenleaf specifically argued that a goal for higher education institutions, if they are ready, is simply "to prepare students to serve, and be served by, the present society." He went on to explain that "a college, operating through the program its faculty chooses to design, will influence its students to be a more constructive building force in society and do this in a way that helps them find their own legitimate needs, psychic and material, better served, than if they had not participated in the college program."

Plainly put, Greenleaf (2002) argued that teachers and college professors have the ability and power to promote servant leadership in their students. He also argued that the potential of servant leadership was present in virtually all youth. This sentiment is crucial and undergirds much of the work in this book. Colleges have the ability, and perhaps the duty, to serve their students, promote servant leadership in their students, and help their students contribute to society.

Buchen (1998) wrote an early article that outlined some recommendations for faculty members to integrate servant leadership. He argued that there were five areas where faculty could accomplish this task: identity formulation, which calls for faculty to restrain their ego; empowering students; doubleness, or the leaders' potential to create more leaders out of followers; relationship building; and the future. For the consideration of the future, Buchen (1998:134) utilizes Greenleaf's maxim and asks, "Does the institution serve its students and faculty, help them grow and is it future focused?" I would also ask if the institution is helping society grow.

The literature and practice of servant leadership in higher education continue to grow (Keith 2012). Most recently, Farnsworth (2007) and Wheeler (2012) have both written books on the topic of servant leadership. These works form a foundation for the present work.

Farnsworth (2007:xi) writes mainly about "educational leadership as service." As service, Farnsworth argues that educational leaders, most notably college presidents, must never use their positions to enhance themselves. Farnsworth (2007) critically notes that American higher education needs a new type of leadership. He (2007:6) bluntly states that "a number of qualities and promises of academic life that we view as most sacred stand as major impediments to our abilities to adjust." He then elaborates on certain characteristics that can be barriers for the advancement of higher education.

The characteristics he poses are intellectualism, collegiality, professional protections, social and cultural isolation, technical naïveté, and traditional leadership models (Farnsworth 2007:7–9). For intellectualism, Farnsworth

(2007) argues that traditionally, higher education long considered itself the bastion of human knowledge; higher education also believed it held the answers to society's problems. Now, however, Farnsworth questions these assumptions. Farnsworth notes how collegiality or the ability for faculty to help govern the university has been a strength of higher education; collegiately can become a barrier because it allows faculty to buck against necessary change. Similarly, Farnsworth (2007:8) argues that professional protections can create "feelings of invulnerability in the face of the need to change." Farnsworth (2007) also argues that many faculty are isolated from the practical workings of the society in which they research and write about; they are mainly theorists with little real-world experience. This isolation limits higher education's ability to see the world as it really is (Farnsworth 2007). Citing Willard Daggett, Farnsworth argued that higher education is reluctant to accept technological innovations. Finally, Farnsworth (2007) notes how universities usually adapt leadership models that do not promote change; instead, the traditional leadership models of higher education are centered on power and control.

As for servant leadership, Farnsworth (2007:12) argues, "A commitment to service removes the blinders of self, of control, and of predisposition to method. It assumes that all paths may be explored." For Farnsworth (2007), servant leadership may be able to help higher education adapt to the turbulent and changing environment in which it now finds itself. Writing from a faculty perspective, I take issue with some of Farnsworth's arguments; nevertheless, many of his ideas of servant leadership are important and grappled with in this book.

Wheeler (2012:xiv) notes how his book is mainly written for higher education administrators at various levels, such as "presidents, vice-chancellors, deans, and chairs." Wheeler (2012) argues that leadership in higher education cannot continue as it has because many people in the institution have a role to play in facilitating organizational change, yet only a few do. He goes on to argue that if administrators do not draw on others in their leadership, administrators may become increasingly alienated (Wheeler 2012). Wheeler pointed out how he expected nonprofit institutions to embody servant leadership, but was surprised to see that it was the for-profit sector that really embraced it; yet the reason was largely as a means to profit. He argued that higher education would benefit from an understanding of servant leadership and thus the reason for his book.

Wheeler, drawing on his earlier research, interviewed identified servant leaders, consulted his own experience in higher education, as well as literature on servant leadership, and from this elaborated ten principles that servant leaders can use to guide their actions. These attributes are service to others is the highest priority, meeting the needs of others, fostering problem solving and taking responsibility, emotional healing, recognition that the means are as important as the ends, keeping one eye on the future and one eye on the present, embracing paradoxes, leaving a legacy to society, modeling servant leadership, and developing more servant leaders (Wheeler 2012). Dean (2014) criticized Wheeler's idea of emotional healing because she argued that emotional healing is too time consuming and impractical, and that most leaders lack the proper training. These points are well taken, but I think emotional healing can simply mean leaders being attuned to the emotional needs of their followers.

Wheeler (2012) and Farnsworth (2007) both raise critical points that all in higher education institutions need to grapple with. Further, they both argue that the notion of servant leadership can help higher education institutions in this regard. This book works from that assertion, that the ideas of servant leadership can help higher education institutions grapple with the issues and problems that they will most likely face in the twenty-first century. Wheeler (2012) also argues for higher education institutions to serve society. This is an important point, one that undergirds this book as well. The present work builds on these two books and other relevant literature in servant leadership, but this book takes a different approach. Presidents and administrators in higher education are the main audience of Wheeler's and Farnsworth's books. A large portion of this book, by contrast, is aimed at faculty (however, I do have sections for administrators); thus I see this work as a complement to Wheeler's and Farnsworth's work. The decision to write not only for administrators and appointed leaders in higher education was not simply to broaden the appeal of servant leadership, although that was one motivation. Rather, by speaking to everyone in the organization, and giving everyone the tools to be a servant leader, the hope is to make servant leadership an idea that is more organic and deeply felt by all members of the organization.

The Aim of This Book

In a draft of an earlier paper on servant leadership, I referred to servant leadership as a task. A reviewer called attention to this word usage and asked if servant leadership was indeed a task. This comment gave me reason to reflect on the nature of servant leadership. As Wheeler (2012:13) notes, "Servant leadership is not a set of techniques or activities. It is a way of being, a philosophy of living and influencing." Servant leadership can best be described as an ontological and epistemological disposition, a state of being in and knowing the world. Service to another becomes part of an individual's psyche. This aligns with Dennis and Bocarnea (2005), who drew on DePree (2002) and Patterson (2003) in arguing that leaders need values and ideas to guide their action. DePree (2002:94) argued for a "defining thought" that can give leaders "a way to think about leadership and moral purpose." Servant leadership can be a thought, an idea that can help leaders act as a servant. Organizations, guided by servant leaders, may also need these types of guiding thoughts, and this can be accomplished by all members of the organization truly grappling with the ideas of servant leadership.

Following the idea above—namely, that of engraining servant leadership and thus making it a mental guide—can help to make servant leadership have staying power in individuals *and* organizations. As noted earlier, Spears (2004) and others such as Sipe and Frick (2015) argue that servant leadership is by no means a simple or quick action that can magically fix an organization. It is not a panacea or cure-all for all individual and organizational ills (Northouse 2016). Another consideration is follower acceptance of servant leadership ideas. As Northouse (2016) notes, research has shown that the receptivity of followers to servant leadership is a determining factor in the success of servant leadership (Liden et al. 2008). If followers do not want to be led by a servant leader, servant leadership will be that much more difficult to pursue (Northouse 2016).

Patterson (2010:76) argues that servant leadership is difficult because it is easier to simply be an authoritarian; by contrast, servant leadership is a "tough road for leaders." Implementing servant leadership requires a serious commitment to understanding one's values and reflection upon them (Sipe and Frick 2015). Further, this implementation is fraught with setbacks, self-doubt, and self-questioning. The true adoption of servant leadership and the integration of it into one's psyche is a lifelong process, yet one with profound effects. The aim of this book is to give some insight into how servant leadership can be implemented in the realms of pedagogy, faculty research, strategic planning, accountability, and assessment. Yet in order to truly understand how to implement servant leadership, there must be some understanding of what we are implementing and how we can know if it is working.

Considering the uncertainty of servant leadership research sketched out earlier, I believe that we need to imagine servant leadership differently. This is not so much a new definition, but rather a new way to think about and understand servant leadership. The notion of constellation thinking, which largely derives from the German thinker Theodor Adorno, may be able to accomplish this task. As O'Connor (2013) notes, Adorno, following Benjamin, argued that objects are multifaceted; they are a "constellations of concepts." An object can never be known in its totality and can only be understood by examining a number of concepts and ideas that comprise it (Adorno 1966/1973; O'Connor 2013). Each concept helps to illuminate an object, but is only a part of its understanding. As Adorno (1966/1973) argues, "the concept does not exhaust the thing conceived." Essentially, this means that when we think about something and label something, the label does not contain all the meaning. Adorno (1966/1973) explains that "its own inevitable insufficiency" drives human thought. Human thought is driven by what it does not know; it is constantly trying to understand reality. Further, as Buck-Morss (1977) points out, Adorno relished in contradictions. Adorno (1966/1973) explains that identity (or the process of thinking or labeling) is linked with the notion of contradiction. Reality was a constellation of contradictory concepts (Buck-Morss 1977). Contradictions drove reality forward; they allowed for new ideas and movement (Adorno 1966/1973; Buck-Morss 1977). Moreover, constellations had to be understood in their particular and unique context; similar and identical elements take on different meanings in different contexts (Buck-Morss 1977).

The constellation analogy, while not perfect, does help to reframe servant leadership. Attention to the inability to define servant leadership definitively as well servant leadership's contradictions offers an opportunity. There is much unity in the dimensions of servant leadership, as evidenced by the research. Even the unity of servant leadership dimensions, however, may play out differently in different settings. Further, servant leadership is not static; its unknowability, contradictions, and uncertainties are a source of perpetual growth. Buck-Morss (1977) also points out that Adorno's treatment of constellation thinking is not overly systematic and is not meant to be rigidly applied. Following Buck-Morss's (1977) ideas, if we use constellation thinking to describe servant leadership, it cannot be understood rigidly or applied in some lockstep manner.

As DePree (2002) rightly notes, leadership does not have a blueprint; rather, leadership is more akin to a quest without end (DePree 2002). Constellation thinking defies any leadership blueprint and can help to open new ways of seeing on the quest of servant leadership. This vision of constellation thinking, however, may create a sense of uneasiness or uncertainty. Yet this may just be the natural terrain of servant leadership. Sipe and Frick (2015) note how comfort with complexity is essential for servant leaders. They (2015:139) argue, "Everything is related and everything is part of a system. A Servant-Leader is a fragment of many systems." Researchers of servant leadership should heed this advice as well. There are many facets to servant leadership, some of which may not be empirically verifiable, but rather only understood in the context of discussion and thoughtful arguments. We as researchers must be comfortable in this complexity.

Prosser (2010b) poses a relevant question for our purposes: is servant leadership a theory or philosophy? Prosser (2010b:10) argues that a theory is much more constraining; a theory must "be considered specifically and applied accordingly, and . . . risks losing its focus on the crucial concept of service." A philosophy, on the other hand, is much more wide ranging. Following Grayling (1998), Prosser (2010b) notes that a philosophical understanding can enable one to obtain an understanding of such ideas as reality, meaning, and truth. Prosser (2010b) notes that a philosophical understanding can help to probe the complexity of servant leadership and Greenleaf's thinking, and he argues that many respected thinkers (many of whom are cited in this book) see servant leadership in philosophical terms. He also notes how the creation of many of the models and measurement instruments of servant leadership follow from a philosophical, not a theoretical, orientation.

If we label something servant leadership and we use specific definitions and dimensions to describe it, those definitions and dimensions can never describe the entire phenomenon. Rather, the idea of servant leadership is too complex to be described in its entirety. Servant leadership may need to be seen as a constellation where the line between leaders and followers, actions, individuals, and organizations becomes fluid. Following Leary and Hoyle (2009), van Dierendonck and Nuijten (2011:250) similarly note that "it should be acknowledged that no single measure can fully capture and operationalize complicated constructs—like servant leadership—and that it may be sensible to have a broader range of instruments available." Expanding on the above, servant leadership cannot be defined in a few (or many) studies; rather, all the studies illuminate and unlock different aspects of the complicated and complex notion that is servant leadership.

Servant leadership as a constellation, however, can have an anchor, or a core. Despite the variability in servant leadership research, Prosser (2010a:37) argues that there is a foundational tenet to servant leadership: "the commitment to being a servant." Prosser (2010a:37) notes that despite this nonnegotiable, servant leadership is not a one-size-fits-all notion; rather, it is "sensitive to different styles and different requirements." So Prosser's (2010a) notion can form the anchor of the servant leadership constellation; service can be defined and practiced and conceived in a multitude of ways, but the idea of serving another human being, whether through performing physical acts or serving someone by helping them create new ideas or understand information, is the key to the constellation.

Of course, as many scholars point out, the questions surrounding servant leadership can inhibit its understanding and application (Lynch 2012; Winston and Fields 2015; van Dierendonck 2011). If the constellation view is taken, the vagaries of servant leadership do not necessarily have to be seen as a detriment, but as a source, or, more precisely, an opportunity for forging understanding. Yet this understanding does not have to be unified. For instance, servant leadership in a small Catholic university will look much different in a large public research university. Yet both will be part of the same truth—servant leadership is anchored in the idea of serving and empowering others, just in different ways.

The next question, then, is who actually implements servant leadership? My answer to this is simple (if not a little lofty): everyone. As Prosser (2010b:37) notes, "it is possible for someone to be a servant-leader without holding any formal leadership position within the organisation." This aligns with Northouse's (2016) notion of emergent leadership. Emergent leaders are those in organizations who hold influence despite not having an official leadership title or position (Northouse 2016). Following these ideas, faculty, while not having designated titles, can still become, and indeed might *need* to become, influential leaders, and their leadership can be grounded in service.

Throughout the centuries, exemplars of servant leadership like Jesus and Buddha have become famous, but really servants exist all around us, from our parents to our teachers. It is important not to lose sight of this fact, that servants are everyday people, not just famous figures. As noted above, Greenleaf argued that all students have a servant leadership potential in them. This belief is central for implementing servant leadership in higher education settings (even if it is not true, we can still aspire to it). So, when implementing servant leadership, implementers should understand that service is not just the province of leaders, but it can be the province of all. All serve all, and all are served by all in a multitude of ways. Thus, this book is aimed at all in higher education, not just formal leaders such as administrators. In essence, all members of an organization can be seen as leaders, or at least possessing some leadership qualities, even if many of these people will not ultimately be leaders (Bennis 2009; Letizia 2017a). Nevertheless, leadership can become organic and woven into the DNA of an institution.

While servant leadership may not be prominent in higher education, it could plausibly be argued that the ideas of servant leadership are embedded in the DNA of all education institutions, both K–12 and higher education. Education institutions are literally built on service. Shaker (2015) argues that many faculty members go beyond their official job duties to serve their students in a variety of ways. Shaker (2015:4) further argues that this is a type of "philanthropic" work on the part of faculty that ultimately strengthens the public good. Following this sentiment, it is not a stretch to argue that millions of teachers and professors, and countless staff and administrators, serve their students and their communities every single day. Further, the financial rewards for this service, for most of these servants, is not very enticing. And that is what makes this book different. Servant leadership is not a practice; it is not only the province of CEOs and college presidents. It is the province of every single person on a campus, acting in concert with each other, attacking problems and creating solutions. Ideas of servant leadership should not be applied to campuses, but rather become part of their identity, part of their ontological and epistemological disposition. Organizations, however, cannot be seen as an abstract entity. They are populated by people, by individuals who make the systems and rules (Covey 2002; Greenleaf 2002; Sipe and Frick 2015). Thus, this penetration of servant leadership must be rooted in the individual psyche of employees, not just held at the abstract institutional level. Greenleaf (2002) argues that "not much will change until the *builders within institutions*, those who have competence and strength, begin to move." He further notes that in order to build and sustain servant institutions, individuals in those institutions must take it upon themselves to accomplish this task (Greenleaf 2002). McGee-Cooper and Trammell (1995:120) also note "a servant-leader makes time for people—even when there isn't any." As such, individuals in institutions will have to spearhead this change and make the necessary time for it.

Many different people on campus must have a role in implementing servant leadership. The next question is: how will we know if it is working? To answer this, a number of researchers have sought to measure servant leadership (Parris and Peachey 2013; Pousa 2014). As Giroux (2016) argues, however, many in the university are preoccupied with measuring student outcomes and data, yet Giroux notes that these ideas are not easily measured. How do you measure things such as compassion, honesty, or virtue? As such, the idea of servant leadership must contain an element of ambiguity because how could the notion of service truly be quantified and measured? This does not mean it should not be measured, but rather always measured with caution. Thus, the literature of servant leadership serves a necessary and important function by giving us proxies of what servant leadership may be; the research has yielded linguistic markers by which we can label and understand servant leadership, but this understanding can never become ossified. Concepts could never totally define objects (Adorno 1966/1973; Buck-Morss 1977). Thus, researchers may need to embrace the inability to name if servant leadership is understood as a constellation and not a fixed concept. As such, aside from traditional qualitative and quantitative research methods, another way to have some type of measurement and understanding of the constellation of servant leadership may be through the use of created products.

The use of student products is not new in K–12. Brookhart (2013) notes that the evaluation of student products, such as written pieces and essays, is one way to evaluate students. Baumann, Millard, and Hamdorf (2014) further argue that student writing and other types of student products like posters and projects can be important and valuable ways to measure students' civic learning and understanding. Elsewhere, I have argued that the creation and assessment of student products can help to showcase the ideas that students produce for democracy. Specifically, I argued that the assignments that students produce in the classroom can actually be viewed as a student's contribution to democracy (Letizia 2017a). The use of products can be extended to servant leadership.

In a wider sense, Marginson (2010) argues higher education institutions (among other sites) play a crucial role in idea creation. Marginson (2010:11) writes, "It is in the institutions of higher education, scholarship and research . . . that we have the capacity to consciously imagine the future in terms of sequence and duration, which is essential to us." Weerts, Rassmussen, and

Singh (2015) and Weerts and colleagues (2015) also argue that the notion of creation, of creating ideas and things, is crucial for higher education to take on the increasingly complex issues society faces. Weerts and colleagues (2015) call for institutions to become "hubs of relevant creativity." Pink (2005) also calls for organizations, such as schools, to help foster creativity, which he argues is crucial for the present age. I situate the call for reimagining servant leadership research in the backdrop of this call for creation.

Wheeler (2012) asks department chairs what they will leave to the department. One particular notion that is usually brought up is academic products, such as research papers, curriculums, and academic programs. Wheeler (2012:129) specifically notes that "servant leaders expect that if their behavior is focused and consistent and a positive culture is developed, then faculty members can focus on their work and together, the products will result." In an earlier piece, Smith (1995) argued that one of the characteristics of a servant organization is ownership. Smith (1995:208) argues "that people within the organization must develop ownership—ownership of ideas, of process, of accountability, of relationships and so on." Smith (1995) goes on to note that ownership must now belong to all; it can no longer be only the concern of the few at the top of the organization. And as Smith (1995:208) notes, "there are no blueprints" to promoting ownership in servant-led organizations; it is an obstacle that individuals and organizations have to contend with.

Following these ideas, a variety of academic products (student assignments, strategic plans, and assessment reports) can be seen as evidence of servant leadership in a variety of forms. In a wider sense, these products can help all organizational members take some sort of ownership of the ideas and processes of the organization. The product-based research stream I am calling for aligns with Winston's (2010) call for more qualitative studies on servant leadership in some ways. Winston (2010) rightfully notes that while we have a number of measurements that measure things important to servant leadership, such as hope and trust, these characteristics are shared with other leadership paradigms and that servant leadership is still largely unknown. He posits that qualitative studies can help us truly understand what servant leadership is. I similarly contend that the products of servant leaders and their followers can help researchers better understand servant leadership. Products are joint creations of servant leaders and their followers; they may represent servant leadership in unique ways.

In a larger sense, these products, along with traditional qualitative and quantitative research, may be further concepts in the constellation of servant leadership. The products of servant leadership are not just means to understanding servant leadership, however, but ends in themselves. While the products may not garner extrinsic rewards and praise, Wheeler (2012) notes that true servant leaders do not seek these types of rewards. The products of servant leadership may be intrinsic rewards. Wheeler (2012:169) writes about the importance and value of intrinsic rewards "being a part of something bigger and empowering others to meet their potential." Wheeler (2012) argues these are the ultimate rewards of servant leadership. Dean (2014: 275) takes umbrage at this statement, however; she laments that "academe has a long history of under-recognizing and under-rewarding women and minorities and equates legitimate concerns for salary, promotion and resources with narcissistic ambition." While I do not dispute these arguments, I simply think Wheeler was implying that genuine service and care for another human being are not given accolades, and those who choose to care should not expect extrinsic rewards. Moreover, Greenleaf (2003:78) succinctly notes that "the ultimate test of the servant motive is what one does with one's optional time for which one is not paid." The products that servant leaders and followers create together can be these methods of empowerment and larger visions, and they are most likely things that professors and administrators will not receive monetary compensation for undertaking. Nevertheless, they may be the true test of servant leadership. Servant leadership can be measured by promoting the creation and subsequent evaluation of products that leaders and followers create in different contexts, such as student papers, faculty research, strategic plans, and assessment reports, to name a few. The products that servant leaders and followers produce can be a type of measurement alongside traditional qualitative and quantitative research.

For instance, the method discussed in chapter 2 encourages professors and students to engage in conversation, in a lengthy dialogue over the course of weeks or the semester in an effort to have students create new insights in student papers. Professors must serve students, and the efforts of this service should lead to new student insights and creations. All of the chapters rely on some type of production, whether it is the production of a strategic plan, research, assessment report, or student work. The products of one class or institution cannot be readily standardized or quantified. Rather, the research on servant leadership can help to spark conversations and help design methods and strategies to facilitate the creation of new ideas and new insights critical to the functioning of higher education and the larger society. It is this evidence that this book seeks to promote. The ideas and products that people create can be one way to measure servant leadership. This notion of idea and product generation forms a core tenet of this book.

Therefore, servant leadership can be defined as a constellation, with the anchor of service to others, implemented by a number of different individuals and measured by the creation of ideas and products. My aim is to use servant leadership as a beginning, as a tool to initiate growth and development in various areas of higher education, specifically in pedagogy, faculty research, and strategic planning, accountability, and assessment. This book uses servant leadership to reframe some of the core purposes and activities of higher education for all appointed leaders in higher education, but mostly for faculty and those without true leadership titles. In addition, some studies look at servant leadership within organizations. Certain chapters follow this and deal with promoting servant leadership within higher education institutions, but other chapters argue for higher education institutions (and really for faculty in higher education institutions) to assume the role of servant leaders toward society at large. Other chapters blend both of these actions. Again, this echoes Greenleaf's (2002) call to create servant institutions.

To achieve the task of implementation, I draw on all types of literature of servant leadership from the last four decades. All of this research has helped us *begin* to label and understand the phenomena of servant leadership, but this is only a beginning.

Why Servant Leadership and Why Now?

Greenleaf wrote in the early 1970s, but the ideals of servant leadership may be more pertinent and needed now than they ever were. It might be an understatement to say that our age is volatile. One of the more pressing questions of our age is the question of the individual. And servant leadership can be instrumental in answering this question. What is the individual? Is the individual an entity with unlimited freedom or simply a part in the much larger web of society (Letizia 2017b)? Most likely, the answer to this is not one or the other, but rather somewhere in-between. Yet today the answer seems to lean toward the former. Giroux (2011:9) bluntly argues that, at present, there exists "an almost rabid individualism" due to the destructive theories of neoliberalism. Neoliberals essentially uphold a society driven by market values and centered on the individual (Harvey 2005). Giroux (2016) notes that the proponents of neoliberalism are attacking higher education and the conception of higher education as a public good. He further argues that higher education is crucial in the fight against this destructive vision of the individual (Giroux 2011). I have also dealt with servant leadership, education, and neoliberalism in another work (see Letizia 2014).

Servant leadership may be able to add a new dimension to higher education as a public good and help to create a more balanced and healthy vision of the individual. Bennis (2004), in regard to traditional leadership, argues that servant leadership is the antidote to this type of individualism. Bennis (2004:xi–xii) writes: "We recognize more and more that servant-leadership serves as a check; a counterbalance to the glorification, deification, and lionization of leaders who have actually neglected or forgotten why they're there;

to serve the people who are affected by the organization. *That's why servant-leadership matters.*"

Following this line of reasoning, servant leadership can help administrators and faculty work against rabid individualism by elevating the notion of service to others.

The theories of servant leadership can also help higher education institutions act. So much very important literature and research have focused on exposing the problems of higher education. Greenleaf (2002) argued that criticism was important and needed, but too much criticism was paralyzing. At some point, people must act (Greenleaf 2002). Following this, criticism is crucial because researchers must have a deep working understanding of organizational issues and problems, and how those organizations are situated in the larger society. Now, however, it is time to *act*. This book is a move away from analyses and criticism, and toward a plan for action (Weerts et al. 2015). And there is no shortage of problems in higher education, such as decreasing state appropriations and increased calls for accountability, questions of academic quality, to wider social concerns such as income inequality and the role of the individual in society, to name a few. Integrating servant leadership is a way to take action toward some of these pressing problems.

It is not my contention, however, to argue that servant leadership can save higher education or magically change the minds of policymakers and reformers who are skeptical or downright hostile to the more civic and socially minded purposes of higher education. Rather, servant leadership, if embedded into the structure, discourse, and behaviors of higher education, and measured by the products produced by a number of hands in higher education, may be a small but powerful first step in transforming higher education institutions in the age of neoliberalism. Using servant leadership in higher education is more than simply a question of making higher education more efficient or responsive. It is a visionary question, one that seeks to challenge and reimagine higher education in a volatile and even hostile era. Writing a book on servant leadership is ultimately about putting forth a new plan for higher education institutions so they can continue to serve the public good in a volatile era.

The notions of organizational stewardship, community building, meaningful work, and empowerment, to name a few, derived from the literature of servant leadership, may be able to help higher education institutions serve students and society in this volatile time. Again, these facets are not the end of service; they are only what can be measured at the current time. As such, they are the beginning of service.

The Author

Creswell (2013) and Merriam (1998) argue that qualitative researchers must take heed of their position and biases in the research process and how this position may have affected their research. I think it is important to do something similar here. Writing about servant leadership was a transforming experience for me; yet this transformation was not always easy. Further, as I wrote this book, I transformed, which affected the book further during revisions. Many times I was forced to confront things about myself, and I realized many areas where I need to change. For one, writing about servant leadership made me scrutinize my own leadership capabilities and behavior. I wanted to believe I am a servant leader in my professional and personal life. But am I really? Further, if one proclaims that he or she is a servant leader, does this lack of humility negate his or her servant leadership in some way? Can one even decide if he or she is a servant leader, or does this judgment have to be made by someone else? I do not have definitive answers to these questions. I do not think that one can proclaim herself or himself a servant leader. I do think, however, that an individual can say she or he is striving to be a servant leader, while always recognizing her or his own fallibility. As noted earlier, Sipe and Frick (2015) argued that many servant leaders will never fulfill all the lofty attributes of servant leadership. This is where I fall. I do not claim to be a servant leader. Rather, I strive to be a servant leader, but I also recognize that I have fallen short in many ways, that I could have done better and that I need to keep trying. Perhaps the most important area that servant leadership made me examine was my treatment of subordinates. I revisit all my actions with students: Was I short with this student? Did I get annoyed with this student? Did I really make an effort with this student, or did I simply brush her off? This is no less true in my personal life. Was I too short with my children? Did I pick a fight with my wife? To say you are a servant leader is one thing, to act it is another. And I think that one's relation with others, especially subordinates (such as students and children), is a true indicator of how well one is a servant leader. This is an area to which I am highly attuned now, and where I will continually strive to get better. In one instance, I realized that I had been using an idea my student had given me without giving him the proper acknowledgment. I never meant to steal his idea, but I realized that I needed to rightfully acknowledge him and his contribution in my own work (which I do later in this book). Essentially, servant leadership taught me to scrutinize areas where you think that you do not need to be scrutinized. And now I proceed which a much clearer understanding.

The point is that writing about servant leadership made me scrutinize all of my professional and personal actions and made me become much more aware of some of the issues examined in the preceding two paragraphs. In the widest sense, writing about servant leadership made me truly define my moral compass. This is not an easy process, but it is crucial. It is transforming, but it can be painful because you realize things about yourself that you did not think were wrong, but upon further inspection, you begin to understand you could have probably taken a better course of action. I hope all my readers undergo a similar transformation. As Nash and Murray (2010) note, however, ethics should not be rigid and absolute; there is always flexibility. The uniqueness of judging ethical situations is an important responsibility for servant leaders.

Something else that writing about servant leadership made me more attuned to was humility. For me, after I earned my PhD, I felt on top of the world. I do not think I ever acted in a brash or cocky manner, but I did feel I had reached a pinnacle of intelligence. I especially prided myself on my research. After about a year where I was riding high because I had a number of publications and a new job as a university professor, it hit me. I began to find small methodological and conceptual flaws in some of my research. I knew that this probably happened to many professors, but I became despondent. What did this mean? Was I not the scholar I thought I was? After much painful reflection, I learned two important lessons. First, always be humble! Realize that you are not as smart as you think, and that you will make mistakes. Second, do not dwell on mistakes. Rather, admit them and, most important, use them to improve. This is not original advice, but it is humbling when it happens to you. In a wider sense, my mistake, and mistakes in general, can be reframed as an existential phenomenon. What is a mistake? It is an evolutionary event, a transformative process that allows one to grow. As Nietzsche (1889/1954) famously remarked, what does not kill you, makes you stronger. Yet in order to truly take advantage of this growth capacity, one must be humble, and servant leadership can teach us to be humble. Again, I hope my readers begin to examine their own professional and personal lives and begin to reframe and understand their lives in new ways. Servant leadership should have this effect if it is to truly change the world!

Reflection Questions

This book utilizes reflection questions to help the reader reflect about the ideas presented in the chapters (Sipe and Frick 2015). Another purpose of the questions is to highlight the fact that this book is just a beginning. The ideas in this book should never be seen as the final authority on servant leadership. I have simply started a conversation about how servant leadership can affect higher education. Following this idea, the questions are meant to continue the conversation. I also do not want to present servant leadership as a panacea. Rather, there are downfalls and drawbacks to implementing even seemingly empowering ideas such as servant leadership (Kezar 2001). There are also serious criticisms of servant leadership (Dean 2014; Preiss 2014). Thus, each chapter contains questions asking the reader to think about how servant leadership may actually hinder the function of higher education that the chapter proposes. The reflection questions for the first chapter are:

1. In what other ways can servant leadership be researched, promoted, practiced, and understood outside of the traditional modes of qualitative and quantitative research? How can qualitative, quantitative, and other modes of research be harmonized?
2. What other functions of higher education, besides the ones described in this book, can servant leadership be used to reframe?
3. What are some ways servant leadership may hinder or hurt the understanding and execution of the functions described in this book?

2

Servant Leadership and Pedagogy

Neumann (2014:249) argues that one of the foundational freedoms in America is the "freedom to learn," even if this freedom is not directly stated in the Constitution. Furthermore, she argues that this freedom underpins many other freedoms. Yet attending an institution of higher education may not be enough to truly exercise one's freedom to learn (Neumann 2014). Neumann (2014:250) argues, "Once 'in' a student must be positioned, by way of teaching, to access the skills, knowledge, and ways of knowing likely to lead to deep substantive understanding and insight." But what exactly does learning entail? Neumann (2014), following a number of authors, argues that the act of learning is the integration of old ideas with new ones, grounded in cultural contexts and prior knowledge shaped by family and community concerns (Dewey 1902, 1916; Bransford, Brown, and Cocking 2000; Ladson-Billings 1995; Shulman 2004a, 2004b). She continues that learning is a struggle for the brain as the brain comprehends new and unfamiliar ideas in the context of what is already known. This definition points to the difficulty, as well as the tremendous opportunity, in advancing teaching and learning on college campuses. Neumann (2014) also notes that learning must center on content, on actual material covered in classes. Citing Bransford, Brown, and Cocking (2000), Dewey (1902, 1916), Schulman (2004a, 2004b), and Schwab (1978), Neumann (2014:251) argues that "subject matter matters." She notes that if the content was irrelevant, why have different courses? As such, I argue that professors, who are experts in their various disciplines, are in the prime position to be servant leaders to their students in the struggle that is learning. And this is not just in the abstract, but in specific subject areas.

This assertion, while intuitive and maybe even obvious, can and must be expounded on. The seeming obviousness of the assertion that professors should be servant leaders to their students' learning begins to become more complicated when we ask questions such as: How exactly can professors be servant leaders to their students? How exactly can servant leadership be used to bolster student learning? What is the exact nature of this service? What types of service are desired and appropriate?

Noland and Richards (2015) performed a study that examined how servant leadership was linked to college teaching; they termed this servant teaching. Their study began to answer some of the above questions. Noland and Richards (2015) adopted Liden and colleagues' (2008) scale to examine servant teacher behaviors. They found that cognitive learning and student engagement are positively correlated with a servant leadership approach. Noland and Richards (2015:28) argue: "Servant teaching is focused on student development and putting the needs of students ahead of that of the teacher." Fitzgerald (2015) argued that Spears's ten attributes of servant leadership could be employed in the classroom. Fitzgerald (2015) points out that teachers must truly hear their students, engage in foresight and reflection (as opposed to simply reacting to events), and promote the growth of all students. Nichols (2011) calls for servant leadership to transform K–12 teaching in a number of ways. Nichols (2011) specifically argues that servant leadership can influence teaching by fostering a sense of stewardship in students. Teachers must help to sustain a sense of community and stewardship in their students in a society that does not readily praise these values (Nichols 2011). These works help to shed light on the possible roles, actions, and impacts of servant teaching. Pousa (2014) also notes how teaching is a prominent method of fostering development in people.

Epstein (2014) argues that there is always an element of the particular in teaching and learning in K–12 classrooms. She goes on to argue that universal prescriptions for learning may not capture the complexity of teaching. I believe this holds true for college teaching as well. In addition, different approaches will be necessary for different disciplines. However, all disciplines, especially as they are taught in a college setting, have commonalities. One major commonality in almost every discipline is academic writing. Students are asked to write term papers, reflections, and increasingly blogs and wikis in order to demonstrate their knowledge and understanding of concepts of various disciplines. This chapter reviews a method of academic writing that can be used in a wide variety of courses.

A fruitful research base to start with in order to integrate the ideas of servant learning with student learning is the research on self-authorship (Evans et al. 2010). Self-authorship was employed by psychologist Robert Kegan (Evans et al. 2010). Later, Marcia Baxter Magolda, a higher education researcher, furthered the ideas of Kegan in a student development context (Evans et al. 2010). This chapter reviews pertinent literature on self-authorship and integrates these ideas with servant leadership in order to create the beginnings of a strategy by which professors can become servants. First, however, a brief description of Kegan's (1994) and Baxter Magolda's work is necessary for background.

Kegan and Baxter Magolda

Kegan (1994) argued for the importance of understanding how adults develop. He delineated what he called five orders of mind through which individuals develop. These orders of mind are not about learning new skills; rather, the different orders of mind signify "ways of organizing experience that are not simply replaced as we grow but subsumed into more complex systems of mind" (Kegan 1994:9). Kegan (1994) argued that from the ages of twelve to twenty, most individuals are transitioning to the third order. The third order of mind entails an individual understanding another person's feelings and expectations as well as the ability to "internalize another point of view" (Kegan 1994:30–31). However, individuals cannot "see the self as author . . . of one's inner psychological life" (Kegan 1994:31). This sentiment is crucial. If individuals do not see themselves as authors, then they see themselves as being driven by external forces. The fourth order of mind that Kegan (1994) put forth is self-authorship. In this order of mind, individuals begin to see themselves as authors, as creators. Specifically, in the realm of learning and school, in the fourth order Kegan (1994:303) argues that individuals set their "own goals and standards," they see themselves as "co-creators of the culture (rather than only shaped by culture)." In the third order of mind, individuals cannot reflect on or truly question the ideas and notions that guide their lives (Kegan 1994). Yet there exists a transitional state between orders of mind, what Kegan (1994) called a holding environment (Evans et al. 2010). A holding environment is an "evolutionary bridge" that allows for individuals to move from one order to the next (Kegan 1994:43). Mentors and teachers can provide support in holding environments that allow individuals to progress to self-authorship (Kegan 1994). Of course, many adults do not operate from fourth-order consciousness (Kegan 1994).

Baxter Magolda (2004b, 2009) described a similar movement from a phase marked by what she calls external formulas, to the crossroads where people begin to question these formulas, and finally to the phase of self-authorship, where individuals no longer use these external formulas to guide their lives. In the crossroads, people begin to build what Baxter Magolda (2009:4) calls the internal voice, which allows individuals to understand their own beliefs and the external forces pushing on them. In self-authorship, individuals use their internal voice to guide their life (Baxter Magolda 2009). Baxter Magolda (2004b) further argues that the college years can be and should be used to promote student growth and get students on the path to self-authorship. Of course, many students will leave college not reaching self-authorship (Baxter Magolda 2004a, 2009). The model that Baxter Magolda proposes, the learning partnerships model, which is built in part with the ideas of Kegan, is meant to move students toward self-authorship (Baxter Magolda 2004b). However, Baxter Magolda (2004b) does note that due to entrenched norms in higher education, transforming the educational process to one that truly promotes self-authorship is still hard to accomplish, yet it is achievable. Some major universities, such as Miami University and Virginia Tech, have implemented ideas from the learning partnerships model (Hodge, Baxter Magolda, and Haynes 2009).

The learning partnerships model views learning as a social process (Baxter Magolda 2004a). As such, the learning partnerships model calls for a great deal of support for students in various phases of learning (Baxter Magolda 2004a). Professors and student affairs professions are integral to providing this support. Since knowledge is a social process, learning is more than a cognitive endeavor (Baxter Magolda 2004a, 2004b). Learning entails an intrapersonal or identity dimension and an interpersonal or relationships dimension (Baxter Magolda 2004b). Baxter Magolda (2004b) points out that self-authorship requires growth and maturity in all three of these facets, and all three of these facets are linked. Baxter Magolda (2004b) also points out that all three phases help to promote citizenship. In addition, Baxter Magolda (2009) notes that the journey to self-authorship is not linear, but heavily predicated on personal and environmental factors.

Specifically for fostering effective writing, Haynes (2004), who used the theories of self-authorship to help build an interdisciplinary writing program at her university, argued that professors could truly help their students write more effectively when they tended to the interpersonal and intrapersonal dimensions. She recounted that many times students struggled with questions of self-confidence, and with understanding their own values and bad habits that they picked up along their educational path. Dealing with these concerns helped to create better writers (Haynes 2004:81). As van Dierendonck (2011) points out, strong relationships and trust are important mediating factors in servant leadership as well.

Here I believe that the ideas of servant leadership can be integrated with self-authorship theories. Professors can guide students to reach the shores of self-authorship. Moreover, following Baxter Magolda (2004b) and Haynes (2004), I argue that service toward students, especially in the context of their writing, must not artificially divorce the cognitive from the interpersonal and intrapersonal. Rather, all facets of learning must be seen in a holistic context. This may constitute the ultimate act of service to the students and the wider society that students will help to mold.

Servant Leadership and Writing

Student writing in college courses may be an ideal vehicle to achieve a number of ideas related to servant leadership, such as (but not limited to) empowerment, stewardship, persuasive mapping, and, most important, meaningful work. Writing can be a method to fostering these dimensions. Attention to writing can foster stewardship because writing can be seen as an act of care for the next generation as it helps to develop the minds of the young. As noted earlier, persuasive mapping is "mapping issues and conceptualizing greater possibilities" for organizational members (Barbuto and Wheeler 2006:319). Writing can allow students to see these greater possibilities in academic disciplines. Writing can also allow students to see how they can use the ideas of the discipline in wider society. Finally, Sendjaya and colleagues (2008) argue that servant leaders must make the work of their followers meaningful. If students create new ideas, professors can highlight how these new ideas are meaningful for society. The above facets of servant leadership are by no means exhaustive in describing how writing can be used to promote servant leadership.

The next section uses my own research (Letizia 2016a, 2016c, 2017a) as a starting point to explore the intersection between servant leadership and writing. Kegan (1994:284) specifically argues that when students write from the fourth order, the professor stands "over the shoulder of a fellow inventor ready to comment upon their independent invention, on what *they* are making." When students write from the fourth order, they do not write to please the teacher or write to meet a standard; they write for themselves (Kegan 1994). They create new ideas. My own research extends Kegan's (1994) ideas of writing from the fourth order and Baxter Magolda's (2004, 2009) theories of self-authorship and holding environments/crossroads.

I have developed a framework to guide student writing. The framework centers on a student's thesis or claim. Booth and colleagues (2003) argue that the thesis or claim of the paper is the basis of the entire paper. The claim frames the argument and structure of the entire paper. I have argued elsewhere that the claim of the paper can be a powerful democratic or civic sentiment. Beyond the structural importance of the thesis, the thesis or claim is the *essence* of the paper; it is the driving thought, the voice (Letizia 2017a). Moreover, this voice or claim is not simply a cognitive one, but in light of self-authorship, this voice or claim becomes something more; it can become part of one's identity or how one relates to others in the world. Yet, following Neumann (2014), the claim cannot be divorced from the disciplinary content of the course. The claim of a scholarly paper, reenvisioned as a democratic voice, can be a new way to understand the importance of student writing, or a new way to frame the importance of student writing and its relation to academic disciplines. However, writing a powerful claim, a truly democratic sentiment, is by no means an act that students should undertake on their own; it requires guidance. In addition, it may not come naturally to most students. The ability to write this claim must be nurtured by faculty. Booth and colleagues (2003) further argue that a claim should be backed by reasons and evidence to make it truly credible. While this chapter only focuses on writing the claim, professors could further serve students by delving into the reasons and evidence that back the claim up.

Cast in terms of servant leadership, helping students to write this claim can be a powerful act of empowerment. Nurturing this democratic voice in students, in the form of a thesis or claim, may be the greatest act of servant leadership. As we watch political discourse devolve (Drew, Lyons, and Svehla 2010), as political discourse degenerates into bigotry and anti-intellectualism, students now more than ever need to be taught how to function in a democracy, and in a democracy that demands that they have command of information. Professors can view themselves as servants who must lead their students to citizenship. The college classroom and, more specifically, the writing assignment can be seen as the holding environment. In this holding environment, faculty need to help and serve students to reach self-authorship.

Writing the claim or thesis, however, is an advanced step in the writing process and in the nurturance of the democratic voice. Before faculty and students can contemplate this step, a student first must grapple with an almost infinite amount of information. The information age, while liberating due to this access, comes with its own perils, which, if not properly addressed, can actually hinder a student's participation in civic life. A dangerous pitfall is that of "information glut" (Fullan 2001:6). As Sharratt and Fullan (2012) point out, the amount of information that we have access to and are exposed to is overwhelming. As a result, many times people will simply gravitate toward what catches their eye, and what is "instantly stimulating," but they miss what is truly important (Sharratt and Fullan 2012:2). Professors, who are creators and disseminators of information, can act as servants to their students by helping them sift through and understand this information. In the widest sense, Fullan (2001) and Sharratt and Fullan (2012) argue how information must be made meaningful for it to truly be useful and impactful. Professors must help to render this data useable and understandable. This is not to say that professors must push specific types of information on their students; rather, professors need to enable students to understand the various types of data sources out there and how to interpret those sources.

Locate-Evaluate

In 1989, the Association of College and Research Libraries issued a statement that proclaimed that information literacy entailed the ability to locate and evaluate information (Addison and Myers 2013). As such, one way professors can help students and guide them through the information of the information age is with a process called locate-evaluate (LE). I have written about variants of this framework elsewhere. (Letizia 2016c, 2017a). I reinterpret this framework though a servant leadership lens. Many teachers in high school and many professors in universities probably use this process in some form. The LE simply gives some structure and a name to this process. It is the first step behind the formulation of a claim because the claim should no longer be a pedantic academic exercise or haphazard process. Rather, it should now be carefully built with evidence and insights that draw on the information available. Of course, there is no one way to structure a writing assignment. As Wheeler (2012) notes, servant leaders must know themselves. When structuring a writing assignment, a professor must analyze the students' comfort level. Will he or she allow students to create their own claim, or will the professor set boundaries on the claim? Essentially, the professor must decide how much freedom students will have to create their own claim. This decision will structure the entire process. Thus, what follows is not definitive; rather, it is only a tentative guide.

The first step of the LE framework is location. This is probably the easiest step and the step with which students are most familiar. Yet professors must radically expand their students' knowledge base. Professors must also reframe how students access knowledge. Professors in different disciplines must show students how to access information from various sources. At this stage, the effort revolves around quantity. Professors must expose their students to a number of credible sources. Here faculty can guide their students through various information tools such as JSTOR, ERIC, and Google Scholar, to name a few, as well as more discipline-specific ones. Faculty can also show students methods to access information such as using different search terms to maximize effectiveness. Faculty cannot assume that students simply know where to look; rather, they must guide them through various access points. Here it is also important to listen to students. Students may know sites that faculty do not. A crucial tenet of servant leadership is listening to followers. In this case, students who have been raised in the information age and with access to technology their whole lives may have information that faculty do not.

Students can access information with ease, yet the task of evaluating that information is crucial as well (Addison and Meyers 2013; Stoddard 2014). Here the role of faculty is essential. Fostering problem solving is paramount for servant leaders (Wheeler 2012). The influx of information is a problem in the sense that there is so much information, and without proper instruction in evaluating information, students will literally be stranded. Here the pitfall identified earlier as information glut and the subsequent use of only superficial or trendy knowledge is always present (Fullan 2001; Sharratt and Fullan 2012). Students who are raised on computers and Ipads are still not necessarily good consumers of information. In the barest sense, evaluation can be a form of empowerment. Armed with evaluative capabilities, students can begin to sift through information and understand what information is credible. Teaching students how to evaluate information also guards against faculty *giving* information to students.

Yet what exactly does this evaluation entail? Obviously, there is no set agenda for this task. Some questions to consider are: Who wrote the piece (was it a professor, journalist, blogger, and so forth)? Where is the information found (in a journal, book website)? Is there a political bias to the piece? Are there any contradictions between your sources? Do they all agree? What points, if any, are omitted from these pieces that you can glean by reading other pieces? Another crucial question centers on peer review. While it does have problems, peer review is vital for the research process (Beall 2013; Booth, Colomb, and Williams 2003; Perna 2016). Professors could explain the peer-review process and show why, despites its flaws, it is crucial for knowledge generation. Professors could help students understand the process of academic publishing and its relation to knowledge. Professors can discuss with their students how some journals and book publishers have higher or at least different standards for research and how this dictates knowledge creation. In addition, professors could discuss how predatory publishing has affected knowledge creation. Many times this work is not properly peer reviewed (Beall 2013; Truth 2013). What is the implication for knowledge creation if authors are paying for their work to be published? Another major issue is who actually funded the research. Powerful organizations many times fund specific research in an effort to advance an agenda. This is not to say that research from organizations is worthless. Many times this research is excellent and valuable. Nevertheless, students should understand the impact that funding can have on research outcomes (Washburn 2006).

These questions can act as starting points for faculty to serve and empower their students regarding the vast amount of information in the information age. Helping students to understand the ever-growing corpus of information may now constitute a type of service for servant leaders in the classroom. If we live in the information age, then servant leaders in the classroom may need to center part of their service on information, on its location and evaluation and eventual usage in academic assignments. This also aligns with Neumann (2014), who argues for the importance of subject-matter content in the learning process. Professors are experts in their disciplines, and most of the information that students are utilizing is the literature from academic disciplines.

Yet these should only be starting points. Any earnest attempt at evaluation should entail earnest conversation and dialogue. Evaluation of information can become an opportunity for growth because students and professors can come to new understandings in their discussions of material. Faculty members also provide a type of emotional healing to students at this state as well. Students may be struggling with understanding and information overload, as well as the pain that comes from criticizing their own long-held dogmas and external formulas. Teaching students how to evaluate information gives them confidence in dealing with information. Of course, the process I am describing is not automatic; there is no set template. Rather, the process is iterative (Booth, Colomb, and Williams 2003; Haynes 2004), students may come to new insights in a variety of ways, and servant leaders can facilitate this process. The framework described here, interpreted through a servant leadership frame of mind, simply tries to make this process of formulating claims more deliberate.

The Writing Framework

Once information has been located and evaluated, the next step is to transform the information into a claim or thesis. Essentially, students must put this information to use. The demands of citizenship have been irrevocably impacted by the growing amount of information (Drew, Lyons, and Svehla 2010). Serving students by helping them locate and evaluate information and then helping them utilize the information in a coherent thought (the claim) may now constitute a new type of citizenship education (Letizia 2017a). Information can be put to use in a democracy by creating new and progressive ideas (Shafer 2013). If information is central to democracy now, servant leaders can help their students transform information into coherent and meaningful democratic ideas that propose new insights, point out and help to remedy injustice, and create meaning for fellow citizens. This act of servant leaders pays attention to individual empowerment but also stewardship concerns of leaving a positive legacy to later generations.

Again, this process may not be automatic or natural. Rather, faculty must act deliberately and intentionally. As noted earlier, Fullan (2001) argues that information must be made meaningful; it must be rendered useful to people to actually understand and employ it. For Fullan, this is the job of a leader. Servant leaders do not just interpret the information for students but help them interpret the information themselves. Again, the most effective way to do this is simply by talking to students and hearing what interests them and how the information they uncovered can be used to generate a topic. By talking to students, professors can also help to situate knowledge in the inter- and intrapersonal realms of their being (Baxter Magolda 2004b; Haynes 2004). Each student will be different, and some will need more guidance than others in creating their claims. Further, people in general want to be heard and acknowledged (Wheeler 2012). Simply talking to students may be one way to give such acknowledgment.

In the writing framework, there are three levels. However, this by no means implies that writing ideas can be neatly pigeonholed into a mechanistic or rigid process (Booth, Colomb, and Williams 2003; Haynes 2004). Rather, the framework, tied to the voluminous research of self-authorship, is only a guide. The first stage of my framework aligns with Kegan's third order of consciousness. Here a student's thesis does not really say anything different or new; it basically repeats what someone else has said before. In addition, the claim at this stage will usually align with what is considered more commonly accepted knowledge; the claim is usually uncontroversial. This stage also aligns with Bloom's (1956) notion of comprehension, which entails an understanding of the material. Of course, there is nothing wrong with using others' viewpoints, and it is a crucial step in formulating arguments. However, when students are only doing this, it may limit their ability to achieve self-authorship because they are relying too heavily on authorities. If a student relies too heavily on authorities, he or she may not be able to be empowered.

This level of the framework should not be seen as a total obstacle or barrier, however. While we do want students moving to a more empowered and self-authored state, students must first be conversant with the information they have. Again, this links back to Neumann (2014), who argues that subject matter is important. If a student is in this stage, they are grappling with subject matter. The student may simply be immersed in information and trying to process it (or he or she may be hungover and unable to complete the assignment!). Conversely, if a professor senses that students are only relying on a few sources or not really exploring what is out there, professors can also intentionally expand the students understanding of information and how much there is. At this point, a student may not be able to formulate a second-level thesis. To be a servant leader in this level, a professor can prompt the student to explore information and can act as a comforting voice for the student as the student locates and wades through the almost limitless information. I would guess that most professors of undergraduates see these types of theses and claims. If and when a professor senses that a student is ready to create a higher-level claim, one where the student must criticize or evaluate existing information and not just repeat it, the professor can utilize the ideas from the second stage of the framework.

The next stage of the framework aligns with Kegan's (1994) notion of a holding environment. In the writing framework, the claim is an extension of the student, of the student's voice. The professor is a steward and one who empowers. At this stage, a professor can help a student begin to say something different and not simply repeat what authorities have said before. A student does not magically pass into self-authorship; it is a process fraught with setbacks or, at the very least, obstacles (Baxter Magolda 2009). In the second phase of the writing assignment, the professor can start to show the student how to question information. This stage aligns with Bloom's (1956) notion of evaluation, which entails judgment. Perhaps the most effective method here is simply to speak with a student and understand the student not just cognitively, but personally as well (Haynes 2004). The professor should not tell the student what is good, but let the student come to this realization himself or herself. Similar to the evaluation stage of the LE process, here a professor shows the student how to question the information. This is the essence of a holding environment, and of empowerment. The essence is guiding students to think critically about the ever-growing corpus of information to which they have access. This stage is evaluative, where a student learns how to question authorities. Due to this questioning aspect, this stage is a necessary one to the path of self-authorship.

If a student is ready to challenge the external ideas he or she has lived by, a professor can work with students to create a claim that criticizes or evaluates existing information. As noted earlier, Neumann (2014) argued that an important facet of learning is when individuals understand their long-held beliefs and work to integrate new ideas. Here the student is not just criticizing information, but formulating a claim, a voice that is critical of an authority. And that is the key to this level: students are challenging authority in a productive way. They are also integrating new ideas with previously held ideas and, in some sense, may be challenging an internal authority. Servant leaders or servant professors can help students come to the realization that their lives are not at the mercy of distant authorities and so-called experts. This does not imply a flagrant disregard for authority, rather, a recognition that students, as citizens in formation, have the ability and the right to challenge authority with proper understandings and evidence. Students become empowered. Faculty can have students consider some generally accepted theories, such as theories dealing with terrorism, the economy, or climate change. From this, the professor can help the student challenge that claim with relevant evidence. Again, the professor does not do this for the student, but allows the student to accomplish this task on her or his own. If students do challenge existing ideas, this may also create pain because they are moving away from what they know, and professors must anticipate this pain and anxiety. As such, professors must be a source of healing. If a student appears to be ready to move from writing an evaluative claim to writing a claim that attempts to say something original, the professor can look to the third phase of the writing framework.

The third stage of the framework aligns with self-authorship. In the third stage of the writing framework, the professor helps to guide the student to create a new insight, one that goes beyond evaluation, one that goes toward creation. As noted earlier, this idea of student as creator follows Kegan (1994) and his call for students to write from self-authorship. Here the professor helps students to say something new. Of course, it is very difficult for students to actually say anything new because there is so much information out there. It would be very difficult for someone, especially an undergraduate, to have enough command of that information to say something totally original. Nevertheless, a professor can serve students by helping them to at least grasp what it means to try to say something original. By saying something original, students can become self-authored. The framework can allow professors to help their students achieve certain ideas and cognitive learning. Wheeler (2012:24) argues that "bureaucratic structures often restrict imaginative thinking and consideration of new ideas." Following Wheeler (2012), the framework can also allow professors to aid their students to create new ideas. How can the subject matter be used to create newer, better, and more meaningful possibilities? Instead of simply relying on the old ideas that have guided your life, how can you use the material of the class and the discipline to create a new idea, a new possibility?

However, as van Dierendonck and Rook (2010:156) ask, what is creativity? Following Amabile (1996) and Shalley, Zhou, and Oldham (2004), van Dierendonck and Rook (2010:156) argue that creativity in an organizational context is "the generation of novel and potentially useful products and ideas." Shalley, Zhou, and Oldham (2004) note that creativity can be defined as the generation of original ideas. Novelty means that ideas are different from what is available at the time. Usefulness entails some type of value for an institution (Shalley, Zhou, and Oldham 2004). Finally, servant leadership has also been shown to help foster creativity (Neubert et al. 2008; van Dierendonck 2011). Bloom (1956:162) argued for the notion of synthesis, which entails combining elements and ideas "as to constitute a pattern or structure not clearly there before." Bloom and colleagues (1971) further note that synthesis assignments allow for students to produce new ideas and products, and to take a sense of ownership in their work. This is in contrast to most schoolwork, where students are to produce a preset correct answer (Bloom, Hastings, and Madaus 1971). Barber (2012) notes that synthesis is a crucial facet of learning. Following the above sentiments, professors can help students understand the originality and usefulness of their ideas.

Van Dierendonck and Rook (2010) argue that servant leaders who embody many of the dimensions described earlier—such as a sense of empowerment, humility, and stewardship, to name a few—can help foster creativity through certain mediating processes in organizations. These processes are providing clear expectations of roles and feedback that is constructive. Next, servant leaders must cultivate genuine relationships with organizational members. When these processes occur, members usually show higher intrinsic motivation (van Dierendonck and Rook 2010). As van Dierendonck and Rook (2010:164) argue, "leadership in creative organizations is a balancing act of providing direction on the one hand . . . and offering freedom to explore on the other." The writing framework proposed in this chapter, as a whole, which culminates in the third level, can help to scaffold the teaching of meaning by providing direction and freedom.

Shalley and colleagues (2004) also note how the type of evaluations supervisors give their subordinates can affect creativity. Critical evaluations, which seek to criticize a person's creation, can stymie creativity, whereas developmental evaluations, which are meant to help a person grow, foster creativity (Shalley, Zhou, and Oldham 2004). As such, professors can use the framework as a developmental evaluation, as a way to help their students grow, not criticize them.

As van Dierendonck and Rook (2010) argued, creativity is crucial for organizations. In a wider sense, however, as John Dewey argued, democracy is a creative endeavor (Dewey 1988; Parker 1996). Democracy is a thing in motion, driven by the actions and ideas of its citizens; democracy is a "creative, constructive process" (Parker 1996:191). Moreover, as noted earlier, Shafer (2013) argued that academic writing is a method for students to create new ideas that can drive democracy. As such, the writing method can help to foster this creativity for democracy. Self-authorship calls for students to evaluate external ideas and utilize their own ideas (Baxter Magolda 2009). The ideas of students must be based on evidence; they cannot simply be unsubstantiated opinions or dreams. However, students also exert their voice for others to use in their own lives. Further, in a democracy, a claim has civic importance as well. In an age of soundbite slinging (Drew, Lyons, and Svehla 2010), when political debates morph into soundbites, an evidence-based claim can be a powerful weapon of truth. Thus, a servant leader must help to bring about this claim.

The student is empowered because the student now has a voice. This can also help to answer Buchen (1998), who, following Greenleaf, asked how a university helped its students grow. Moreover, the professor has performed a duty of stewardship because that student, at least in this one instance, has exercised her or his voice, and this is a great asset to society and democracy in general. Empowerment, growth, and stewardship congeal. The student is learning to contribute to society, to become a citizen. By learning this, and in line with the tripartite division of self-authorship, students can learn about their own beliefs, their own understandings of knowledge, and their own place in society, and how they can contribute to society. All of this may not magically come about because of one assignment, but one assignment can serve as the foundation.

Professors can help and guide students not only to self-authorship but also toward creating meaning. Working toward a higher purpose is a tenet of servant leadership (Sendjaya, Sarros, and Santora 2008; Sipe and Frick 2015). Yet this tenet should not just encompass the servant leader but the followers as well. Students in college are yearning for meaning (Nash and Murray 2010). It is the responsibility of a servant leader to help these students create meaning. Meaning is framed in the existential questions that we all ask ourselves: What is the purpose of my life? Why am I alive? How can I make a difference? Why do I get up in the morning (Nash and Murray 2010; Sipe and Frick 2015). Today, those questions are not readily answered, and many institutions of higher education do not give students the opportunity to engage in these types of questions (Nash and Murray 2010). Society does, however, offer rampant consumerism, hedonism, and easy escape routes such as promiscuous sex and drug use that are extremely prevalent on college campuses (Nash and Murray 2010). And many students turn to these unhealthy and self-destructive areas for meaning (Nash and Murray 2010). Nash and Murray (2010) and Nash and Jang (2013) argue that professors can foster meaning making in a number of ways, such as pedagogy.

The point is that professors can act as servant leaders by helping their students articulate new ideas. Kegan (1994), who worked with adult students, argued that professors can help students to create new ideas through their writing, and not simply write for a grade. Further, following Kegan (1994:284), students can come to own their writing; it can be something that "*they* are making." What a student writes can be something meaningful for the student and for society, and it can be something that the student owns and takes pride in. Following the ideas sketched above, students can write for meaning. Writing a great paper, a paper that actually contributes to knowledge, may be a way for professors to show students how they can own their work. Again, one assignment cannot magically create meaning, but it can be a start. Professors should also fully disclose and detail the entire process to students. Students should know that they are being led to create something. They should truly understand the expectations of creation; if not, they may simply view creating ideas as a command from the teacher, which would defeat the entire purpose! They should be taught to value and understand their own creations and ideas.

The final aspect of the framework to consider is how does or can the idea put forth by the student serve humanity. As Evans and Giroux (2014) note, ideas are not meaningless. They are powerful; they help people take action. Freire (2000) calls for the notion of praxis, which entails a synergy between theory and practice. Weiner (2007) has argued that there is a crisis of imagination (it is the title of his chapter) and that educators must inspire their students to imagine a better world. Weiner (2007:58) further notes that this this "critical imaginary" is not fantasy, but rather a way to "rewrite the categories of the real." McLaren (2007), however, laments that many times, those who work with concepts and theories are derided for being too abstract and out of touch. McLaren bluntly argues while ideas alone cannot change the world, philosophical reflection and understanding the larger social context of issues are crucial for any social movement or transformation. Following these sentiments, professors can help students to ask: What does their created idea do? What does it expose or propose? What actions can it lead to? How can it illuminate actions and make actions intelligible? How does it fit into the larger social context of events? Professors, when helping their students, can promote the notion that ideas are a type of service. Students can serve people with new ideas. For instance, Thomas Jefferson and a number our Founding Fathers served humanity by creating the political ideas that we still live by (Dayton, 2012). Scholarship can be service, and servant professors can help promote this idea with their students. Servant professors can talk through with their students and find ways in which their claims can serve humanity.

Crucial to this entire framework is effective feedback. A professor should continually give feedback throughout the entire process. Conversation is key to servant leadership, and constructive feedback is especially important for fostering creativity (van Dierendonck and Rook 2010). As Brookhart (2008) argues, effective feedback entails students using the feedback to grow. Again, a professor will have to decide how the assignment will be structured; for instance, will students be allowed to submit multiple drafts? In my experience, I found that multiple drafts are crucial to fostering self-authorship because of the opportunity for feedback. A multitude of research confirms this as well (Lickona and Davidson 2005). The multiple written drafts allowed for written feedback as well.

Servant teaching can be thought of as a constellation of sorts. As Noland and Richards (2015) point out, there are a number of facets of servant teaching and teaching and learning in general that need further attention from researchers. Each different facet that Noland and Richards (2015) postulated in their study—student learning, motivation, and engagement—may be a concept in a larger constellation. What I have described in this chapter, evaluation and creation for meaning, can also be thought of as concepts in this constellation. Fostering student creativity, especially in the context of the creation of new thoughts and ideas for democracy, ownership, and meaning, may be especially important concepts in this constellation, concepts that allow for growth and empowerment of students in new and exciting ways for the individual and society. Of course, the framework should not be applied in a rigid manner. For instance, it may be difficult to distinguish between a true level two and level three claim. When does evaluation end and synthesis begin? As such, the framework is meant only to be a loose guide.

Case Study

I will briefly recount my own experience as I implemented this method to highlight exactly how I was able to use informal feedback opportunities to practice servant leadership. While I do not claim that this method is effective because I used it, I will simply recount some of my experiences to help guide future professors and point out other opportunities for servant leadership. The informal one-on-one with students is the glue that holds this method together. The one-on-ones give this method vitality, and truly create possibilities for service to students. This aligns with Fitzgerald (2015), who argued that teachers who embody servant leadership in the classroom should pay attention and be concerned with the development of each student in their care. Haynes (2004) also stressed the importance of meeting with students to support their writing. Specifically, these one-on-one meetings allow a professor to practice Sipe and Frick's (2015) second and third principles: puts people first and skilled communicator. In the widest sense, the framework put forward in this chapter, but especially the personal element, aligns with Patterson's (2010) notion of love. Patterson (2010:72) bluntly argues, "This love is a force, a force so intense that it changes lives—the lives of the followers, the life of the organization, and even the life of the leader." As I have argued, this framework, if truly believed in and followed by professors, can possibly accomplish this change because it is rooted in a type of love. It is rooted in love and deep concern for students and their growth and development not just as individuals but as contributing citizens.

I have used this method in a number of classes with a number of students. Each time I realize where I need more clarity. This is as much a learning process for me as it is for the students. Here I would like to acknowledge one former student by name, Steven Arnold. I taught him in the 2013–2014 school year in dual enrollment American History. I had not quite implemented the full writing framework sketched out in this chapter, but I had implemented certain portions of it, most notably, the personal conferences. Steven wrote an excellent claim. I was so impressed with this claim and, with his permission, used it as an example for his classmates and later classes. The claim became an example for the framework, and I wound up using it in published articles. However, after close to two years of using his claim, I realized that had I had never properly acknowledged Steven's contribution to my own work, so I wanted to publicly acknowledge Steven's contribution to this framework here and thank him. I also wanted to thank him in a wider sense; he taught me the value of student work and that students, if given the chance, can create meaningful ideas.

Again, following the tenets of self-authorship, the cognitive cannot be separated from the interpersonal domain (Baxter Magolda 2004b; Haynes 2004). Thus, this method allowed me to truly get to know my students, not simply in a personal way, but in a personal *and* cognitive way. I got to know how my students truly *thought* about knowledge and various disciplines. Part of this method requires intense one-on-one counseling with each student regarding their topics. There were a number of meetings for each paper the students were required to write. The first meeting was claim formulation. This meeting was essentially a brainstorming meeting. Here I earnestly discussed with students their interests regarding the topic. After reading their assigned chapter and doing class activities, the students and I could begin to discuss what ideas they had on various topics. After this, students were encouraged to come and meet with me to discuss their progress. Many students took me up on this, and I was able to have some excellent conversations.

Here is a great opportunity to listen attentively and build up relationships (Sipe and Frick 2015). Listening and collaborating are quintessential planks of servant leadership (Wheeler 2012). For almost their entire school career students have been trained to listen to their teachers. These one-on-ones can allow teachers to listen to their students, but also collaborate with them to build new ideas and build relationships. The relationships, however, are not the relationships of friends, but of intellectuals; they are based on knowledge and shared ideas.

I do not claim to be a servant leader, or an expert collaborator or skilled listener. However, one instance stands out for me. A student came to me and asked for assistance with her paper. We pulled up her paper on my computer and worked on it for roughly twenty minutes. We spoke about American history. But I listened to her ideas, she listened to mine, and she typed her paper. I watched her rearrange it and incorporate new ideas. I watched her grow. At that moment, I felt that I was becoming a servant leader.

Conclusion

This chapter has introduced a writing framework that professors can use to help students reach self-authorship and, in a wider sense, serve their students and society as a whole. One crucial component to reaching self-authorship may be servant leadership on the part of professors. Academic assignments, especially writing assignments where students have to wade through and evaluate massive amounts of information, can be rethought of as vehicles to reach self-authorship with professors as their guide. For this assignment, there is a continuous line that can be traced from the first time a student locates a source to the finished paper. (Notice I said continuous and not straight, it may be squiggly! As has been stressed, research is a complicated endeavor!) The purpose of the framework is to create opportunities for professors to practice servant leadership with their students through pedagogy.

Reflection Questions

1. In what other ways can pedagogy be framed as service? Specifically, what pedagogical methods can be utilized to serve students?
2. In what other ways can pedagogy help students to create meaning?
3. How may servant leadership hinder pedagogy at the college level?

3

Servant Leadership and Research

This chapter examines how some of the ideas of servant leadership can reshape the norms of faculty research across various disciplines and fields. Many faculty and administrators may object to changing the norms of academic research, however. In addition, research norms are still largely entrenched (Basken 2016). There are some disclaimers before I proceed. I am not arguing that all the norms and practices associated with academic research are outdated or wrong. In fact, many of these norms and practices have served academia for almost 150 years. I am arguing that some of the norms and practices associated with academic research may need to be rethought, and servant leadership can act as an excellent starting point for this change. Implementing any change to these norms and practices will most likely prove extremely difficult. Nevertheless, it may be time to have this discussion (Basken 2016; Denzin and Giardina 2009). As evidence of this changing position, the *Chronicle of Higher Education* in January 2016 ran a special issue examining the changing visions of research. The piece specifically examines how researchers may need to take a more active role in using their research to effect change (Basken 2016). Climate change, wealth inequality, and technical change continue to intensify and change our lives (Zizek 2009). In this volatile time, academic research should help to promote justice (Denzin and Giardina 2009).

Before making this argument, however, it is important to understand the historical roots of the modern university and professoriate. In addition to understanding the historical roots, it is also important to understand how the research ideal has changed over the course of the twentieth and twenty-first centuries. I have devised four different conceptions of academic research. In the language of servant leadership, these four conceptions can act as guiding thoughts or ideas for faculty researchers (DePree 2002; Dennis and Bocarnea 2005).

Research Typology

These four conceptions are not mutually exclusive but rather overlap and coexist. The first is the traditional vision of scholarship and research, which I have labeled the research for knowledge strand. The second strand of research is almost an inverted form of the research for knowledge strand. It is the research for prestige and promotion strand. In this strand, scholars pursue research not so much for the sake of knowledge (which is still present) but for purposes of prestige, promotion, and tenure. A vision of research that has developed over the last forty years, and is in direct contrast to the strand of research for knowledge but is somewhat congruent with the notion of research for prestige and promotion, is the research for revenue and profit strand. In this strand, as the name suggests, research is not seen so much as advancing knowledge but rather as a means of revenue for individuals and institutions.

The fourth strand is the research for service strand. Again, this strand overlaps with the research for knowledge and research for revenue and profit strands in some ways. Many research initiatives over the last few decades have had service as their aim. This chapter builds off these ideas and calls for service to be embedded into the DNA of faculty research and made completely explicit. I also argue for a new facet of the research for service strand, which I have dubbed intellectual service or research for meaning. Intellectual service entails a view of service that is not as centered on the physical and tangible attributes of service (such as partnerships or helping underserved populations, for instance), but rather service as ideas. The overriding question of the intellectual service strand is how can ideas serve humanity and give meaning to human endeavors, and not just now but for posterity as well.

As with any typology, the one above is by no means exhaustive or complete. In many cases, individuals and institutions will pursue simultaneous strands. While an understanding of historical events and ideas is important in the understanding of research in American higher education, this typology is not meant to be a chronology, as many of the research strands overlapped in the past and continue to overlap. The typology is intended to be a loose guide situated within a historical context to better understand some of the different conceptions of academic research. Another important aspect to be cognizant of is that "research" is a large term. Here, I aim to include all types of research, from the sciences, social sciences, and humanities, as well as from different professional fields, but there are variations between different disciplines.

Research for Knowledge

Research represents a core component of American college faculty responsibility. This was not always the case, however. As is well known, German thought heavily influenced higher education in the United States in the beginning of the nineteenth century (Boyer 2015; Veysey 1965). Of course, as Turner and Bernard (2000) point out, American universities did not adopt a German template and apply it wholesale to American universities; it was adapted for the American context. Different advocates in America picked and chose what they wanted from German higher education (Turner and Bernard 2000; Veysey 1965). At the same time that the German influence was beginning to take hold, other influences were affecting American higher education, such as the utilitarian influence and the liberal arts influence; as such, the German influence was filtered through these conceptions (Turner and Bernard 2000). Nevertheless, the nineteenth century does represent a sort of seismic shift regarding the conception of higher education, and the German influence was decisive in many ways (Geiger 2000; Veysey 1965).

One of the main tenets of German higher education was the idea that knowledge should be pursued not for practical ends but simply for knowledge itself (Veysey 1965). During the 1860s and 1870s, many American academics visited German institutions and brought back their ideas with them. However, as Veysey (1965) points out, the reality and the perception of German higher education were not always in line. Veysey (1965) specifically points out that many Americans, in their zeal for all things German, neglected the more spiritual components of German education and research and rather saw Germans squarely focused on empirical and scientific research (which simply wasn't the case). Nevertheless, the ideals of the German university left an indelible mark on the trajectory of American higher education in one way or another (Geiger 2000; Veysey 1965). And the most dramatic German influence was the pursuit of knowledge for its own sake (Veysey 1965). Boyer (2015) argued that the initial focus of colonial colleges was on teaching. By the nineteenth century, many colleges had incorporated service as part of their mission (for example, land grants). Finally, by the twentieth century, research had become prominent (Boyer 2015).

There was also some question as to what constituted scientific research, however (Veysey 1965). Some saw only the natural sciences as scientific, but many in higher education included natural sciences, social sciences, and the humanities. As Veysey (1965) notes, all disciplines could incorporate research. Geiger (2016:21) similarly notes that while "research universities are most readily measured by science indicators," all disciplines, including the social sciences and humanities, were included in this new "academic revolution." Geiger (2016:21) goes on to point out that "more Americans studied humanities and social sciences at German Universities than natural sciences." Whatever the discipline, this vision of research was not impacted by practical demands or the wider concerns of society (Veysey 1965). The German model perpetuated the vision of academics in the ivory tower, pursuing research for its own sake and rarely engaging with the wider society. Academics and their research were supposed to be above politics as well as the daily concerns of the polity, and they were supposed to enjoy freedom to pursue these aims (Veysey 1965).

This vision of pure research aligns closely with Boyer's (2015) notion of scholarship for discovery. Boyer (2015:69) argues that "no tenets in the academy are held in higher regard than the commitment to knowledge for its own sake." Further, as Boyer (2015) notes, this type of scholarship requires the freedom to undertake it. Bok (2015:342) stated that pure research "was said to be inspired by the desire of investigators to find new knowledge without regard for practical use." The knowledge obtained in this way was to become a collection to draw on to solve social ills; this more practical use of knowledge was termed applied research. By the Second World War and throughout the Cold War, research became an important part of US policy making (Bok 2015). The notion of basic research was promoted largely by Vannevar Bush. As Ramaley (2006) notes, Bush argued that basic research should come before applied research, that basic research was research unencumbered by practical or commercial demands (and teaching), and that this was the primary responsibility of universities, whereas more practical research was the responsibility of industry and government laboratories (Ramaley 2006; Slaughter and Rhoades 2004).

Slaughter and Rhoades (2004) argued that by the 1990s, many began to question the viability of Bush's model, which posits basic research prior to applied research. Many began to call for a more complex understanding of research, where "entrepreneurial science was privileged" (Slaughter and Rhoades 2004:49). Bok (2015) similarly argues that the distinction between pure and applied research has become fuzzy for a number of reasons, due in part to government and industry influences and suggestions of topics to research, interdisciplinary research, as well as the desire by many scholars to put their scholarship to use solving social issues.

Nevertheless, the strand of pure learning is very much alive. As Saltmarsh (2016:50) argues, and following Lynton, by the twentieth century basic research exercised a "reign of tyranny" over the university. As Basken (2016) notes, there is still a reluctance on the part of many researchers to be involved in politics or social causes. This sentiment echoes the perceived German ideal of research. Whatever its origin, research was to remain pure. So, while frayed and fuzzy, the research for knowledge conception still impacts higher education in a variety of disciplines.

Research for Prestige and Promotion

As research universities began to grow in the United States throughout the twentieth century, and scholars from all different disciplines began to pursue research, research in some ways became business as usual. This leads to another strand of research, a much less flattering one, research for prestige and promotion. Pusser and Marginson (2013) argue that research productivity of faculty is measured in some way by all prominent higher education ranking systems. Research and citations generate prestige, and those faculty members who can publish in prestigious journals and garner citations bring prestige to the university. Faculty members, especially at but not limited to research universities, must then constantly publish. The publication bar is consistently raised, and the amount of research multiplies.

In a scathing examination of current faculty research trends, Farnsworth (2007) argued that that majority of academic journals emerged so faculty could publish in them. Essentially, academic journals and other publishing outlets exist not for the sake of advancing knowledge but for academics to gain promotion. Terosky and Gonzales (2016a), in their study of faculty research production, noted how many faculty members they interviewed argued that researchers in large research-intensive institutions could not follow their true desires in research. Rather, the participants argued that these faculty members largely neglected their own desires and passions in research so they could increase their publication numbers. In addition, Gonzales and Terosky (2016) also note that all publications are not the same. Journal type and whether publications are viewed as too radical or activist can also affect how research is viewed (Gonzales and Terosky 2016). The top-tier research journals usually garner the most attention (especially during hiring time), whereas many other solid but less prestigious publications may not generate the same type of attention from hiring committees. Ward (2012) explains that since journals are quantifiable through rankings, the most prestigious journals are usually prized over books and lesser-known journals. Publications in top journals also bring the university prestige and increase rankings in a number of ranking systems (Pusser and Marginson 2013). Yet little attention is actually paid to the potential impact of the scholarship. In this view, research is no longer about the lofty ideal of advancing knowledge for knowledge sake but for faculty to advance themselves. The growing corpus of research and knowledge becomes businesses as usual for higher education.

When research becomes a vehicle of prestige and promotion, it tends to foster a publish-or-perish mentality (Bok 2015; Miller, Taylor, and Bedeian 2011). In this climate, the quantity of publications reigns supreme over quality

(Bok 2015; Glassick, Huber, and Maeroff 1997). Miller and colleagues (2011) note that the publish-or-perish mentality can lead to research that is devoid of significance and meaning. Bok (2015) argues that the vast majority of articles that are published are never cited. He goes on to examine some lamentable statistics: citing Cheney (1991) and Hamilton (1991), Bok noted that roughly 75 percent of articles in the social sciences are never citied and that a whopping 98 percent of all published articles in the humanities have never been cited. Hamilton (1991) further notes that over 72 percent of articles in engineering were not cited, while almost 56 percent of articles in mathematics were not cited. Only a small number of articles are actually cited, which means that most articles sit idly in journals and do not advance knowledge. Following Cole and Cole (1972), Bok notes how most citations in the sciences come from a small cadre of scholars, whereas the vast majority of scholars are not cited. Thus, only a small group of scholars in the sciences advances the progress of science (Bok 2015).

Bok (2015) examined relevant studies and surveys over the last few decades and noted how the pressure to publish has increased dramatically in many institutions. O'Meara and Terosky (2010) also argue how, over the last two decades, faculty have had to deal with ever-growing publication requirements. Articles are churned out so faculty can be promoted, but as Bok and Farnworth point out, the research is usually not of high quality or relevant. Bok (2015) did, however, echo an argument made by those who defend the proliferation of research. No one can foretell what articles will become valuable beforehand; thus, a large stock of articles is important to widen the pool of possibilities. However, as he then states, how much is too much? What Bok (2015) does note is that increased research demands may leave less time for teaching, but not impact teaching effectiveness in a negative manner. The staggering amount of uncited research, the focus on quantity over quality, and the seemingly ubiquitous research ideal have prompted many to decry the research game. Boyer (2015:65) similarly noted that research norms have "created a shadow" over the university.

Giroux (2014b) recounts how in the discipline of English, many times doctoral students are encouraged to take on projects and dissertations that will not offend anyone or disrupt the status quo. He noted how these dissertations are filled with jargon and simply reiterate whatever theorist happens to be in vogue at the moment. Darder (2016) similarly notes that research and the tenure process act as a means to dampen the ability of young professors to question the elites and produce knowledge that can truly influence society. Terosky and Gonzales (2016a) concluded that when research is not a forced requirement, the faculty members in their study pursued research interests closer to their heart; they pursued their research with vigor and passion. Even a casual glance at many of the leading journals in my discipline yield a number of methodologically sound but ultimately irrelevant studies. While this is purely my subjective opinion, there seem to be many articles that simply do not tell us anything worthwhile; rather, the authors explain some arcane or pedantic point.

In the widest sense, following all of the above ideas, the act of requiring research may actually undermine its power and ability to challenge and question. This is not to say that the research is worthless; even a safe article or dissertation may tell us something that can be used or cited later. Nevertheless, these criticisms of research going nowhere and telling us nothing are important. The publish-or-perish mentality, especially at large research institutions, is alive and well, and many times it does encourage quantity over quality. However, at many institutions there is little or no pressure to publish. Smaller public institutions and liberal arts colleges usually do not have this intense pressure to publish (Brown 2008). Yet the publish-or-perish mentality still affects many institutions in a variety of ways, even institutions that are not considered research institutions or smaller research institutions (Bok 2015; Boyer 2015). Many research-minded administrators who have pushed for this research ideal in universities where research was not prominent usually believe that research can attract grants, prestige, and rankings (Bok 2015).

A very real limitation of the research for prestige and promotion ideal is that this type of research can limit truly beneficial research that has the ability to benefit society in a myriad of ways. Nelson, London, and Strobel (2015), following a number of authors, argue that the publish-or-perish mentality can deter faculty from involvement with applied research and community issues. Nelson and colleagues (2015:25) argue that the "incentive structure of research universities that prizes peer-reviewed academic publications" presents a very real barrier for faculty who wish to engage in research partnerships with communities and pursue community engagement.

In the widest sense, when research is valued for prestige and promotion, there tends to be a disregard for the actual impact of that scholarship. The ability of scholarship to help solve problems or make life better is neglected, and research publications become an end in themselves, and not the means to a better society or to advance knowledge.

Research for Revenue and Profit

The next strand of research is that of research for revenue and profit. After the 1960s, many conservatives sought to rebut the growing radicalism of higher education by casting higher education as a market endeavor (Newfield 2008). Newfield (2008:10) argues that by the 1980s, the traditional mission and purpose of public universities, that of promoting "broad cultural and human development," had been adversely impacted by the dictates of the market because universities were increasingly beholden to outside funding and influence. Newfield (2008) highlights certain questions that arose as university missions began to shift toward a more market vision. The main question is what would happen to the university in regard to its traditional research pursuits for basic knowledge and making the world a better place since these pursuits cannot be commercialized (Newfield 2008). Giroux (2014a) similarly argues that universities have become accomplices to this corporate regime in a number of ways, specifically by giving less and less support for research that does not bring in revenue.

Slaughter and Rhoades (2004) articulated the theory of academic capitalism, which they argued emerged by the 1980s. Essentially, academic capitalism tries to explain the relationship of higher education institutions to the emerging global economy and information society, as well as to governments (Slaughter and Rhoades 2004). As universities continually lose state funding, research becomes an increasingly attractive revenue stream. In 1980, the Bayh-Dole Act passed, which allowed universities to retain the profits made from research that was federally funded (Slaughter and Rhoades 2004). This act provided an opportunity for universities wishing to profit from federally funded research. Slaughter and Rhoades (2004) note that academic capitalism, and specifically the notion that research can be used to garner private funding, has fundamentally affected higher education. Universities and the actors in them, however, are not passive or unwilling entities who simply pursue funding, but rather are active partners in a complex system and network of actors (Levin and Aliyeva, 2015; Slaughter and Rhoades 2004).

As Bok (2015) and Ward (2012) note, higher education institutions have been brought closer to industry and the private sector in a variety of ways, such as by acting as consultants to business, licensing activities, and seeking corporate funding and sponsorship. Further, many times professors create their own companies that universities can then have equity in and which serve as opportunities for venture capitalists (Bok 2015; Ward 2012). Moreover, Ward (2012) argues that patenting has now become part of the tenure process at some institutions. Of course, Ward (2012) points out that federal grants and support are still the main source of funding for scientific research, yet even federal grants are geared toward projects that are more practical.

Yet as Slaughter and Rhoades (2004) also argue, academic capitalism, while becoming prominent, has not totally subsumed the older vision of the university as an organ of the public good; these visions exist alongside each other and interact. Slaughter and Rhoades (2004) also caution that they do not seek to return to some mythical past golden age of higher education. They point out that not even a century ago, colleges only really served the interests of white men, and females and African Americans were marginalized. They further note that much of the activity of higher education research was focused on weapon building and defense and was intimately tied to the

Cold War. Nevertheless, in the current state of academic capitalism, research is largely seen as a method to generate revenue. Bok (2015) argues that many of the fears regarding commercialization—namely, that the emphasis on profitability would shift resources from basic to applied research—have not materialized. However, Bok (2015) does note that commercialization may undermine the traditional pursuit of free and open science, as well as the trust in science due to financial conflicts of interests between scientists and corporations. Further, Bok (2015), citing Thursby and Thursby (2007), notes how despite the National Research Council's declaration that universities should use their partnerships with industry to foster the public good and foster scientific knowledge for the public good, most technology transfer administrators confessed that the main desire is to increase profit and revenue. In addition, Peters and Giroux (2014:193) also note that universities and business are forming closer alliances and that research has turned "entrepreneurial."

Levin and Aliyeva (2015) sought to investigate how neoliberalism and academic capitalism have affected the behavior of faculty. They concluded that neoliberalism does affect faculty behavior and research activity in subtle ways. Levin and Aliyeva (2015:548) argue, "At UC [University of California], the primary role of full-time faculty is both oriented toward and articulated as research. In turn, research provides the production of knowledge, which is in demand in the economic marketplace."

Basken (2016) notes how the push for profitable and patentable research has impacted university research. He recounts how certain research is funded and more highly valued because of its potential for profit. He argues that what is funded is what is usually immediately profitable. Basken (2016:3) sums it up: "cash-strapped universities, bolstered by sympathetic government policies and public and private grant programs, are working hard to develop ways of monetizing their research."

The above analysis points to a growing movement to view research in terms of profit and monetary terms. Alongside of research for knowledge, research for promotion and prestige, and research for profit and revenue is another strand, research for service.

Research for Service

The research for service strand posits that research is a type of service to humanity that faculty are in a unique position to undertake. Faculty can be servant leaders through their research, or *servant researchers*. The notion of using research for service is by no means original to this book. While the term "servant leadership" is not used directly, the last twenty-five years have seen an emerging conversation that aims to recast research and connect it more fully to practice and use it to help society and teaching, inaugurated largely by the work of Ernest Boyer (Moser and Ream 2015). As Veysey (1965) notes, conceptions of applied science, where research was made practical and useable to society, had begun developing in the nineteenth century. Later, the Progressive era gave a tremendous boost to applied science, and many scientists endeavored to demonstrate how their research could be applied in society (Veysey 1965).

By the 1990s, Ernest Boyer and Ernest Lynton, among others, had helped to reframe the idea and purpose of scholarship (Saltmarsh 2016). As Saltmarsh (2016) noted, Lynton (1996) argued that knowledge should help to improve the community; faculty must use their disciplinary expertise to tackle increasingly complex social challenges. Further, Lynton (1994) argued that the knowledge should not only move from university to community, but rather a two-way communication should be established (Saltmarsh 2016). Saltmarsh, drawing on Lynton, argued the "tyranny" of basic research was evidenced by the linear conception that knowledge only flowed one way, from the university to the community (Saltmarsh 2016:48). Lynton (1994) called for a much more dynamic and fluid vision of knowledge, where it was the purview of many parties (Saltmarsh 2016). Lynton (1994:11) saw knowledge as an "ecosystem," moving in a number of directions and feedback loops and connected in various ways. Essentially, the university was to be only one point in a bigger knowledge-producing web. Boyer (1996, 2015) proposed four different types of scholarship: the scholarship of discovery, the scholarship of integration, the scholarship of teaching and learning, and the scholarship of application—all of which, as Lynton (1994) pointed out, overlap and mesh in the abovementioned ecosystem. The scholarship of discovery was the quintessential task of universities; it was the creation of knowledge (Boyer 1996, 2015). Regarding the scholarship of integration, Boyer (1996:17) argued that there was "an urgent need to place discoveries in a larger context." The next type of scholarship was the scholarship of teaching or the scholarship of sharing knowledge (Boyer 1996, 2015). Here, Boyer (1996:17) argued how scholarship is a "communal act"; it must be communicated to wider audiences and specifically to students. Application entailed utilizing the knowledge gained from research to improve society (Boyer 1996, 2015). Boyer's vision of application was expansive; it did not simply entail a technical or utilitarian application of knowledge. Boyer (1996:18) argued that "by making knowledge useful, we mean everything from building better bridges to building better lives, which involves not only the professional schools, but the arts and sciences as well." I expand on this sentiment shortly and reframe it in light of servant leadership.

Boyer's vision of scholarship sparked a discussion about the value and uses of university research (Beach 2015; Huber 2015; Moser and Ream 2015; O'Meara 2015; Saltmarsh 2016). Boyer saw an important function of research as linking with the community and students. This is the essence of the research for service ideal. More recently, St. John (2013:xv) has called for research that "generates actionable knowledge that informs efforts to equalize opportunity for and improve the quality of educational and life opportunities, especially for those underrepresented among college graduates and practitioners across professions." Similarly, Denzin and Giardina (2009:13) sound a call for qualitative research to impact society in tangible ways when they write, "we seek forms of qualitative inquiry that make a difference in everyday lives by promoting human dignity and social justice." They note how qualitative research can expose injustice and critique injustice in society.

Nelson and colleagues (2015) examined a successful partnership between university researchers and community members that in many ways aligns with the research for service ideal. Of course, as noted earlier, Nelson and colleagues (2015) also argue that the publish-or-perish mentality can deter these types of partnerships. Nevertheless, echoing the title of their article, they call for "reinventing the role of the university researcher." One specific way to do this was not to approach community members with "a set research agenda that addressed knowledge gaps in the academic literature," but listening to community members (Nelson et al. 2015:21). Nelson and colleagues (2015) concluded that successful community partnerships entail fruitful dialogue and, above all, trust. The ideas of listening, dialogue, and trust all align with servant leadership (Greenleaf 2002; Spears 1995; Wheeler 2012). To truly serve people (or, in this case, communities), academic researchers must listen to the needs, problems, and desires of the community and not impose ideas on them. Researchers must engage in a dialogue with community officials as well. Terosky and Gonzales (2016a) also found that some researchers in their study saw immense value in working on issues in the community by applying their research expertise.

The research for service strand follows the above thinkers in calling for research to serve society in a variety of ways. Some universities are beginning to embrace what I have termed the research for service ideal. The University of South Florida (2017) has a research initiative called Research that Matters (RtM). Its website states: "We seek to support and spotlight academically rigorous research that addresses the causes and consequences of real world problems, that seeks solutions to these problems, and that is carried out in partnerships with community stakeholders." Lehigh University has a similar research initiative. The above examples all demonstrate how research can be utilized for service to humanity.

As noted earlier, Boyer (1996) called for applied research to have a broad and in some ways existential impact on society. I expand on this below.

Research for Intellectual Service/Research for Meaning

Many of Greenleaf's (1998) ideas also can help to reframe research as service. Greenleaf (1998:69) argued: "A requirement of maturity is that one *learns to find his own significance*, even under circumstances in which powerful forces may seem to operate to deny it." This quote can easily extend to what I call the research for intellectual service or research for meaning strand. Research can serve humanity by being a vehicle to help students, faculty, and citizens find and create meaning. However, Greenleaf (1998:70) further argued that "so often, too, significance is blocked by compulsive drives for goals that do not provide fulfillment." This thought is telling and sheds light on research. What if the academic community is seeking fulfillment in the wrong thing, such as promotion and profit? Again, I do not argue to dispense with these ideas totally, but to make service (and service defined in a complex and encompassing way) central to research. Research must be tied to significance, and not just significance in a utilitarian sense but also in a much more existential and social sense.

The focus of the research for intellectual service strand is not simply on using research to effect social change. This is one component of the research for service strand, and the more practical component. The other component entails a more intellectual focus. As noted earlier, Boyer (1996) called not just for professional schools to improve our lives but also for the arts and sciences as well. This is a powerful idea, and one that can be reframed in terms of servant leadership. Following Boyer (1996) and the above sentiment, service should also consist of intellectual service, a service through ideas. Here, I must note that I am not advocating to value traditionally esoteric and abstract ideas for how well they can promote more practical endeavors such as businesses and workforce training (Jay and Graff 2012; Kleinman 2016). In a society that is dominated largely by profit and consumption, only ideas that materialize into profit are deemed useful, but this may miss the point. Ideas, thoughts, insights, and interpretation of all sorts are powerful; they cultivate awareness, criticism, and creation. As Evans and Giroux (2014:101) argue, "ideas are not empty gestures, and they do more than express a free-floating idealism." Rather, as Evans and Giroux (2014) go on to argue, ideas (as well as technology and public spaces that make them possible) are crucial because they help people to think in new ways and give people the fortitude needed to change.

Following Evans and Giroux (2014), ideas can act as a starting point for new discussions and creations. As noted earlier, Weiner (2007) argued that there was a crisis in imagination; this may hold for faculty and their research as well. Researchers, even and especially researchers who pursue more intellectual and esoteric research, may now have an obligation to use their research to help remedy these threats and to envision new possibilities. This is how all faculty research, especially humanistic and esoteric research, can service humanity. In the information age, access to and understanding of information is now a necessity for citizenship (Drew et al. 2010; Letizia 2017a). Following this sentiment, academic research is integral to democracy; it becomes knowledge that citizens must utilize as they participate in the Republic. Research is integral to democracy. All research must be brought into the fold, not just research that is believed to drive the economy.

Yet I add another facet to democracy, that of meaning. Nash and Murray (2010) describe meaning simply as the reason one gets out of bed; it is what drives a person. Nash and Jang (2013:2) argue that students "need strong background beliefs and ideals to shore them up during these times when religious and political wars plague entire societies; when the natural environment continues to deteriorate; when the fluctuations of the global economy results in recession, inflation, and in the inequitable distribution of scarce resources." It is no exaggeration to state that we live in volatile times. Following Nash and Jang (2013), the ideas of meaning can be an anchor in this volatility. Nash and Jang (2013:3) further note that "we have found that no matter the age, stage, wage, or any other difference, all of our students have a need to make meaning of their lives." While Nash and Jang (2013) work primarily with students aged eighteen to thirty-five, this desire for meaning is present for almost everyone, especially in the volatile times in which we find ourselves. Zohar and Marshall (2000) argue that individuals seek meaning and want to be part of something larger. People crave spirituality and wholeness (Zohar and Marshall 2000). This also follows Sendjaya and colleagues' (2008) call for servant leaders to help create and foster meaning.

Nash and Murray (2010) demonstrate how much of their students' meaning making is done in concert with other individuals and society as a whole. For instance, relationships and civic pursuits are integral for meaning making. Nash and Murray (2010) go on to note that meaning making is important for the sustainment of humankind. Nash and Jang (2015) further argue that service to others is intimately tied to meaning-making. Extending these sentiments to research, the meaning that research can promote must be considered in a larger social context and not as simply an individualistic endeavor. Faculty must start grasping the questions of meaning that face society and use their research to begin to answer those questions—and pose new questions. This can be a deep type of existential service to society at large.

Perhaps the most important aspect of the research for intellectual service facet is posterity. Research can be viewed as an evolving foundation upon which the future can be built. Historically, research has helped humanity evolve; it has helped us build physical things, understand the universe, and create legal systems and a host of other innovations. Of course, most of humankind's achievements have taken place outside the university (here, think of our humble beginning creating tools and mastering fire), but as humanity has progressed, the university has played an increasingly important and now indispensable role. The collection of human knowledge in a general sense has set humanity apart as a species. Faculty research can be recast as building blocks in this awesome process of human knowledge creation, and, in a wider sense, connecting our past to our future. Research is a link and a bridge to something better. Following this sentiment, the question is not only how can research be of service to society, but perhaps most crucially, what does this research leave behind for posterity? Borrowing from the research as knowledge strand, if research is seen as ever expanding, and as an attempt to create more knowledge for humanity, the most important question to ask, then, is what contribution does my research leave behind? How can my research be used by later generations? What meaning or purpose does my research have? Every piece of research, no matter how seemingly inconsequential, is a stepping stone, a notch, in the evolving construction of the universe. What if there is no inherent purpose to human life? Research can help to make life purposeful. Humanity, both in the present and in the future, can use research to help build meaning. The research itself can help to create meaning, but all types of research are meaningful because they can give a purpose to human endeavors and human existence. The research produced is a piece of knowledge that was not around before the researcher created it. It can point in a direction for humanity, and specifically later generations, to follow and to create meaning with. This is the ultimate vision of research for intellectual service. Researchers may not even be aware that their research has this awesome potential; it may take others to point it out.

Faculty can reframe and assess their own ideas before, during, and after the research process with some simple questions:

In what ways can my research, my ideas, and my insights serve humanity?
What does or can my research leave behind for posterity?
How can my research become information for citizens to use in a democracy?
How can my research help citizens to communicate?
What new insights can I create?
What conversations can I start with my research?
How can research help people find significance in their personal lives?
How can my research help society create meaning collectively?
How can my research be used by posterity to create new ideas and new meanings?
Which injustice can I expose?
Who may I anger or attract as an enemy? Is there anyone or anything I should anger or disrupt and why?

These types of questions can perhaps guide researchers in new ways, ways that at least get them thinking about the larger purpose of their research. Institutional type also may play a role here. Researchers at large research-intensive institutions may not have the luxury of entertaining these types of questions, mainly because they must abide by research for prestige and promotion and research for revenue and profit norms. Yet researchers in other institutions, such as smaller public institutions, teaching institutions, and even liberal arts and religious institutions, may have more freedom to experiment and truly create revolutionary research (Gonzales and Terosky 2016; Terosky and Gonzales 2016a).

The research for the intellectual service ideal aligns with a number of notions put forth in servant leadership literature, specifically those of stewardship and creating value. Wheeler (2012:127) writes: "In servant leadership, the stewardship focus is on service over self-interest and a commitment to the long term, which makes a difference to future generations. It's holding something important in hand for those yet to come." Wheeler (2012) argues that units and departments on campus should highlight how their research, especially the more abstract research of the physical and social sciences, benefits society, even if, and especially if, those contributions are not as readily apparent to a world that desires immediate payoff. (Wheeler's ideas of stewardship will be taken up in the chapter on accountability as well.) Following these ideas, how can research help later generations to be good stewards of society and leave a legacy for society? The notions of stewardship and value are at the heart of the research for intellectual service strand and seeing research as a type of intellectual service to humanity that creates meaning for later generations.

These considerations are by no means exhaustive. They may not apply to some or most researchers. However, they may lay some foundation, or at least help to start a conversation. What exactly is the value of research, and, specifically, more abstract and esoteric research? Here, there could even be a blending between research for knowledge and service. How does abstract research become useful for humanity? Researchers could work not only on research but also on showing how their research can be recast as a vital stepping-stone to meaning. These questions can help direct researchers to pursue research with intellectual service in mind.

Next Steps

The next consideration is actually making research have an impact. Many university tenure and promotion systems are based largely on quantity of publications and not what impact research has on society or the state of knowledge (Basken 2016; Bok 2015; Nelson et al. 2015; Terosky and Gonzales 2016). Terosky and Gonzales (2016b:106) note that "basic or traditional research publications continued to be rewarded and prioritized." Gonzales and Terosky (2016) argue that research is one of the main levers of legitimacy in the academy; research is how faculty are judged.

However, as Basken (2016) notes, it may change with age, especially as younger professors fill the ranks. The *Chronicle of Higher Education* posed the following question to a number of experts: "What can universities, governments, journals, and private funders of research do to ensure they are making the greatest possible efforts toward solving society's most pressing issues?" (Basken 2016:10). Some suggestions entailed being cognizant of and prioritizing "long-term preventative strategies over short-term cures," which the experts saw as the main responsibility of political leaders and foundations (Basken 2016:10). Other answers dealt with revisiting journal formats. Specifically, a suggestion was made to create a new section in journals, one for application. Another suggestion called for universities to create "centers for responsible innovation" that help to foster recognition of the "social value of research." To promote servant research, the journal section idea could be expanded to include not just application but, where applicable, existential meaning. New journals could also be started for this purpose as well. In addition, centers for meaningful research could be created on campus. This last recommendation also aligns somewhat with Nash and Jang's (2013) call to create meaning-making centers on campus. However, those are focused more on pedagogy, where what I am proposing is more focused on faculty research.

Gonzales and Terosky (2016) also point out some ways that research norms can be changed. These different methods include rethinking hiring practices by having committees consider applicants from different institutions besides traditional research universities. Gonzales and Terosky (2016) argue that this consideration can help to recognize different types of scholars and ideas. Another method deals with scholarly conferences. Conference planners can try to include a diverse array of scholars in the conference planning process (Gonzales and Terosky 2016). In addition, Terosky and Gonzales (2016a) also argue that much of this socialization regarding research norms starts in graduate school (Eddy and Hart 2011). Professors inculcate these research ideals to their students. As such, Terosky and Gonzales (2016a) argue that professors and advisers should also start preparing their students to work in a variety of institutions and not hold up research-intensive universities and the research model, which prizes quantity or publication in top-tier journals, as the gold standard (see also Brown, 2008). Terosky and Gonzales (2016a:264) argue that their participants realized that there were "multiple ways to be a 'legitimate' academic and scholar at multiple types of institutions." This sentiment can help pave the way for promoting the notion of intellectual service. If there is a concerted call to recognize new ways to look at research, new visions of research may begin to take hold.

Hutner and Mohamed (2016) argue that we may be experiencing the onset of a new type of Gilded Age, which has brought upon us severe global inequality. Following this, Hutner and Mohamed (2016:16) call for public universities to respond to the emergence of this new Gilded Age by helping to promote and cultivate the "the democratic arts of the twenty-first century." This call should be extended to all universities. I contend that a necessary facet of these democratic arts for our times may now entail a promotion of meaning. In a meaningful democracy, citizens are not only focused on justice and equity, but ultimately on creating a sense of meaning together in a collective sense (Letizia 2017a). Research can provide citizens with the necessary resources to pose, answer, and pursue these types of questions.

While my vision of research for intellectual service entails all disciplines, the articulation of meaning does closely align with many of the imperatives of the humanities. Yet as Kleinman (2016:86) argues, the humanities as well as the liberal arts have come under attack "as economically irrelevant, unaffordable luxuries." It stands to reason that framing research and ideas of meaning may face similar criticism. Economic and vocational impact largely determine what is deemed useful and necessary (Kleinman 2016). Kleinman (2016) examined four governors who criticized humanities education. He argues that a proactive defense of the humanities is necessary, aimed at the polity and citizens, not simply at people inside the university. Kleinman (2016) goes on to argue that this defense should highlight how the humanities help to promote workforce development and economic growth by showing how more and more employers are calling for liberal arts majors and how liberal arts majors actually wind up, over time, earning comparable wages (sometimes higher) than more supposedly economically useful majors. While I do not disagree with this strategy totally, I think that the strand of research for intellectual service must be much more holistic and not simply look at the economic possibilities of humanities research. Giroux (2016:32) bluntly argues that "educators must go on the offensive in defending higher education as a public good." Essentially, educators must not wait to be attacked, but get out in front of it. Following Kleinman (2016) and Giroux (2016), advocates of this type of meaningful research must pursue a proactive strategy, focused on various stakeholders, and which highlights the immediate and long-term effects of intellectual service, specifically the creation of meaning for society. This is no easy task. Ward (2012) argues that these big intellectual questions are the antitheses of neoliberal research norms.

Following Kleinman, as a proactive strategy, advocates of the research for intellectual service would not be reacting to attacks, but instead helping to articulate a new narrative, a new vision of research that can help bolster democracy with a sense of meaning in this new Gilded Age. For this vision, they can draw on some of the ideas articulated above; specifically, advocates can begin to take the meanings that researchers articulate and weave these into their campus communications with students and faculty and their communications to policy makers and the general public.

Different institutional types can pursue different kinds of scholarship (Boyer 2015). My call for research as intellectual service is not aimed primarily at research universities. While all faculty who do research can consider the claims I have raised, faculty at universities that do not have research requirements or that are not as research intensive may actually be in the best position to pursue this type of research. Faculty research agendas at non-research-intensive institutions can shed light on different ways to view research (Terosky and Gonzales 2016a). Faculty who do research at other types of research institutions many times can pursue creative research topics and not have to worry about meeting a specific research quota; they can research what they are passionate about. In short, these researchers have a freedom that their counterparts in larger research universities may not have (Terosky and Gonzales 2016a). These faculty members can perhaps really pursue different types of research and in the process perhaps start a new conversation on the purposes of research. They can become servant researchers who lead society through their research. As universities foster citizenship, they can also foster this notion of meaning. Further, from a servant leadership perspective, institutions can be servant institutions in the sense that they serve society by helping that society create meaning for itself and for future generations with their research.

In a wider sense, all of strands of research I identified may be concepts in the constellation of academic research, as well as others that are yet unknown. These different concepts do not necessarily harmonize and many times may be at odds with each other, but some connectedness can be sought. Yet these connections will most likely not be without tension, and further, will mostly likely be affected by institutional types and outside contexts.

Bringing the Strands Together

I articulated four strands of research—knowledge, prestige/promotion, revenue/profit, and service—and put forth a new facet of the service strand, that of intellectual service. All strands can be weaved together and bolster each other, foregrounded by the research for intellectual service strand.

The research for service strand can help to temper the research for knowledge strand by making research more practical. Yet the research for knowledge strand simultaneously tempers the research for service strand by valuing research and knowledge itself. Thus, a simultaneous connection between the utilitarian valuing of research and research for knowledge sake can be promoted. This is how the research for knowledge and the research for service strands can strengthen each other and work to reinforce each other.

The other two stands, however, are not as easily integrated but nonetheless may still have certain useful features. While the research for prestige and promotion strand can cheapen research and turn it into "business as usual," with little inherent value, the research for prestige and promotion strand does at least make research a valued component of academic life. It can help to motivate and drive faculty to publish and pursue diverse areas of research. Again, taken to its extreme, research for prestige and promotion does cheapen the value and quality of research, but tempered with research for knowledge and research for service, the research for prestige and promotion strand can help to keep faculty engaged with research, always with an eye on quality. Boyer (2015) argues that all faculty must engage with research in some fashion.

In addition, as noted earlier, the research for service strand coupled with the research for prestige and promotion strand can help to redefine new faculty reward systems that not only promote quality publications but also promote ways in which research can serve humanity. The research for revenue and profit strand usually comes under scrutiny from within higher education, usually the more liberal and humanist camps. Yet research for revenue and profit can heighten the awareness to make research more practical. Again, under the research for revenue and profit strand, the practicality and usefulness of research are not geared toward the public good, but toward profit, and this is the major shortcoming. Nevertheless, the research for revenue and profit strand can at least heighten the potential for research to improve society in more practical ways.

Thus, all strands of research can coexist, and can strengthen and reinforce each of the positive points in each other. The research for intellectual strand can further augment this synergy, and following some of the experts' suggestions on making research more attuned to the pressing social issues, the research for intellectual service strand may be able to help reframe much of the current research. As researchers, the federal government, universities, journals, and private organizations look to the larger concerns facing society and the short- and long-term solutions to those issues, they must look not just toward the present but toward posterity, and not just in a practical or utilitarian sense but in a much more holistic and meaningful sense. What types of research and research combinations can help to create meaningful solutions? Climate change is of the utmost concern, but why save the planet? What is the point of caring for and saving the earth? What makes life worth saving? Why build better schools? Just to train students and ensure they get jobs? How can the educational system help prepare people for lives worth living? What research would contribute to these types of questions and answers? These deep questions of meaning (Nash and Murray, 2010) must be interlaced into the more practical concerns of the above problems (for example, how many degrees should the earth's temperature be lowered?). Meaning as service is not the articulation of abstract, esoteric, or radically personal meaning, but meaning related to social issues, research questions, and the ability of researchers to answer these questions. Providing these types of questions that relate to meaning, and meaning in a social and civic sense, is a type of service that researchers can promote. Indeed, this type of research can help others grow and develop. This is how researchers can be servant researchers and lead society.

Of course, the search for meaning can be downright terrifying. People may come face to face with questions of meaninglessness (Nash and Murray 2010). In promoting research for intellectual service, some of these questions will undoubtedly arise, but this should not stop researchers from pursuing and positing them. Rather, researchers should confront them honestly and boldly. Further, researchers should try to illustrate what a world without meaning may look like. Why is it important to pursue and create meaning? What is the point of all of daily actions, our research, our teaching, our good grades, our voting, if life does not have meaning? These are questions that most likely will never be answered and will garner controversy, but they can at least begin to start conversations that are desperately needed. My argument is to make research central to these questions of meaning. Further, this is not simply personal meaning. Rather, research can help citizens forge a collective sense of meaning in a variety of ways.

All who do research can ask themselves these questions. Of course, many researchers will most likely not ask themselves these questions for a number of reasons. They may not be comfortable with esoteric questions like these, and they may not see the relevance of these questions or this exercise. Some may argue their disciplines should not broach these questions. While individual researchers can ask themselves these questions, researchers can also ask these questions of other research as well. Those in the humanities and liberal arts can start to delve into questions of meaning for other types of research, such as in STEM fields with more practical applications as well as professional fields like business and nursing.

As O'Meara (2015) argues, Boyer created new ways to talk about research and reward systems. My intention is similar. Following the ideas of DePree (2002) and Dennis and Bocenera (2005), I seek to provide guiding thoughts and ideas for faculty who are undertaking research (indeed, some of these values may be aspirations, and some may be deterrents). Specifically, by considering the research for intellectual service strand, faculty can see themselves as emergent leaders of society, or servant researchers who serve society and posterity through various types of research (both traditional publications such as articles and books as well as the more progressive types of scholarship that Boyer outlines). Through their scholarly work, servant researchers can help grapple with questions of meaning, pose new questions of meaning, and, in the widest sense, help to *create* meaning and purpose for now and posterity.

Case Study

This case study was created from conversations with colleagues and my own experiences. It centers on a hypothetical promotion situation, yet illustrates many of the ideas of this chapter. A faculty member had just earned the rank of full professor. However, there were many obstacles. Some in the department did not look favorably on her research. Her research was not mainstream; it dealt with more esoteric topics that the mainstream journals did not readily publish. She had published some books with decent presses and a few articles in some well-regarded journals. Nevertheless, the department wanted her to publish in more recognizable and mainstream journals in the field. This pressure existed largely because the university sought to move up in the research rankings. As such, department heads were pressuring their faculty to publish in what were perceived to be prestigious journals to boost university rankings.

Before we extrapolate from this example, a caution is in order. No two institutions are the same. Further, no two disciplines are the same (there are even great differences across subdisciplines). A Google search of "tenure requirements at _____" (insert type of university) reveals dozens of variations. There is also variability between the same types of universities. Again, no two universities are the same. What is valued at one institution (that is, peer-reviewed journal articles) may be slightly different at other institutions (which may also value peer-reviewed books as highly) and across disciplines.

Nevertheless, this hypothetical experience is telling. This professor thought that her research was not valued because it was not mainstream; it was not what the top journals published. She believed that this research played a vital role in criticizing society and social institutions in an effort to improve them and create meaning. She thought that her research was just as important as more mainstream research that was lauded in the top journals. In some ways, she argued that the top-tier journals were predicated on nepotism and cronyism. While it is beyond the scope of this book to take up this claim, I will say, anecdotally at least, and in my small field, that some of my colleagues do hold this perception, which is telling. She sparred with her dean over journal types, acceptance rates, impact factors, and the places of publication, among other things. In the end, as noted above, she did receive full tenure, but felt resentful of the process.

I think this situation is illustrative of certain questions that this book has raised. What, exactly, constitutes good research? Who determines what is meaningful research? There is no one answer to these questions. I have argued that service and meaning should play a role, however, in answering these questions. As such, servant leadership can provide guidance in this instability. Research that serves faculty, society, and posterity can be valued and sought after. How can research truly become a vehicle of service? How exactly can it serve? Can it empower faculty, society, and posterity? Can it expose and rectify injustices? Can it provide meaning? Can it provide new questions that help society create meaning? Of course, engrained habits are hard to break, as is the hold of rankings, but some institutions may be able to buck the trend, and some already are.

Reflection Questions

1. In what other ways can research be framed using servant leadership?
2. In what other ways can research serve universities, society, and posterity?
3. In what ways may servant leadership actually hinder the understanding of university research?

4

Servant Leadership, Organizational Theory, and Strategic Planning

Organizations face unprecedented issues and problems today (Bryson 2011; DeGraaf, Tilley, and Neal 2004). This is especially true for higher education institutions. Strategic planning, while it has its pitfalls, nevertheless can help higher education institutions plan for a volatile future (Keller 1997). Further, the volatility of higher education due to funding concerns and globalization, to name a few issues, has made strategic planning crucial (Sullivan and Richardson 2011). Many higher education institutions undertake strategic planning (Mueller 2015). However, building on the literature, Sullivan and Richardson (2011) argue that higher education institutions must link the institution's strategic plan and vision with the actual day-to-day functioning of the organization.

Bryson (2011:7–8), who draws on Olsen and Eadie (1982), defines strategic planning as "a *deliberative disciplined approach to producing fundamental decisions and actions that shape and guide what an organization (or other entity) is, what it does, and why*." Olsen and Eadie (1982) further note that strategic planning deals primarily with the creation of organizational strategies in relation to its resources, opportunities, and external environment. In the widest sense, strategic planning helps organizations create value for society (Bryson 2011). Working from this premise, I argue that strategic planning may also be an excellent vehicle to integrate servant leadership; service can be an integral part of the public value these institutions produce. Moreover, even if a person will never sit on a strategic planning committee, having familiarity with the notions of strategic planning, most notably organizational mission, and vision, and how these ideas shape the basis of an institution, is of immense importance and can allow the individual to understand her or his organizational context. Further, organizational members, while they may not partake in formal strategic planning, will most likely have to make strategy, assess strengths and weakness, and evaluate strategies, even if just informally in their subunit. Therefore, the information in this chapter will be useful for a variety of roles and actions in an organization.

Spears (2004) argued that foresight was an important characteristic of servant leadership. DeGraaf and colleagues (2004) examined Spears's original ten characteristics of servant leadership as they relate to organizational life. The notions of conceptualization and foresight may be especially important for planning. DeGraaf and colleagues (2004) describe conceptualization as the ability to understand the larger picture, and foresight as the ability to create a plan to achieve that picture. They (DeGraaf, Tilley, and Neal 2004:150) stress how important these notions are for a servant leader because a major criticism of servant leaders is that they "abdicate their power and lose the opportunity to truly shape the organization by their own vision of the future." By paying attention to conceptualization and foresight, servant leaders can retain their ability to create a vision (DeGraaf, Tilley, and Neal 2004).

Likewise, Kim (2004:203) argued that foresight is not the ability to discern the future (which he notes is not possible); rather, foresight is the ability "to perceive the *significance and nature of events* before they have occurred." Kim (2004:209) outlines five ascending levels of perspective: events, patterns, systemic structures, mental models, and vision. In order to truly exercise our foresight, Kim (2004) stresses that we must not focus strictly on the day-to-day events. If we do, we only react. Rather, we must be able to see the larger patterns that ungird experience; then the "systems, structures, processes, and policies that are producing the events and patterns," which are social; next, the mental models, which are psychological or deep beliefs that we hold and that determine how we see reality; and finally, a vision of the future shared with others (Kim 2004:211). Servant leaders must operate from the higher levels (Kim 2004).

Kim (2004), following Fritz (1989), also examines how the notion of choice relates to vision and leadership. Choice allows one to connect to a vision and purpose (Kim 2004). Fritz (1989) argues that there are different types of choices. The "fundamental choice" is the foundation from which all other choices spring; it is a choice that is rooted in a "state of being" (Fritz 1989:188). As Kim (2004) notes, the fundamental choice is rooted in purpose. From this choice, other choices flow, such as choices that deal with strategies (Fritz 1989; Kim 2004). One must have a clear picture of who one is, of one's purposes, in order to know how one will act (Kim 2004). Kim (2004:220) holds that the articulation of an organization's "core values, purpose and vision" can provide stability in chaos and act a foundation for action. Moreover, Kim (2004) points out how Greenleaf charged that not exercising foresight is essentially an ethical failure because if we do not exercise foresight, those who come later will suffer. In order to serve, we must exercise foresight; we must take care of the future (Kim 2004).

As noted earlier, Sipe and Frick (2015), who also followed Spears, argued that foresight and systems thinking were pillars of servant leadership. A systems thinker "thinks and acts strategically, leads change effectively and balances the whole with the sum of its parts" (Sipe and Frick 2015:6). Sipe and Frick (2015), similar to Kim (2004), argue for different levels of perception, beginning with a foundation of beliefs, moving to culture, then to strategies, and finally to day-to-day events. While the levels are termed differently than in Kim's (2004) scheme, the idea is similar: leaders must look beyond the seemingly logical and day-to-day events toward a more holistic and systemic understanding of the reality they face. In addition, Barbuto and Wheeler's notion of persuasive mapping may relate to planning as well. Barbuto and Wheeler (2006:319) describe persuasive mapping as "mapping issues and conceptualizing greater possibilities" for organizational members. Strategic planning can be a vehicle by which new possibilities are articulated and defined, especially possibilities that organizations can use to practice servant leadership.

Spears's (2004), DeGraaf and colleagues' (2004), Kim's (2004), Sipe and Frick's (2015), and Barbuto and Wheeler's (2006) ideas point to the fact that planning and charting a future direction for the organization are essential for servant leaders. Servant leadership is not only about empowering others; in some ways, it is an act of balance between empowerment and vision (DeGraaf, Tilley, and Neal 2004). Strategic planning can offer a concrete way to achieve this leadership and vision, and, just as important, concrete methods to go about achieving it.

Strategic Planning

Bryson's approach to strategic planning is called the strategy change cycle. As Bryson (2011) notes, however, the strategy change cycle is centered predominantly on planning but also entails elements of management and implementation, which makes the entire process more feasible. He notes that strategic planning is only a tool; successful strategic planning requires the work of dedicated organizational members. Moreover, Bryson (2011) argues that leadership cannot be replaced with a strategic plan; leadership is crucial. In a wider sense, Bryson (2011) argues that strategic planning, and specifically the strategy change process, is teleological, or goal driven; there is an end purpose in sight

(Van de Ven and Poole 1995). As such, strategic planning allows organizations to achieve certain goals. These goals are not automatically achieved as a result of following the plan, however, but are won through learning, dialogue, feedback, and making choices (Bryson 2011). This focus on learning, dialogue, and feedback to achieve goals aligns well with the ideas of servant leadership.

The strategic change cycle is broken down into ten steps: initial agreement/stakeholder analysis, identification of mandates, clarification of organizational mission and values, identification of external and internal environmental considerations, identification of strategic issues, strategy formulation, strategy and plan review and adoption, description of the organization in the future (vision), implementation, and strategy and planning process reassessment (Bryson 2011:44–45). Bryson cautions the reader that while the process looks linear on paper, it rarely works this way in real life. Rather, the process is "iterative." It may not start at the first step, there may be much deliberation on certain points before decisions are rendered, and in some cases organizations may have to repeat the entire process or large sections of it due to new mandates or environmental pressures (Bryson 2011:69).

The ultimate purpose of strategic planning, and specifically Bryson's vision of the strategic change cycle, is that it is meant to aid a public organization in the creation of "public value," which Bryson describes as "producing enterprises, policies, programs, projects, services . . . that advance the public interest and the common good at a reasonable cost" (Bryson 2011:11). Following this sentiment, this chapter argues that strategic planning for educational institutions can be used not only to create public value but, more specifically, to frame this public value as service in a variety of forms. Strategic planning is now crucial to accomplish this task. Yet it may prove nearly impossible if no attention is paid to the pitfalls of representation.

In a world soaked in communications and technology, there is a question as to what represents what. Information, in the form of advertisements, think-tank reports, newspapers, and Internet news stories, to name a few, surround us. We structure our lives around this information in the assumption that it is true. Yet information is now viral; it spreads across all sectors of society. Truth can be precarious to say the least. Trying to plan in a world where information does not represent what it claims to represent is obviously a challenge. Planning to serve in such an environment is even more difficult. Following Bryson's strategic planning, each component of strategic planning is reframed in terms of service and representation. Here I draw on some of my past research that examined strategic planning in light of the crisis of representation (Letizia 2013, 2015).

Representation and Strategic Planning

The French scholar Jean Baudrillard grappled with the ideas of representation in the late twentieth century. As Poster (2001:1) argued, "Baudrillard has developed a theory to make intelligible one of the fascinating and perplexing aspects of advanced industrial society: the proliferation of communications though media." Baudrillard's ideas, while ambiguous (Poster 2001), can at least force planners to consider new and sometimes frightening aspects about the information age in which we find ourselves. Baudrillard argued that we as a society had passed into hyperreality, which is "a world of self-referential signs" (Poster 2001:6). As Baudrillard (1981/1994:6) notes, "Representation stems from the principle of the equivalence of the sign and of the real." There is no longer a correspondence between sign and real in hyperreality, there is only simulacrum, where there is "no longer a Last judgment to separate the false from the true" (Baudrillard 1981/1994:6). In hyperreality, simulacra take precedence (Poster 2001). Simulacra are not lies; rather, simulacra work by "absorbing the real" (Poster 2001:6). As such, Baudrillard (1981/1994:43) argued that we were experiencing the "death pangs of the real" and the loss of referents. Society is immersed in simulacra; they are copied and mass-produced, and they appear on television and advertising and surround us (Baudrillad 1981/1994; Hatch and Cunliffe 2013; Poster 2001). We no longer even have history with an intelligible sequence of events; now there is only a void where all sorts "events, ideologies [and] retro fashions" emerge to fill the emptiness (Baudrillard 1981/1994:44).

Hatch and Cunliffe (2013) argue that Baudrillard's notion of simulacrum can shed light on organizational theory. They cite Enron's creation of fictitious partnerships and elaborate accounting schemes as an example. They also highlight how corporations utilize elaborate images and marketing to sell their products. These things became simulacra, truth with no referent. They were taken as truth, and in some sense were truthful, but really, they did not correspond to any referents (Hatch and Cunliffe 2013). For Baudrillard (1981/1994), there were no more referents. There were only simulacra that become truth. This situation creates tremendous volatility. One cannot help but feel this volatility in almost every aspect of one's life. Information from the media, from think tanks, from advertisers bombards us. Organizations, especially higher education institutions, seem to operate in a perpetual state of flux and chaos. What is true in this state of affairs? More important, do the ideas we take to be true correspond to any stable, underlying reality?

Again, Baudrillard is highly controversial and extreme. Yet his ideas, while extreme, do help to illuminate some of the issues of representation (Kellner 2015; Poster 2001). His ideas may also be able to reframe planning, or at least problematize it and make planners aware of some of the pitfalls they may face.

The absence of truth and accurate representation is the most pressing issue. How can an organization plan for the future in this volatile environment? How do we plan when what we take to be true is in constant flux, or if there is no discernable or knowable truth? I do not think there is a definitive answer to this question. However, I believe that if planners are at least cognizant of the perpetual flux in which we find ourselves, planners may be able to create a more realistic plan. As such, a strategic plan informed by servant leadership and cognizant of the pitfalls of representation may offer higher education administrators and faculty a way to redefine their organizations as organizations that are truly dedicated to service and to the growth of students and society. In the widest sense, the plan itself may actually be able to become a truth in the void. Of course, the plan cannot become ossified or rigid; it must be a fluid truth (Letizia 2015). Nevertheless, the plan can be a foundation to build truth upon. Service, in all its forms, may be a method to forge some stability in hyperreality. Kellner (2015) notes that Baudrillard is maybe better thought of as a thinker who can challenge prevailing ideas than as one who offers concrete methods and applications. As such, I do not wish to follow Baudrillard in a rigid sense, but rather use his ideas as a loose guide.

Planning to Serve

The first step is the initial agreement or stakeholder analysis (Bryson 2011). As Bryson (2011) points out, the process must start with someone. Once the process is initiated, a stakeholder analysis must be performed. Bryson points out that this is crucial. Groups and individuals who may potentially partake in the planning process must be identified. The beginning of the planning process entails the formation of a small group that sets a course for the process. Then a larger group meets and reaches out to other potential stakeholders. One question that members in groups should decide is who should be, and who should not be, involved (Bryson 2011). Bryson (2011) notes that organizational factors will most likely dictate the size and scope of these groups. In larger organizations, for instance, the number of people involved in this process will most likely be greater, whereas this may not be the case in smaller organizations (Bryson 2011).

In this initial step, certain considerations can be given to service. For one, when initiating strategic planning, planners can consider if service is desired and germane to the organization. Next, when performing stakeholder analysis, planners can pose certain questions, such as: How should service be framed? Specifically, what types of service are on the table? Is it the service of service learning; is it more direct and practical service? On the other hand, is it a conception of service rooted more in ideas, such as the notion of intellectual service, as described in chapter 3? Is it multiple types of service or a combination?

Who is to be served? Other questions about who can actually serve within the organization and who is willing to serve should be considered as well. Another similar question is who can and is willing to help the organization serve? Further, who might oppose service? Will service be seen as paternalistic? This is a crucial question when considering stakeholders. Again, these questions may be more complex when different types of service are discussed.

Mueller (2015) notes that one of the pitfalls of strategic planning is that while the notion of organizational values is usually said to drive the plan, there is usually little agreement as to what organizational values actually are. Following this warning, if servant leadership is to become an organizational value, it must be clearly defined. Moreover, in light of the above arguments, if it is not clearly defined, it runs the risk of becoming a simulacrum.

The questions of representation will further complicate the stakeholder analysis. For one, service itself can become a simulacrum unless it is sufficiently defined and articulated among stakeholders. The potential for service to become a simulacrum can emerge if stakeholders hold simplistic views of service or if service is seen as some type of ready-made idea. Specifically, service cannot simply be equated with customer service in a business sense. The service of servant leadership is much more; it is much deeper and more complex. During the initial agreement, stakeholders should dig deep into how they want to define service (and how it can be defined in hyperreality) and how their organization is best poised to deliver what type of service. Having true deliberation about service, really penetrating what service is for an organization, can guard against it becoming a simulacrum, or a trite, hollow maxim that means nothing to organizational members.

Steps two and three of the strategy change cycle entail the articulation of the mandate and the mission, which, in a wider sense, is the public value of an organization (Bryson 2011). Simply put, mandates are what is required of an organization. There are formal mandates of policies and regulations, as well as informal mandates such as norms or expectations of voters (Bryson 2011:121). Bryson (2011) notes that many times organizational members are simply unaware of what the organization can and cannot do. As such, Bryson (2011) points out that many organizational members assume that the organization cannot do certain things when, in reality, they are not forbidden. The point of this step is for organizational members to determine what their organization is forbidden to do and what it is allowed to do, and from this, begin to articulate a course of action.

Specifically pertaining to mandate, strategic planners can consider what types of service are allowed. For instance, a Catholic college cannot serve its students or the wider public with advice or service regarding abortion. The question here is how can planners reframe service to fit formal and informal mandates? Yet many times policies that affect organizational behavior are simulacra themselves. This is especially true with educational policy. Educational policies increasingly cast higher education institutions solely as market entities without regard for their civic potential (Giroux 2016). Planners and stakeholders should understand this complexity when planning. How can we perform service to humanity and posterity in light of higher education policies that only cast higher education institutions as market entities? This no doubt complicates matters.

The third step entails understanding the organizational mission. An organizational mission articulates the purpose of an organization, why the organization exists. The mission gives organizational members meaning and purpose for doing what they do (Bryson 2011:127). Mission statements should be short, activist, and an inspiration (Bryson 2011). Bryson outlines six considerations for understanding mission and notes that articulating the answers to these questions is time consuming and can be downright grueling (Bryson 2011:138–143). These questions can be specifically tailored to planning for service.

First, organizations must ask: "*Who are we?*" This is an identity question (Bryson 2011:138). Here, it may make sense to understand service not as an action or skill, but as an identity, as intimately woven into an organization's mission. How does service reflect and drive the very existence and purpose of the organization? How can it? And of course, what type of service is being considered? This aligns with Kim's (2004) notion of choice and servant leadership. If an organization has a strong purpose and truly embodies it, the organizations' choices will reflect this purpose (Fritz 1989; Kim 2004). Thus, embedding a notion of service in the organizational mission, or making a latent service mission explicit, can truly give organizational members a source of meaning and a guide to their actions.

The second question that Bryson (2011:140) proposes is: "*What are the basic social and political needs we exist to address?*" Bryson stresses that organizations are not ends in themselves; rather, they provide the means to a stated end. Here, the end is service. Service in a variety of forms can help create public value in a variety of ways. Yet planners must always guard against promoting a vision of service that is a simulacrum. Service cannot be an abstract or vague term. Service should also not be canned in the sense that institutions adopt a ready-made idea such as customer service in a business sense. Rather, service must be tailored specifically to an organization's mission and mandates, and the notion of service should be genuine and authentic in the sense that the people promoting it believe in it and can truly articulate what they mean by it. If this cannot be done, the notion of service may simply be a simulacrum, an idea that does not truly represent anything.

I have condensed Bryson's (2011:140–141) third and fourth questions: What do we do to recognize and respond to the needs in the previous question, and how should we respond to stakeholders? For servant leadership, these questions can be reframed as how can service help the organization respond to those needs? Again, this notion of service that is promoted by the organization must not only align with mission and mandates but also be able to actually help the organization respond to needs, and be responsive to stakeholders; it cannot simply be what organizational members think will work. The needs in America and societies all over the world are pressing and great, needs that deal with acceptance, tolerance, understanding, and the just use of knowledge, to only name a few. True authentic service can help to respond to some of these needs. If service does not, if it does not help society to heal and progress, it may no longer be "true," or correspond to the actual needs of society; service would be simulacra.

The fifth question is: "*What are our philosophies, values and culture?*" (Bryson:141). Here, planners must consider whether the idea of service they are planning for is conducive to the aforementioned philosophies, values, and culture. Bryson (2011) cautions that a discussion of philosophies, values, and culture may necessitate some uncomfortable discussions regarding the organization's true and unstated public purposes. However, these discussions may also help to mitigate against simulacra because planners and organizational members must ensure that they are not pursuing ideas that do not align with the truth of their organization, the truth embedded in the deeper philosophies, values, and cultures. Alternatively, if the university or department does adhere to politically unacceptable (but unstated) philosophies, as Bryson (2011) notes some organizations do, can these be changed or at least exposed? The exposing of these problematic values can be a type of service itself.

The final question is: "*What makes us distinctive or unique?*" (Bryson 2011:142–143). Here service, defined in a specific way, can help to make an organization unique. Planners should consider exactly how their detailed notion of service makes their institution unique, or how it can make their institution unique. This is crucial. In an environment where institutions are seeking to distinguish themselves, service can help. However, service should not be a gimmick or some way to sell the university; service must be embodied and believed in.

Bryson (2011:140) notes that an institution must "actively stay in touch with the needs it is supposed to fill." He notes that institutions tend to disregard outside voices, and this can lead to a type of organizational isolation. As such, organizations must be in contact with stakeholders to ensure their mission, their existence, serves the needs they are meant to serve. There must be ongoing attention to the changing needs of the society that a higher education institution is supposed to attend to (Bryson 2011). This constant conversation and revisiting can help to ensure that the mission remains fluid and does not ossify into a simulacrum, into something that does not align with formal or most likely informal mandates or the underlying philosophies, values, and culture of an organization, as well as the wishes of stakeholders.

Eden, Ackermann, and Gallimore (2011) note that an organization's mission (or vision, discussed shortly) can be conceived as goals. They also note that goals are not singular or in a vacuum—rather, they are linked in a variety of ways—and that planners and organizational members must work through and discover these linkages. The mission or vision then "can be a summary of a goals system" (Eden, Ackermann, and Gallimore 2011:122). As such, if aspects of servant leadership are embedded into a mission (or vision), planners and organizational members must understand how different goals in the mission related to servant leadership may or may not be linked. There may exist a synergy between different goals in the mission (or vision), and planners must try to articulate them. Will servant leadership enhance another goal? Detract from it? Can servant leadership be enhanced by another goal? Or be impeded by another one? These are some questions planners may need to consider if mission (or vision) is conceived as goals.

The next step in the strategy change process entails an understanding of environmental concerns. Bryson breaks this step into two parts. The first part calls attention to the external environment that the organization finds itself in and to "the opportunities and challenges (or threats) the organization faces" (Bryson 2011:51). The second part of this step calls attention to the internal environment of the organization in an effort to enumerate the strengthens and weaknesses of the organization (Bryson 2011). Taken together, both parts of step four entail what Bryson calls a SWOC/T analysis (strengths, weaknesses, opportunities, challenges/threats). Constantly examining both environments and the internal and external factors that affect organizations can aid the organization in understanding its opportunities and challenges (Bryson 2011:52). Bryson argues that too many times organizations place too much emphasis on the negative, on the threats; instead, organizations should also begin to focus on the positive and their opportunities (Nutt 2001). Keller (1997:168) argues that higher education institutions especially must pay attention to the outside environment when planning, because higher education institutions can many times "be amazingly narcissistic" and ignore their wider environmental context and outside pressures and concerns.

When assessing their internal situation, or strengths and weaknesses, planners may ask: does service align with the organization's strengths or is service a weakness? If it is a weakness, can it be made into a strength? Is this feasible? Another key consideration of internal situations is organizational culture. Following this, planners may ask how their vision of service aligns with organizational culture. Bryson (2011) notes that culture is essential, but, following a number of authors, is largely misunderstood by organizational members. Yet culture may be crucial to truly integrating the ideas of servant leadership in the actual DNA of an organization (Rasmussen 1995).

Schein (1998:12) defines culture as "*a pattern of shared basic assumptions that the group learned as it solved its problems of external adaptation and internal integration.*" Further, culture is "*taught to new members*" (Schein 1998:12). Schein (1998:17) argues that culture exists on three levels: artifacts, espoused values, and underlying assumptions. Artifacts are "the phenomena that one sees, hears, and feels" when a person engages with a new organization (Schein 1998:17). The information conveyed from this level, however, may be difficult to understand and interpret for observers (Schein 1998). The next level, the espoused values, gets closer to the organizational culture. However, if these values are not truly engrained or learned, if they are only spoken but not believed, they do not truly convey organizational culture (Schein 1998). The final level is basic assumptions. These assumptions are taken for granted and unquestioned among organizational members; they give direction to member's actions (Schein 1998). In the widest sense, these shared assumptions give stability (Schein 1998). If planners want to embed their ideas of servant leadership in an organization, it will have to be at this level.

Yet the changing of culture is an arduous task, but if planners want to embed the ideas of servant leadership in their organizations, they need to grapple with culture change. Schein (1998), following the well-known thinker Kurt Lewin, argues for a process of unfreezing, cognitive restructuring, and refreezing to change organizational culture. As noted above, culture provides stability. Yet if leaders wish to change culture or embed the ideas of servant leadership in their organization, they need to follow Schein (1998) and disrupt organizational members' stability or equilibrium by presenting data and evidence that make organizational members question if their shared assumptions are still effective. However, this process will be full of anxiety, and Schein (1998) stresses that leaders must provide a sense of direction. In the next step of the change process, new ideas related to the core ideas of an organization are learned by organizational members, and finally, these ideas must be refrozen, which is the last step (Schein 1998). An idea is refrozen when it provides stability and lessens the anxiety of organizational members (Schein 1998).

Rasmussen (1995) illustrates how Schein's cultural framework can be used to examine and promote a servant culture in organizations. As Rasmussen found with her analysis, the leaders of the organization she analyzed were committed to servant leadership in words and actions, and this commitment help to create a servant-oriented culture. Rasmussen (1995:284–285) argues that leaders should follow Schein and employ embedding mechanisms (rewards, resource allocation, hiring, promotion) to initiate culture change and reinforcing mechanisms (rituals, myths, and stories) to continue this change. Rasmussen (1995) found that leaders in the organization she examined embedded and reinforced servant leadership in a number of ways. Overall, Rasmussen (1995:295) concluded that "the leaders' commitment to and follow-through in consistently role modeling the desired values is the single most important lever for influencing or changing an organization's culture." She noted that if leaders in organizations say one thing and do another; their espoused actions do not become embedded in the organizational culture.

Following Schein (1998) and Rasmussen (1995), planners can consider how the ideas of servant leadership can be used to disrupt shared assumptions. Is there a corporate culture that sees students primarily as a source of revenue? Can this assumption be exposed and proved faulty with the notion of servant leadership? Once this is done, how can the new ideas of servant leadership be learned? What actions should leaders take to embed servant leadership? How should leaders role model servant leadership? What policies, symbols, and rituals should they create and uphold to help reinforce servant leadership? Moreover, considering the variability of servant leadership research, which ideas from servant leadership can be used? Most important, how can the ideas of servant leadership provide stability for organizational members? Can they? Will there by negative consequences or resistance to the ideas of servant leadership?

If understood through organizational culture, servant leadership may have much more permanence and staying power than if it were simply empty slogans from leaders. This is perhaps the most crucial point. Following Schein (1998) and Rasmussen (1995), how can the desired ideas of servant leadership be frozen and embedded into an organization's culture? Can a preferred notion of service be used to disrupt organizational members and show them how their organization could be made better? Could the notion of service be connected to a new and better understanding of the organization's purpose or give psychological safety? These are questions that planners must consider if they are to use their ideas of servant leadership in their organization and, more important, if they are to make those ideas impactful.

A number of scholars have noted the relationship between servant leadership and culture. Wheeler (2012:146–147) encapsulates this notion: "Because servant leaders are committed to the long haul, they understand that cultural change is crucial to success but it will take time and commitment of those involved to be successful. There is no such thing as a painless, surgical, cultural change. Those involved quickly see what they are losing in the change process, yet it is usually unclear to them what they will gain."

Similarly, Parris and Peachey (2013), Liden and colleagues (2008), and Laub (2017) all argue that the ideas of servant leadership are related to positive institutional cultures.

Of course, not all institutional members have the power or means to lead a full-scale culture change in their organization. Nevertheless, those with less power (newer faculty members or staff, for instance) can at least begin to observe culture. They can also work on small-scale culture change. Schein (1998) and Bess and Dee (2012) note that many scholars of institutional culture call for the recognition of various subcultures. Following this idea, faculty can begin to look at different subcultures, such as the faculty subculture and the culture of their department. Faculty can begin to pose new ideas at faculty meetings or even in informal conversations with their colleagues to gauge culture and to look for ways to possibly integrate servant leadership in their subunit.

Bryson (2011:160–165) lists a number of external situations and phenomena that will impact organizations in the twenty-first century, such as growing social complexity, technological innovation, growing diversity, questions of legitimacy of organizations in the wake of widespread scandals, and environmental concerns, to name a few. Planners must consider these questions and other external situations that affect organizations. Planners may ask, how can service be used to maximize opportunities? On the other hand, how can service be used to deal with threats? In a more basic sense, how does the preferred notion of service fit in to this rapidly changing environment, and specifically how can the institution utilize service in this environment?

A SWOT/C analysis can also help organizations determine what Bryson (2011:53) calls their "critical success factors." A critical success factor is something that an "organization must do, criteria it must meet, or performance indicators it must do well against . . . for it to survive and prosper" (Bryson 2011:154). Following this, planners can help to define what Bryson (2011) and others called distinctive competencies that allow organizations to act toward the critical success factors. A competency is something than an organization can do, an ability (Bryson 2011). Bryson outlines different types of competencies: distinctive competencies are competencies that are not easy for others to perform, core competencies are integral to the organization's success, and distinctive core competencies help organizations create "more public value than alterative providers" (Bryson 2011:154).

As such, planners can reframe service as a competency of the organization. Planners may want to articulate their notion of service as a competency of their organization that can help to ameliorate threats and exploit opportunities. As a competency, service, however organizational members may define or articulate it, is something that an organization can do. Of course, servant leadership should not be seen as a task to be performed; rather, as a competency, service should be an extension of a changed understanding. This competency, however, cannot be forced. If planners try to promote a notion of service for their organization that is unrealistic or not feasible, or which does not satisfy stakeholders or the mission, that notion of service, as well-meaning as it may be, can turn into a simulacrum because it does not faithfully represent the organizational reality.

Eden and Ackermann (2011) argue that discovering core distinctive competencies can help public organizations truly understand themselves and their abilities. Of course, defining what is truly distinct can be a challenge, but this is crucial for organizational success (Eden and Ackermann 2011). Eden and Ackermann (2011) further note that core distinctive competencies usually exist in networks and bundles. A competency may not be distinctive, but coupled with other competencies, may form a distinctive bundle (Eden and Ackermann 2011). Attention must also be paid to the difference between competencies (which is the *ability* to perform a task) and a competency outcome (the result) (Bryson 2011; Eden and Ackermann 2011). As such, if serving is a competency within higher education organizations, and I would assume most higher education institutions do have service attributes, these must be understood. Planners can work to understand these ideas in their organizations and make them explicit and take advantage of the bundles of competencies they uncover (Eden and Ackermann 2011). Planners can also look to see if there are combinations of different organizational competencies that can help to promote service in pedagogy, research, planning, assessment, or other areas. As such, simplistic or cliché notions of service may become simulacra. Planners must truly dig deep and understand the organizational reality and the synergies that may exist between different types of service.

Following Kim (2004) and Sipe and Frick (2015), those who truly want an accurate picture of the internal and especially external environment should not only look at day-to-day events but also at the larger systems in which these events are situated. For instance, instead of just seeing diminished funding as a threat, leaders may need to go beyond the immediacy of diminished funding and truly understand some of the reasons for diminished funding, which are most likely ideological. Understanding at this more complex and holistic level can help servant leaders to dissect the threats and issues they face, and create more robust and sustainable visions. This reflection on deeper levels of action can help to create much more sustained responses and longer-lasting interventions. When considering these deeper levels of reflection, planners can ask, how does service fit in or buck against larger patterns that organizations find themselves embedded in? How does the preferred notion of service align with mental models that organizational members hold?

Bryson (2011) argues that the first four steps of the strategic planning process culminate in the fifth step. The fifth step, perhaps the most important step in the process, is strategic issue identification (Bryson 2011). Bryson (2011:55) defines strategic issues as such: "*Strategic issues* are fundamental policy questions or critical challenges affecting the organization's mandates, mission and values." A strategic issue should be stated with clarity and as a question, which invites a solution. There should also be multiple answers to the question so that multiple possibilities become evident (Bryson 2011:57). Moreover, the strategic issue should be understood in the context of the mission and mandates and SWOC/T analysis. Additionally, strategic planners should also be able to discuss what happens if the strategic issues are not addressed because consequences can help to drive home the gravity of the issue for organizational members (Bryson 2011).

Bryson (2011) identifies different types of strategic issues; strategic issues can be strategic or adaptive, on the one hand, or operational and technical, on the other. Many issues have both adaptive and operational elements (Bryson 2011; Heifetz, Grashow, and Linsky 2009). Technical issues have answers that are largely already present and known (Heifetz, Grashow, and Linsky 2009). Adaptive issues, on the other hand, are not solved as easily; they require transformed beliefs and an understanding of loss that comes with change (Heifetz, Grashow, and Linsky 2009). As Heifetz and colleagues (2009:19) note, "Making progress requires going beyond any authoritative expertise to mobilize discovery, shedding certain entrenched ways, tolerating losses, and generating the new capacity to thrive anew." Here, planners can examine how their preferred notion of service interacts with strategic issues. How can service ameliorate or further these issues? Can service help to deal with strategic issues and/or operational issues? This may be especially true for adaptive issues and adaptive facets of adaptive/operational issues. If adaptive issues require new ways of thinking and knowing, servant leadership can be employed in this role. Servant leaders can help their followers create new possibilities and create new ideas. Service (however an organization defines it) may not be the answer. It may not help to remedy a strategic issue, if it is made to be something it is not; it may be a simulacrum, a truth without a referent. Nevertheless, if service and servant leadership can help to remedy these strategic issues, planners can consider how and in what ways. If service can help to deal with a strategic issue, can service help to create new concepts or knowledge? Can it help to conceptualize the strategic issues? Can it help to assuage loss (or will it create more)?

It may make sense to pose service and an organization's definition of servant leadership as the organization moves into the identification of strategic issues. The identification of strategic issues can proceed in a number of ways. Bryson (2011) describes what he calls the vision approach. In the vision approach, planners proceed with a vision—not a concrete or detailed one yet, but a rough vision. After considering the mission and mandates, as well as the SWOC/T analysis, planners should articulate how "the organization should look like as it successfully meets its mandates, fulfills its mission, creates public value, and in general achieves its full potential" (Bryson 2011:201). Here, the vision can be a vision of service, and servant leadership. Bryson notes how different planners can articulate different visions, and these visions can be compared, analyzed, and ranked. The ranking system should decide how well the visions meet the mandates and mission and promote public value. Next, members should use these visions and comparisons as a starting point for discussion and deliberation to articulate a unified vision. This vision can act as a "*grand strategy*" and help an organization situate itself in the larger environmental context (Bryson 2011:203). The later strategy creation step can be a way to create more detailed strategies to help make this larger vision materialize (Bryson 2011).

Bryson (2011) does note that the visions approach may work better with nonprofit organizations than with public organizations because public organizations are usually more restricted due to the expectations of diverse stakeholders and more restricting external mandates. While this may be true, service is (or should be) inherent in higher education institutions in some form, and thus all higher education institutions, public and private (nonprofit), can work to harness and promote their visions of service in some way that aligns with the organizational mission and mandates.

The sixth and seventh steps are usually entangled. The sixth step is the creation of strategies to deal with the strategic issues, while the seventh step is the adoption of these strategies. Bryson (2011:219) argues, "Strategy therefore is the extension of an organization's mission, forming a purpose-driven (and sometimes purpose-revealing) bridge between the organization and its environment." While both steps are entangled, Bryson argues that there should be separation. Formulating strategies usually entails creativity, whereas strategy adoption usually entails bargaining politically (Bryson 2011). Strategies are created to attend to the strategic issues (Bryson 2011). Further, if organizations use the vision-centered approach described earlier, the strategies formulated are created as a means to fulfill and achieve the vision (Bryson 2011). Bryson (2011:223) outlines different types of strategies, ranging from a grand organizational strategy to strategies for subunits and individual programs.

The preferred notion of service that the planners want to promote can be formulated as a type of strategy. It is important to note the crossover between steps here. I have advocated for service to guide and inform many parts of the strategic planning process (for example, seeing it as part of the mission or as competency). Here, I argue that service should now be codified as a strategy (either a grand strategy, subunit, or program strategy). Bryson (2011) outlines questions that planners can ask when formulating strategies. (I have condensed and modified the questions.) These questions can be applied to a preferred notion of service that planners wish to promote: What are the practical visions we can pursue to address the strategic issue? What are the possible barriers? What actions can existing staff take to implement the vision or strategy? What actions should be undertaken in the following few months (Bryson 2011:235)? Again, the notion of service that an organization wants to pursue must be understood here by everyone so feasible strategies can be made.

If servant leadership is pursued as a strategy, there could be pushback. Ackermann and Eden (2011) note how strategies are disruptive: they disrupt the status quo and the way things are functioning. As Eden, Ackermann, and Page (2011:15) state, "If strategic management [implementation of strategy] does not change the way organizational members think, and so act, strategy can only have any real impact through coercion." If leaders and planners established servant leadership by means of coercion, this would negate it! Genuine negotiation and feedback must be obtained for any strategy; strategy making is a "social affair" (Eden, Ackermann, and Page 2011:14), and this may hold especially true for servant leadership. Strategies are methods of change (Ackermann and Eden 2011). Planners must be cognizant of this potential pushback.

The seventh step is the adoption of strategies. Bryson (2011:244) argues that planners must be able to take advantage of "a *window of opportunity*," which is "an occasion when action favoring change is possible." During this window, proper support can be gained. Since this stage entails bargaining and trade-offs, however, planners must consider whether a big win or incrementalism will be the best method to achieve their notions of service (Bryson 2011). However, in their political dealings and compromises, planners may not want to surrender too much in their vision of service and turn it into a simulacrum that does not align with the values or mission of the organization. During the sixth and seventh steps, the idea of service articulated by planners may start to become real and tangible. Again, as noted earlier, I have argued for this definition of service to inform many steps of the planning process, but as a strategy, service may become action. Again, since this step entails politics and bargaining, planners must ensure that their strategies are acceptable and feasible (Ackermann and Eden 2011; Bryson 2011). A research collaborator and I were once putting together a manuscript on servant leadership, and my collaborator asked me if we were being "too pie in the sky" with our proposal. I thought about this and responded that servant leadership may always entail pie-in-the-sky ideas. This pie-in-the-sky quality may prove somewhat difficult at strategy adoption step. To employ another often-used adage, the strategy adoption phase is where the rubber meets the road and the ideal must meet the practical. Therefore, planners must heed Bryson's advice and aim for feasibility, but not sacrifice what makes their idea of service unique. Indeed, this step may prove the most challenging for leaders wishing to implement service. Those wishing to practice strategic planning must also guard against what Dickeson (2010:20) terms "disconnected planning." Disconnected planning occurs when planners create grand plans but do not account for where the actual resources will be obtained to carry out the plans. Keller (1997) similarly stresses that planners in higher education must be realistic when considering initiatives and the resources needed for them. Implementing servant leadership in many cases will most likely not require massive expenditures; rather, it is more of a cultural and attitudinal phenomenon. Nevertheless, if resources are needed, planners must be cognizant of this fact to ensure that they can actually carry out what they call for in the plan.

Bryson argues that the eighth step, the formulation of vision, is optional. However, vision is integral to servant leadership (Farnsworth 2007; Kim 2004). Thus, I would argue that this step should not skipped. A vision articulates what an organization looks like when it functions well (Bryson 2011). Here, those wishing to implement servant leadership must think about what their organization will look like in the future when the ideas of servant leadership are woven into the fabric of the organization. Implementing this vision, however, may not seem likely, but that may be all the more reason to work for it. Eden and Ackermann (2011) note that visions, by themselves, do not give a plan for action. Rather, it is strategies that help to make visions materialize. The vision of service cannot be a superficial notion of service; it should be something specific to the organization lest it become simulacra. Creating feasible strategies can help to make this vision more attainable. However, a vision does not have to be a bland statement of the future.

Kouzes and Posner (1995) argue that a vision entails possibility and not probability. In short, probabilities entail evidence, whereas possibilities entail hope (Kouzes and Posner 1995). Probabilities are about what will most likely happen; possibilities are about what can happen (Kouzes and Posner 1995). Kouzes and Posner (1995:97) note that "all new ventures begin with possibility thinking, not probability thinking." Further, Kouzes and Posner (1995:100) argue, "Visions are statements of destination, of the ends of our labor; they are therefore future oriented." Visions are ideas for the future; they are blueprints for accomplishing dreams and building the future, and they eventually become real (Kouzes and Posner 1995). Yet this vision is not the sole action of a leader. Rather, as Kouzes and Posner (1995) argue, leaders must bring others into the vision; it must be a group effort to achieve this end.

Following the pie-in-the-sky warning articulated earlier, planners could seize on Kouzes and Posner's (1995) distinction between probable and possible. Will servant leadership be probable? Maybe not. However, could it be achieved through hard work and the creation of a vision to which organizational members could work toward? Perhaps. This notion of bringing others into the vision is crucial. The vision, as Kouzes and Posner suggest, cannot simply be for a few people; others must take ownership and buy in to it. This ownership may be the necessary ingredient in carrying out a possibility and making it more feasible. Promoting the notion of ownership of the vision may be a type of service in itself.

Farnsworth (2007) argues that when creating a vision rooted in servant leadership, the vision must have substance; it cannot simply be an empty, but ultimately meaningless, feel-good statement. I concur, lest the vision of servant leadership become a simulacrum. Further, Farnsworth (2007) argues that a discussion of values must ensue when servant leaders create a vision. He (Farnsworth 2007:49) goes on to note, "Without a discussion of values, there can be no discussion of purpose, of meaning, or of the reasons to be of service." This is a crucial point. Whatever the vision of service and servant leadership, it should engage with values, and ultimately meaning and purpose. In the corporate model of the university, which many universities adhere to now, it is my hope that a vision of servant leadership can reinvigorate, and recast, these long-dormant ideas.

Vision is integral to servant leadership. As such, planners must truly articulate a servant vision for their organizations if they want their organizations to be servant organizations. As noted earlier, strategies can help to bring the vision to life (Eden and Ackermann 2011). Strategies rooted in various types of service, from pedagogy to research to assessment, as well as combinations of these notions, can help to actualize a vision of servant leadership.

The final two steps of the process entail the implementation of the plan and reassessment. For the ninth step, implementation, Bryson (2011:64), following Simons (1995), argues that "implementation should include ways of building capacity for sustained implementation." Essentially, successful implementation is not a one-time deal; it must be built in to organizational practices. Further, planners must anticipate and expect difficulties, note when they occur, and try their best to account for them as implementation ensues (Bryson 2011). As such, constant evaluation is crucial (Bryson 2011). One way to evaluate the results of the plan is by outputs and outcomes. Bryson (2011:289) describes outputs as behaviors or results of changes, whereas outcomes are benefits of changes and, in a wider sense, "larger meanings" associated with outputs.

The distinction between outputs and outcomes may be useful to measure the implementation of servant leadership. For one, planners can try to assess how the behaviors and actions within the organization have changed. Depending on what type of vision of service planners implemented, planners can look to pedagogy, research, and student engagement on campus or combinations of the above. Next, planners could begin to look to larger organizational changes, or the outcomes, to assess how well their plan is working. Has the culture of the organization changed? Are there wider changes in the organization or its immediate environment that can be discerned due to the implementing of servant leadership ideas? Here, planners can look to the different notions of accountability which will be sketched out in a later chapter.

As Bryson (2011) cautions, however, that measurement must proceed with caution. Citing a number of authors, Bryson (2011) notes how many times measurements and evaluations cannot truly capture the complex effects of changes in a number of areas. Giroux (2016) argues the same in regard to student learning. Ackermann and Eden (2011) similarly argue for the need of both qualitative and quantitative measurements of performance. This holds especially true for service. Following this, how exactly can service be measured? If measured in narrow terms, service may become simulacra because the notion of service no longer corresponds with what needs to be done. For instance, the barrage of standardized testing under the No Child Left Behind act (since repealed) turned learning into a narrow test score. Service cannot be made into a score.

As for the final step, reassessment, Bryson (2011) bluntly argues that things change; stakeholders, priorities, conditions, situations all change. As Bryson (2011:317) notes: "Not all strategies continue to work as well as they should. These strategies must be bolstered with additional resources; significantly modified or succeeded by a new strategy; or else terminated." As such, the plan and its vision cannot ossify. If any solution or idea becomes permanent and immutable to change, it becomes simulacra, even a good notion like service. This insight is crucial for the entire strategic planning process. The notion of service and servant leadership that leaders wish to promote and implement cannot be out of touch with the actual conditions on the ground, with the external and internal conditions of the organization. Bryson (2011) also warns of unintended effects. If the vision of service is implemented, will it push out any other programs? Will it divert resources or cause friction? There must be a process of ongoing reflection and reassessment to ensure that this does not occur.

Following a number of authors, Sullivan and Richardson (2011:3) argue that the actual effectiveness of strategic plans in "higher education institutions have met with mixed success." Sullivan and Richardson (2011) offer some ideas to give strategic plan more staying power in higher education institutions. One way is to have frequent conversations about the ideas in the strategic plan, especially at meetings. This conversation can help to keep the ideas of the plan fresh and relevant. Another method is to build individual ownership in the plan. Sullivan and Richardson (2011) argue that if organizational members see themselves as being able to contribute to the plan, this will increase the plan's effectiveness. Those wishing to implement servant leadership and use strategic planning as a vehicle to achieve this task can pay attention to Sullivan and Richardson's (2011) recommendations. The idea of paying attention to an individual's role in the plan may also align with Sendjaya and colleagues' (2008) notion of meaningful work. Leaders can ensure that the ideas of the plan are meaningful for organizational members.

Case Study

Below is a story that was recounted to me by a colleague in K–12 education. I have altered some details, but the message will be clear. The story is illustrative of how aspects of the planning process can be viewed with skepticism and downright cynicism. The tale offers a warning—namely, strategic planning cannot be seen as a bureaucratic mandate. In her building, the administration tried to revamp the mission statement. The previous mission statement had been written much earlier, was composed of cliché language, and simply hung on the wall in a cheap plastic frame in an obscure part of the school. She remembered seeing this sad and crooked thing all the time. The principal had decided that it was time for a new statement. Therefore, he convened a committee to accomplish this task.

Yet the mission statement never was linked to their daily activities and to the daily functioning of the organization. Despite the committee and the reworking of the mission statement, it was still (and always was going to be) just a paper hung on the wall. Many teachers rolled their eyes and grumbled that this action was just another way to feign caring and involvement on the part of the administration. Further, some teachers felt the committee members did not even really care about their task. Whatever the truth of these accusations, they were still sentiments held by the teachers that colored (at least for some) the views of the planning process. My colleague never inquired further about the mission statement. Years later, the new mission statement hung on the wall like the old one.

At the same organization, all teachers had to fill out a goal sheet every year. For this process, in the beginning of the year, all teachers were required by the principal to write down specific goals that they had for the upcoming year. However, my colleague and many other teachers always felt this process was a sham. Half the time the principal would tell them what goals to write! Sometimes teachers would propose more qualitative goals, but these were usually met with ambivalence in favor or more quantifiable goals. She knew that the real goals she had for students, which were not always measurable by easy quantifiable standards, would never be entertained. Therefore, she just wrote down the goals she knew the administration wanted to hear, which always involved raising test scores at the end-of-the-year test. The entire process never seemed genuine; rather, it seemed forced. It seemed like another hoop to jump through.

Nevertheless, these planning exercises illustrate some of Bryson's warnings of how strategic planning can just be formalities. At worst, these situations show how strategic planning, if done for the wrong reasons, can breed mistrust and resentment. The administration at this school perhaps could have started to use servant leadership to reframe some aspects of the planning process. Many employees in the school were skeptical of reform efforts because they all felt they were not genuine, so truly integrating servant leadership would have been an arduous task. Nevertheless, this is what it takes and perhaps when it is needed most. More than just using servant leadership, the administration could have truly committed itself to it and embodied this change by linking planning efforts to employee, student, and organizational progress in real tangible ways. Planning should have been cast as integral, not another hoop. In the examples my colleague recounted to me, planning could be seen as simulacrum that represented nothing, save for wasted time and administrative hoops. Planning may have mollified some administrators, but it only served to garner resentment from the people it was supposed to help. Following servant leadership, planning did not empower anyone, it did not help subordinates grow, and there was no real vision to aspire to. There are some parallels between leading a strategic planning process and leading an assessment process on campus, as will be clear in chapter 5.

Conclusion

As Bryson (2011) stresses, strategic planning is not a linear process. Rather, it is iterative. He also notes that organizational members should be responsive to ideas that are not in the plan but that emerge along the way. Not all steps of the plan will be undertaken in that exact order. Planning will also vary according to the complexities of institutions and the people in them (Bryson 2011). The process that he outlines is simply a rough guide. If members of organizations try to follow the plan in lockstep, if they try to fit their organizations to the plan instead of fitting the plan to their organizations, the plan and the process itself can become simulacra because the plan and the process may no longer represent truth. Again, it should also be noted that no idea can represent the true state of affairs, as the volatility and constant change and pace of modern life make this impossible. Nevertheless, planners should be open to this change and construct their plans accordingly, especially in regard to their preferred notion of service.

This chapter has presented a method for implementing servant leadership in strategic planning. Following Kim (2004), having a vision is crucial for servant leaders. Likewise, instead of simply empowering others, having foresight and vision allows servant leaders to lead and create something (DeGraaf, Tilley, and Neal 2004). This book can be used as a resource for those visionary servant leaders. They must create a vision, but following Farnsworth, this vision cannot be superficial. Leaders can look toward pedagogy and student creation, research for meaning, or as will be discussed shortly, assessment and localized accountability, and combinations of these ideas, to create new and unique visions of servant leadership for their organizations.

Strategic planning is a constellation of sorts. As Bryson (2011) explains, there are so many factors that make up strategic planning. Further, these elements are not to be undertaken in a rigid or lockstep manner, and they will look different in different organizations. Adding servant leadership to strategic planning creates another level of complexity. Servant leadership (a constellation in itself) may be a concept in the constellation of strategic planning; this creates further interactions and complexities and contradictions in the planning process but also more opportunities to integrate servant leadership in various facets of higher education institutions. Servant leadership considerations should not be an add-on to strategic planning, but rather enmeshed and intertwined with planning, as a fundamental plank of its constellation.

Reflection Questions

1. What other models of planning may be compatible with servant leadership?
2. How might servant leadership hinder the execution of strategic planning or cloud some of the issues with which planners must deal?

5

Servant Leadership and Accountability

The concept of accountability dominates conversations in educational policy making (Zumeta and Kinne 2013). Burke (2005), following the *Webster's* dictionary definition, notes how the notion of accountability entails obligation. Burke (2005:2), following Schedler (1999), further argues that accountability can be thought of as "answerability" (Schedler 1999:14). According to Schedler (1999:14), those in power must be able to "*inform*" and "*explain*" regarding their decisions and actions. Along with answerability, there is also usually an enforcement piece to accountability as well; harmful actions are to be punished, positive ones rewarded (Schedler 1999). Schedler (1999) further notes that accountability is not simply ensuring that power is kept in check, but, in a larger sense, that it follows the ideas of the Enlightenment, which seek to ensure that power is restrained by the notions of reason and rationality. Burke (2005:2) argues that accountability creates six conditions for organizations: entities must appropriately exercise their authority, they must be working toward the stated mission, they must be transparent, they must be efficient and effective and demonstrate quality, and finally, they must "show they serve public needs." Ultimately, higher education institutions must be accountable to society, specifically to "students, businesses, governments, and social and civic organizations" (Burke 2005:3).

Following the above terminology, higher education institutions must answer to the society they serve. A large part of the notion of accountability, however, increasingly centers on how effective an institution is in training workers for the economy (Burke 2005; Dee 2006). Due to this preoccupation with the economy, Dee (2006), following Alexander (2000) and Salter and Tapper (1994), notes how many policy makers believe that higher education is too crucial to be left to the universities and academics. Zumeta and Kinne (2013) posited a similar argument. Burke (2005) notes how the demands for accountability have largely come from external parties such as legislators and business leaders who see it as crucial, whereas many in the academy see it as a type of outside interference. As noted earlier, Giroux and Peters (2014) forcibly argue that universities are now largely in line with corporate interests in many aspects of their functioning.

Dee (2006) argues that determining an acceptable balance between accountability to the state and total institutional autonomy is a challenge. On the one hand, autonomy is necessary for an institution to pursue questions of knowledge (Dee 2006; MacTaggart 1998; Newman 1987). On the other hand, calls for accountability from external audiences have increased for a number of reasons, one of which is because, as pointed out above, states want to ensure that higher education institutions are responsive to economic and workforce needs. To bridge this difference, Dee (2006) calls for an accountability system that judges universities not on achieving narrow performance criteria, but rather on how campuses promote the public good within their communities. Dee (2006) states: "The focus shifts from compliance and measurement to mutual obligations toward revitalizing neighborhoods, tackling health care disparities, improving K–12 schools, and promoting the use of sustainable resources, to name but a few examples." This statement encapsulates a true vision of accountability, of how campuses can truly answer to the publics they are supposed to serve. Questions of accountability largely pertain to public universities. Nevertheless, this fact may actually offer private universities a space to take it upon themselves to demonstrate how they are accountable to society, which could open the door for the public universities as well.

At this juncture, however, when universities find themselves being held accountable largely to economic interests to the exclusion of many other interests, the ideas of servant leadership may not seem feasible, but this may be all the more reason to pursue and institutionalize them. Following Burke (2005), if accountability is framed as answerability (Schedler 1999), as serving the public needs in an effective and transparent way, then the ideas of servant leadership, however out of vogue, may be extremely necessary due to the volatility and downright terror that many are experiencing. Zumeta (2011) argues that sometimes higher education institutions must demonstrate a special accountability to the public good by not kowtowing to policy makers and those in power. Rather, Zumeta (2011:140) argues, higher education must "educate them . . . as to what they *should* want." As Zumeta (2011:140) also notes, this will not be easy in the "current climate that emphasizes performance-based accountability and measurement," but it is necessary in a democracy. Society needs more than economic benchmarks and highly skilled workers right now; society needs empowerment, guidance, and healing. It needs servant institutions. Institutions cannot ignore the baser and more superficial accountability concerns imposed on them by the state. Rather, institutions should meet them, and go past them (Letizia, 2017b). Institutions can work to influence the wider environment instead of being subservient to it (Peterson 1997). They can do this by being examples and providing new and more profound definitions of accountability. This may be easier for private institutions that do not have the same accountability requirements.

Greenleaf (2002) saw servant leadership not just invested in the actions of individuals, but in organizations (Laub 2010). His goal was to create servant institutions. He saw higher education institutions as one of the most important and influential institutions in society. Laub (2010:106) echoed Greenleaf's call for servant institutions and issued a warning that points to the importance of organizations: "We can be strengthened and lifted up by our organizational experience, or we can be driven down, oppressed and depleted." As such, servant institutions are of the utmost importance.

Greenleaf's (2002) call for servant institutions aligns with the vision of accountability put forth by Dee and Zumeta. Universities are not merely training centers, as they are largely considered now (Giroux 2016), but servants that must answer to society in a variety of ways. If we go back to Greenleaf's (2002) initial formulation of servant leadership, where servant leaders are measured by how much their followers grow, this can help reformulate accountability with a simple question: Does society grow? Does society grow as a result of higher education institutions? Again, this must be more than a simple monetary measurement of wages (Giroux 2016). Growth of society is obviously not a neutral measure either; it will consist of values, and different groups of people with different values will view growth differently. That is okay, because those types of hard conversations, which will ensue over different values, may become a fecund foundation for growth (Sandel 2009). It may make sense to define and measure growth on a set of theoretical axes. These axes could be cognitive, economic, political, diversity/tolerance, and existential. Moreover, these axes are not discrete entities, but overlapping. Nevertheless, these axes, instead of being discrete measures, could serve as starting points for assessing deep and profound growth.

Greenleaf directs his analysis of institutional change at trustees. While the impact of trustees and leaders at the top cannot be discounted, this chapter seeks to complement this notion of top-down change with more organic changes. Greenleaf (2002) even argues something along these lines. He posits that alongside of formal top-down structures in organizations there exists an informal movement in organizations. This informal sphere allows for risk taking, creativity, and innovations that cannot be achieved within the formal framework of the organization (Greenleaf 2002). It is the informal sphere where true leadership emerges, as opposed to administration in the formal sphere, both of which are necessary (Greenleaf 2002). Therefore, while many initiatives can be undertaken by formal leaders to create a servant institution, there may be other, more organic changes that can also affect organizations.

Servant leadership is well suited to the concerns of accountability, or at least to the deeper, more profound accountability not solely concerned with economics and workforce training that I term deep accountability. One of Wheeler's (2012:127) servant leadership principles for higher education is leave a legacy to society. This principle is rooted in the idea of stewardship, which Wheeler noted is essentially a concern for posterity. The principle of stewardship can be reconceived as deep accountability.

Wheeler (2012) then discusses stewardship at an institutional, departmental, and individual level. For stewardship at the institutional level, Wheeler draws on Greenleaf's ideas of institution as servant, which were outlined above. Wheeler (2012:130) argues that "trustees and higher administrators should be asking questions that address what the needed service is to make a better society." Wheeler (2012) does note, however, that institutional rankings may complicate matters.

On the unit level, Wheeler (2012:133) argues that stewardship is visible when "the unit emphasizes contributions to society," and when "citizens become informed," among other things. For contributions to society, Wheeler (2012) specifically argues that units must highlight what they leave to society and posterity, in regard to their teaching and research or both. Citizenship formation is also at the center of unit stewardship (Wheeler 2012). At the individual level, Wheeler (2012) notes that, among other things, individuals must model citizenship. Wheeler argues that another way individuals must be stewards is by considering an ideal vision of the future and working toward it. I view accountability as something an institution does on a number of levels.

Wheeler's (2012) treatment of stewardship can help to reframe concerns of accountability. Deep accountability, similar to stewardship, is centered on truly transforming society and leaving a positive legacy. Further, this should be the ultimate goal of higher education institutions. Wheeler's tripartite division helps those in institutions pursue this deep accountably on different levels. Instead of only looking at accountability at the institutional level, or as an agreement between the state and campuses, it may make sense to break accountability down into more localized spheres as well. Higher education institutions, even smaller ones, are really conglomerates of smaller entities such as schools (for example, business schools, education schools), which are in turn conglomerates of even smaller entities such as departments. Even departments many times are comprised of smaller units. For instance, my own department, in a small university, consists of a graduate and undergraduate unit, both of which are autonomous and operate independently. With this in mind, accountability can be framed at the institutional, school, department, and even unit level. Different schools and different departments within organizations may be able to promote growth on the axes above in different ways, and if accountability is seen at more local levels, at the unit and individual level, faculty and administrators may be able to have more understanding and control of the ways they affect their society. In short, accountability can be reframed from the bottom up.

The rest of this section uses the research on servant leadership to create a template, a framework to help higher education institutions integrate servant leadership and use it to reframe how they can be accountable to society. Perhaps the most important consideration of accountability is the public good. How specifically are universities affecting the public good and wider society (Dee 2006)? Of course, the idea of the public good is not easy to articulate. As Calhoun (1998) and Mansbridge (1998) argue, the public good is not a thing to be discovered; rather, it must be created. Mansbridge (1998) and Calhoun (1998) argue that this can be done through deliberation. However, as Mansbridge (1998:12) points out, the groups must be on equal footing, on things such as knowledge of "information, contacts, verbal skills, and feelings of potential efficacy." When assessing and promoting local accountability, this notion of different groups deliberating can be useful. One powerful question can be, "How am I, as a professor, or are we, as an institution, helping to prepare people and groups, helping to equalize them, who must deliberate to create the public good?"

Tripartite Accountability

One way for institutions to start thinking about accountability may be to convene an interdisciplinary team to truly understand the university's role in fostering the public good. But this may not be feasible or possible in some universities, so, in keeping with the local vision of accountability put forth in this chapter, accountability can simply be something that individual professors and others on campus are cognizant of. Again, some of this may be too pie in the sky, and frankly, who will want to undertake more work? But as noted earlier, much of the work of servant leaders takes place without formal recognition and rewards (Greenleaf 1998; Wheeler 2012). With that practical limitation in mind, I put forth these ideas as guides; some campuses are asking these questions, and some may want to start. Further, if accountability is framed as a department or individual initiative, it does not have to be too onerous; it can simply be an informal way of thinking about accountability that can help to guide the actions of individuals and departments. Again, accountability is cast as an action. As public servants (this applies to those in private universities as well), whether we think about it or not, we are all agents of accountability, we are paid to make society better, and we may need to start considering this in our day-to-day operations. Considering and promoting this type of accountability may also be one the intrinsic rewards of servant leadership that Wheeler (2012) discusses.

This chapter is closely related to the previous chapter on strategic planning. Institutions and their members must plan effectively; they must plan in the backdrop of hyperreality. Many of their strategies and goals, and their visions, may all align with accountability. These strategies, goals, and visions can help members of higher education institutions understand and pursue accountability. This chapter, however, reframes accountability as localized accountability, and this type of accountability can be pursued by faculty and administrators at the individual, unit, and subunit level. Therefore, strategic planning is more of an institutional effort, while localized accountability takes some of those ideas and allows individuals to pursue them. This chapter is also a standalone chapter; institutions do not have to undertake strategic planning for individuals in institutions to be accountable to the public good. Accountability can be undertaken informally without a strategic plan. As noted at multiple times throughout this book, Dennis and Bocarnea (2005) and DePree (2002) argue that the ideas of servant leadership can provide guiding thoughts for servant leaders to act. Following this sentiment, accountability can simply be a guiding value that helps guide individual action toward service.

What follows are new visions of accountability based on the tenets and dimensions of servant leadership. These new visions should not be rigid or detailed descriptions. Rather, they are loose guides. The ideals of servant leadership will need to be adapted to the public good according to localized and unique institutional contexts.

Persuasive mapping and conceptual skills can help to reframe accountability. Persuasive mapping and conceptual skills are components of servant leadership that can help leaders help their subordinates understand and perform accountability. Barbuto and Wheeler (2006:319) describe persuasive mapping as "the extent that leaders use sound reasoning and mental frameworks. Leaders high in persuasive mapping are skilled at mapping issues and conceptualizing greater possibilities and are compelling when articulating these opportunities. They encourage others to visualize the organization's future." Liden and colleagues (2008:162), following some of the existing literature on servant leadership, describe conceptual skills as "possessing the knowledge of the organization and tasks at hand so as to be in a position to effectively support and assist others, especially immediate followers." The individuals or teams working for servant leadership and the public good in the university cannot simply elaborate ideas and hope they stick. Rather, individuals or teams must work to help various people and parties in the institution actualize these ideas; they must give people the maps and conceptual skills to pursue a better future for themselves and society. The individuals and teams would do well to articulate these ideas, in concert with members of their communities and regions, on how best to serve them. Next, these teams could discuss what skills and mental models may be needed to achieve their ends.

Persuasive mapping and conceptual skills may be crucial because they provide leadership and a method of action for accountability and improving the public good. Members of these interdisciplinary teams, and especially the formal and informal leaders of these efforts, should not simply go through the motions, but rather truly map out what needs to be done and help others get there to create true, lasting, and tangible change. However, if a faculty member seeks to undertake localized accountability, it may remain a solo effort. Even in this situation, faculty may still need to pay attention to mapping and conceptual skills. If faculty are pursuing localized accountability through their teaching, they may need to map possibilities for their students in a variety of ways. Further, faculty may also need to employ mapping and conceptual skills if they are working with other faculty members informally in promoting localized accountability.

One of the most important facets of servant leadership is empowering followers. Greenleaf's (2002) well-known maxim was that servant leaders are measured by how well those under them grow, and how they help the most vulnerable. The notion of empowerment and helping followers grow can be articulated in the ideas of accountability sketched out above. Here, teams or individuals can try to articulate tangible measures to show how they empower students and those most vulnerable.

One specific way that teams or individuals can begin to conceptualize empowerment is by performing a vulnerability audit. This method was inspired in part by Greene (2013) and Wink (2013). Essentially, teams or individuals could look at who is empowered and not empowered in the community. This vulnerability audit could be performed at the institutional, department, or lower level. This would not just be on a whim, but according to observation. If a larger vulnerability audit is performed, many members of the university could contribute to this, from professors in public policy, to those in economics and social work, to name a few. Team members could observe the community, interview people; they could also perform social actor analyses on policies to see how policies empower or neglect certain people and groups (Saarinen 2008). They could observe town and school board meetings and other civic events to see who is speaking and exercising power. A vulnerability audit may garner political resistance or cynicism by some. Nevertheless, an empirical understanding of who is most vulnerable can be a crucial starting point for empowering the most vulnerable. The next consideration is how can institutions help to fix this? Philosophers, historians, and political scientists can help to articulate new forms of empowerment by looking at theories and past events. Others in the university could try to take some of these abstract concepts and make them more concrete. Statisticians could even devise ways to conceptualize and measure them. Further, some of these can align with Boyer's (2015) and Lynton's (1994) ideas regarding different types of scholarship. Of course, heeding Giroux (2016), we should be wary of measuring such fluid concepts. Accountability should not be hung up on measurement, but rather measurement should be used as a guide and proxy to understand some of the effects of the interventions. This vulnerability audit could also be more informal. Professors can simply take heed of where their students come from, of the needs of the surrounding community. These observations can help to inform their teaching and research.

Another crucial question is how can students be empowered to engage with these vulnerable populations? What must be taught to students, both in and out of the classroom, to empower students to empower others? The insights of all professors can help to inform this conversation. Following the language of servant leadership, what conceptual skills should students be taught for this purpose? Further, if certain groups are found vulnerable or disempowered, they should not be treated as subordinates who need the help of the more educated, but as partners (Beckman 2013). How can faculty and students not simply dictate to vulnerable populations but see them as equal partners? This aligns with notion of covenantal relationships put forth by Sendjaya and colleagues (2008). All people should be seen as equals; servant leaders should cultivate an uncompromising equality. Specifically, relating back to Calhoun (1998) and Mansbridge (1998), if the public good is created by different groups who must speak to each other on an equal basis, then empowerment may be measured by how well members of the community are prepared to participate and create the public good. For instance, have traditionally underserved members of the community been aided by the university in any way? Have people who work with these underserved members been helped?

One specific field that may be able to play a crucial role in helping to empower others is that of business. Business departments can play an extremely important role in empowerment and accountability because the main thrust of the current accountability movement centers on financial concerns (such as how well higher education institutions can train workers and aid the national economy). Following this logic, business departments and professors could work with small businesses in the community in a variety of ways to help bolster the local economy. In a time where mega multinational corporations dominate, businesses departments could work to empower small business owners and those wishing to start small businesses. What information or training could business departments provide to small business owners and those wishing to start small businesses?

Two other crucial tenets of servant leadership that can help to reframe accountability are organizational stewardship and creating value for the community. Creating value for the community similarly calls attention to "a conscious, genuine concern for helping the community" (Liden et al. 2008:162). The aforementioned interdisciplinary teams or individuals acting solo can begin to consider and clarify certain issues for the university and the wider community. Once these issues are clarified, the team can begin to promote these messages to wider audiences. Some points to consider are: What legacy has this institution left to society? Here, the teams or those in institutions can try to get a handle on exactly what legacy their institution has. How is their institution talked about by people in the community? In the state? In the nation? In the world? Historians can try to trace the impact of their institution; they can study documents and testimonies and look at past events where their institution had a role. If the team finds that the legacy is not favorable, the next point to consider is what legacy do we as an institution want to leave? Or how do we change what we are doing? If the legacy is positive, the question can be: How do we sustain or augment it? Is there a mismatch between what organizational members perceive as the legacy and what others outside the organization perceive as the legacy? In order to understand how to change, sustain, or augment the institutional legacy, organizational input is needed. In addition, some of these questions may cross over with the strategic planning process outlined in the previous chapter. Leaving a legacy does not have to be a haphazard thing; rather, it can and should be a deliberate action. Servant leadership calls attention to the role of leaders in fostering this legacy.

What contribution does the organization leave to society? Teams and institutional members can consider what products, ideas, and theories the university creates for society. Here, a type of institutional inventory can be undertaken. Team members can take a hard look at what their university actually creates. This can also be part of the legacy. In my own college, we had to undertake a process of prioritizing campus programs (Dickeson 2010). Some of the ideas from this process can be of use in determining the value of programs. Following Dickeson (2010:66), the criteria that can be used to prioritize programs are history of the program; external and internal demand; inputs, processes, and outcomes of the program; the productivity of the program; the revenue, costs, and impact of the program; and an opportunity analysis. Dickeson (2010) further argues that data must support each of the above criteria. Dickeson (2010) calls for members in higher education institutions not to shy away from measuring nebulous concepts, but to be creative and find ways to do this. A value inventory could follow along the same lines, but the results would be more meaningful, important, and wide-ranging. A value inventory can tell the institutions what it creates and for whom, and how its products (and here the term "products" is not be understood in a narrow consumer sense; rather, products are ideas, theories, and services) affect the community and larger society, and ultimately, what the products that the program creates actually mean to society. This understanding is the essence of servant leadership because the institution serves society with these products.

The next point to consider is how the information from the legacy and value inventory can be transmitted to the wider society and stakeholders and policy makers. How can an institution make wider society care about what it does? Another process that we undertook in my institution was institutional branding. The institution felt that we needed to rebrand ourselves. In this process, I learned a tremendous amount about the science of marketing and how the general public understand institutions. While I would caution against adopting a total marketing strategy (the products, theories, and ideas that institutions produce should not necessarily be sold like consumer items), some tenets from marketing and branding can help the institution to transmit its legacy and impact to the wider society. Institutions will need to position themselves and make society and policy makers understand what they do and how they serve the public good.

Of course, as mentioned earlier, the general thrust of present-day accountability policies is mainly financial in nature. Policy makers may not necessarily care about the theories that a public institution produces; they may only care about how the university aids the economy. In this climate, institutions should not neglect their financial contributions to society, but rather nestle them in a larger, more holistic picture of how they serve the public good. Recasting the contribution of higher education as more complex than simply one of vocational training also can draw on Sipe and Frick's (2015) notion of systems thinker. Being a systems thinker entails the acceptance of complexity and understanding the larger picture (Sipe and Frick 2015). As such, it may be difficult to pinpoint exactly how higher education promotes the public good, and higher education members, as well as society, need to understand this. Indeed, McMahon (2009) attempts to measure, from a human capital approach, the nonmarket and social importance of higher education. His analysis demonstrates the far-reaching and sometimes unrealized contribution of higher education institutions The interdisciplinary team or individual can work despite this complexity and begin to show tentative and incomplete ways in which their institutions work toward the public good. Again, these influences may not be easy to discern because organizations and their impact are so complex. The contribution of higher education institutions is complex and nuanced (Bolman and Deal 1991), and promoting this understanding can be an important part of servant leadership.

Another plank of servant leadership that can be relevant for reframing accountability is that of emotional healing. Along with emotional healing, the related notion of forgiveness is an important plank of servant leadership that may also be able to help reframe accountability. While this may seem too esoteric for accountability, emotional healing and forgiveness still may be able to play a role. Higher education institutions can become emotional healers and perpetuate forgiveness. The interdisciplinary team or individuals can begin to contemplate exactly how higher education can heal and where healing may be needed. This should not be difficult. The twenty-first century has proven to be volatile, and this volatility seems to be on the rise. Servant institutions can work to heal people in the face of this volatility.

Unfortunately, there seems to be many opportunities that call for emotional healing in the modern world. How can higher education institutions become emotional healers? How can they help to bind the wounds of racism, classism, and inequality? These are not easy questions, and the answers will vary depending on one's area and region. Interdisciplinary teams or individuals on campus can try to assess where healing and forgiveness is necessary in their own students, and in their communities, regions, and states. There are obvious cases, but there may be less obvious or less publicized cases across the country, or there may be systemic local happenings. This applies to the individual as well. If a student is sexually assaulted on campus—something that is all too prevalent on American campuses—this would obviously necessitate some type of emotional healing. Can institutions provide healing in the form counseling to individuals and communities alike? On the other hand, can they trace the history of events and make this history public?

Perhaps an extremely important way to frame accountability is by following Wheeler's (2012) tenth principle of servant leadership: developing more servant leaders. Perhaps the greatest test of accountability, and the hardest to measure, would be if an institution is creating more servant leaders. Obviously, only a small fraction, if any, of students will go on to embrace the notion of servant leadership. Nevertheless, why not try? Again, we would not want to fall into a measurement trap, but the creation of servant leaders is a way to continue to ensure service to posterity. One method to create more servant leaders is modeling (Wheeler 2012). Faculty could model tenets of servant leadership to their students and co-workers. Of course, one would not want to be pretentious here and claim that they are being servant leaders; this lack of humility would negate servant leadership. Nevertheless, faculty and administrators could silently model servant leadership behaviors without calling direct attention to them.

Finally, the last way that institutions can reframe accountability with servant leadership is by calling attention to the antithesis of servant leadership, that of egoism and authoritarian hierarchy (Wong and Page 2003). Wong and

Page (2003) argue that egoism is opposed to servant leadership because servant leadership is based on a negation of self-interest, on humility, and on not maximizing power, especially at the expense of others. Wong and Page (2003) further note egoism and competitiveness are larger American values, and thus entrenched. Servant leaders are supposed to overcome self-interest (Wong and Page 2003). Wong and Page (2003:8) argue that "egoism is opposite to SL [servant leadership], which is based on self-giving rather than self-serving." As noted earlier, Giroux (2011) has similarly argued that a type of detrimental individualism continues to affect society, and any regard for the public good is neglected.

This warning regarding individualism can call attention to a tension inherent in any polity: the tension between individualism and collectivism. To what degree should individualism and collectivism be balanced? Obviously, a focus on collectivism at the expense of the individual can crush individual creativity and willpower (there is much dystopian literature on this!). However, equally as detrimental, when individualism is encouraged at the expense of the polity, there may be little emphasis on the public good (Letizia 2017b). The point is to find a happy medium between the two. Here, universities and their interdisciplinary teams can work to understand this tension in their communities and regions. Alternatively, individual faculty members or administrators can informally look at this balance between the individual and the group. They can ask themselves: What can I do to promote this balance? Can I use my academic discipline to highlight certain aspects of this balance in society? What does this balance look like in my classroom? What about my community? What questions should I ask to facilitate this discussion among my students? Again, this may be an esoteric task and not totally suited to accountability concerns, but finding this balance may be a type of necessary service. Higher education institutions can serve their students, communities, regions, and states by working to understand this balance and by articulating ways in which they can bring it into balance.

Defining and Measuring Local Accountability

Defining and measuring growth, especially as I have suggested in this chapter, is no doubt a complex task. Nevertheless, it must be attempted to truly envisage the complex and diverse ways that higher education institutions, and the people in them, are accountable to society, one community at a time. When considering vision, mapping, or empowerment, or some of the items I suggest above, such as a vulnerability audit, the interdisciplinary team or individual faculty member can try to gauge the impact on the different axes mentioned earlier. These axes are cognitive, economic, political, diversity/tolerance, and existential. Institutional, departmental, and individual concerns are juxtaposed against these axes as a way for professors and others in higher education to gauge accountability. Further, the tenants of servant leadership outlined in this chapter—those of persuasive mapping, conceptual skills, empowerment, stewardship, creating value for the community, emotional healing, creating more servant leaders, and reducing egoism—can act as a further set of intellectual guides to help frame accountability against Wheeler's tripartite division and the axes.

When considering the university's or individual professor's actions, how can these actions help students and the community grow politically? How do these actions help the students engage in the political process or give them political knowledge? Similarly, how do the actions of the professors and others in the university help students grow economically? Do these actions empower small businesses? Do these actions help citizens begin to identify and combat economic injustice? What about diversity? How does the institution and individual faculty help to promote tolerance, help to bring diverse ideas, from people with different racial and ethnic backgrounds, into the community? Finally, looking back at chapter 3, how do the university and individual professors help to promote and inspire existential thinking and questions in the community? Anyone attempting to answer these questions will also have to pay attention to the specific economic, political, and demographic situations of institutions and their surrounding communities in order to understand the university's impact. Of course, the political, economic, diversity, and existential considerations are not mutually exclusive; they overlap and feed off each other. Therefore, the most important task may be understanding how these spheres interact with other.

The next question is whether there may be a way to measure growth on these axes without falling into a pathology of measurement. Is there "data" to measure this question? On the other hand, should the answers be seen more as a narrative of accountability that can be shared with different audiences? This narrative, however, should not be seen as a static proof or accountability, but rather as a living dynamic method of being accountable to the wider public. This dynamism is the key. Institutions must evolve in the context of their community, and their community's needs, as well as the wider society. This method of accountability aligns with the notion of accountability put forth by Dee (2006) and examined earlier, where accountability is not rigid adherence to numerical indicators, but rather to actual social problems in the community. In addition, this narrative could be a way to begin conversations among faculty, administrators, and all people on campus, as well as external stakeholders.

Case Study

If accountability is seen as obligation to society and interpreted in a localized sense, if accountability is seen as more than degrees conferred, then we can begin to look at how the actions of professors are giving back, impacting, and making their students' lives better and that of the larger society. This chapter looked mainly at how institutions and departments could practice accountability; this case study focuses on individual faculty members, and how individual faculty members can practice localized accountability. We can start to look at how these students then carry this impact into their daily lives and places of employment. This impact might be easier to discern with graduate students who already hold full-time jobs, and that is the focus of this case study. In this case study, I trace the influence of teaching on the wider society. I want to trace how some teachings may impact students in their workplace and, as result, the wider society. No doubt, many faculty may have similar stories. Indeed, the examples I give (which are fictional, but are drawn from my own experience and the experience of colleagues and students) are examples of dedicated but routine teaching in many graduate classes. But that is the point. I want to show how the normal operations that faculty pursue can be examples of accountability. More than this, however, I want to get faculty thinking about themselves as agents of accountability. This case study is meant to act as a guide for faculty members, to guide them to start seeing their teaching as a form of accountability because it is not some abstract endeavor, but rather something that impacts real people and society in positive ways, and more than just economically.

Jack taught Multiculturalism, a graduate-level course for master's students. In this course, he and his students tackled uncomfortable topics. In this class, there had been some intense discussions, as well as some serious soul-searching on the part of many students. One student in particular, James, a white student and third-year elementary schoolteacher, first learned about the notions of white male privilege in this class. James had never heard the term before until he began discussing it with his professor and classmates. At first, he chafed at it a little. He said, "No way, there might be some disparities in the treatment of blacks and whites, but overall, we are equal." However, James seriously began to toss these ideas around in his head, and, after consideration, he realized that the idea had validity. As he further contemplated the notion of white privilege, it affected not only his own perception but also his relationship with others. His major question became, "What do I do with my white privilege?" After talking to others—to women, to minorities—he realized his task was to use white privilege to speak up for those who did not have it. Most important, he took this new understanding into his school, which is an urban school comprised of many minority groups. James began to see how white privilege can affect his students through teachers' actions and even policies. This type of accountability is an individual accountability, on the diversity/tolerance axes, mediated by empowerment and healing. (Of course, other combinations could be feasible.) Nevertheless, accountability is a constellation, because these new understandings will inform Jack's relations and actions that will influence a wide variety of people.

Betty, a graduate professor of education, taught a class called Research Methods. The class was intense. It was essentially a mini dissertation, and it seriously challenged the students. However, the students left the class with a sense of accomplishment, of having created a research study. Lisa, a veteran classroom teacher and excellent student, immersed herself in this project; she assessed the needs of her students and school and devised a truly meaningful study. The study dealt with implementing a character education program in her school. Upon completion, Lisa brought the study to her supervisor, and it began an earnest discussion about implementing a character education program. Lisa's work helped to start this conversation; it helped to make a positive impact on the school. Lisa was not only able to present this project, but this understanding informed her actions. In a private conversation with the professor, Lisa told her how she now understood how to evaluate sources. She understood that there is bad research out there, and she now has some inkling of how to look at and assess research, which carries into her conversations at school. This is individual accountability, on the cognitive axes, mediated by empowerment and mapping and conceptual skills.

Jerry is a faculty member of education in a small private university. His supervisor, Rae, was approached by a potential student about creating a workshop so the student could gain points for renewing her teaching certificate. Rae asked Jerry if he would be interested. Jerry saw an opportunity to create a servant leadership workshop, which he did. A few local students took the workshop. Jerry had full control of the workshop and was able to create a number of interesting and challenging assignments that asked his students to observe their schools and to think of ways to implement servant leadership. He also asked his students to disagree with the ideas of servant leadership so they could consider its pitfalls and drawbacks. The assignments helped to spark excellent conservations and ideas. Of course, Jerry had no empirical way to measure this, but at the very least a few more teachers now had some inkling of servant leadership, and at least according to their written papers, were now going to try to implement some of those ideas in their classrooms. Further, Jerry's department began to offer this workshop regularly. Again, Jerry had no true way of knowing if he helped to create more servant leaders, but at the very least, some more teachers had knowledge of servant leadership and could use it in their classrooms. This is departmental accountability, on the existential axes, mediated by the creation of more servant leaders' tenets.

All of these vignettes point to accountability in its rawest, most localized form. Ideas learned in the classroom, and not just memorized in rote fashion, but also truly engaged with, helped to guide student actions in their places of employment. This is the essence of accountability, of obligation and impact as attending to the needs of the public. The actions of faculty in their classrooms, the pedagogy and content, the willingness and ability of their students, and their students' subsequent utilization of knowledge are one way for universities to measure and promote accountability. Is this not positively influencing the community or at least a small piece of it? Is this not local accountability?

Again, the scenarios I have sketched above are ideal; many times students are not this engaged, or faculty lessons are less than inspiring. Further, research and service to the university and profession are other areas of promoting accountability that I have not touched upon in this case study. Despite these limitations, it may make sense to start to rethink accountability from the top down and bottom up. However, many of the situations I described do take place, and faculty and administrators must seek these out and highlight them for the university and the public and policy makers. This can be a powerful method of servant leadership, highlighting accountability.

Accountability, conceived as local accountability and able to be practiced by individuals, is a constellation. There is simply so much that is unknown regarding how institutions and individuals influence society. Localized accountability puts some agency into the hands of individuals and may allow individuals to have some ability to influence and promote accountability in an effort to serve society. It also can give faculty some sense of ownership of accountability. Accountability is not done to campuses; rather, individuals, departments, and institutions can do accountability! Yet accountability is not just economic, as many policy makers would have it; rather, accountability is economic, social, technological, just and unjust, global and local, individual and institutional. All of these facets make up concepts in the constellation of accountability. All can be pursued in various ways by organizations and individuals.

Reflection Questions

1. How else can accountability be reframed as service? What other tenets of servant leadership can help to promote a beneficial vision of accountability?
2. How can service impair the understanding of accountability? What are potential negative results of using service to reframe accountability?

6

Servant Leadership and Assessment

Portions of this chapter originate from a paper that my colleague Matthew Fuller and I presented at the 2015 Association of the Study of Higher Education (ASHE) annual conference, as well as a paper we presented at the 2017 American Education Research Association (AERA) conference (Letizia and Fuller 2015, 2017). In addition, we have a manuscript that explores how to apply and interpret some of the ideas of servant leadership and assessment. This chapter differs because I apply the ideas of constellation thinking to assessment.

Servant leadership may be able to help transform cultures of assessment on campus. Fuller and colleagues (2016) argue that the act of assessment on college campuses has increased dramatically over the last decade or so. A major reason for this increase in assessment is that higher education institutions are dealing with growing calls to be accountable from federal and state legislatures (Fuller et al. 2016). A main reason for assessment is to improve the learning of students (Ewell 2002; Fuller and Skidmore 2014; Fuller, Henderson, and Bustamante 2015; Fuller et al. 2016). Sometimes, however, there exists a culture of compliance or fear on campuses regarding assessment (Fuller and Skidmore 2014; Fuller, Henderson, and Bustamante 2015; Fuller et al. 2016). In this state, assessment is usually not seen as a means of growth. Assessment, however, and positive cultures of assessment can enable institutions to positively promote student learning, growth, and attainment (Ewell 2002; Fuller and Skidmore 2014; Fuller, Henderson, and Bustamante 2015; Fuller et al. 2016).

In this chapter, I argue that servant leadership may be able to help recast assessment into this tool of growth. Instead of mandating top-down assessment to fulfill requirements, assessment can be a tool where administrators, faculty, and staff, who are viewed as professionals and equals, evaluate their organization, understand its strengths, probe its weaknesses, and grow. Of course, this is quite a lofty view that probably does not align totally with the reality on many campuses, but it can be an ideal to aspire toward for administrators and faculty.

Ewell (2002:24) noted that assessment had to transition "from a movement into a culture." One method to accomplish this change is for the understanding of assessment to move from one of evaluation and "checking up" to one of promoting student growth (Ewell 2002:24). Ewell (2002:25) further notes that this transformation aligns "with the tradition of robust, participatory and practice-oriented scholarship already established by the assessment movement." Following a number of authors, Peterson and Vaughan (2002) argue that student learning cannot be the sole reason for assessment; rather, student learning should ultimately be a means of institutional growth. This notion of seeing learning not as an end but as a means to growth also aligns with the ideas put forth in chapter 2. Therefore, in a more holistic way, assessment and pedagogy are linked, and the ideas of servant leadership may be able to help foster this link. Assessment conceived as growth and fostered by servant leaders can help to promote true pedagogy and learning, learning that empowers students and impacts society.

As noted earlier, organizational culture is deeply engrained values and beliefs of institutional members that help to guide their actions (Schein 1998). Fuller and colleagues (2016), drawing on a wealth of research, argue that positive cultures of assessment should help to foster beneficial assessment practices on campuses. So, what would a culture of assessment, based on student learning and organizational improvement, actually look like? Fuller and colleagues (2015) used Maki's definition to help answer this question. Maki (2010:9) argues that a commitment to assessment would embody three principles: "(1) meaningfully anchored in the educational values of an institution . . . (2) intentionally designed to foster interrelated positions of inquiry about the efficacy of education practices among educators, students, and the institution itself as a learning organization; and (3) woven into roles and responsibilities across an institution from the chief executive officer through senior administrators, faculty leaders, faculty, staff, and students." It is here that servant leadership may be able to help reframe cultures of assessment. The overarching concern is how can institutional leaders who are in charge of assessment work to create a positive culture of assessment in their institution?

In their Delphi study on cultures of assessment, Fuller and colleagues (2015) found a connection between servant leadership and cultures of assessment. The participants in their study argued that servant leadership could be an effective theory to create and sustain a positive culture of assessment. The experts in the study, however, did not articulate how the ideas of servant leadership could be implemented (Fuller, Henderson, and Bustamante 2015). Fuller and colleagues (2015:347) wrote:

> The notion of a servant leader seems to fit descriptions about how assessment leaders might go about developing positive cultures of assessment while also redefining negative aspects of their campus cultures through collegial involvement and dialogue. Future theorisation could explore how Greenleaf's theory of servant leadership could provide meaning and guidance for assessment leaders in higher education. In the present study, assessment leaders offered scant descriptions of how servant leadership or any other theory informed their efforts to instill cultures of assessment.

This chapter takes the next step and builds off the assertion that servant leadership can promote a positive culture of assessment. The participants in the Delphi study mentioned servant leadership briefly, but, after more examination, many of their responses do align with servant leadership. Using the ideas of the Delphi study and interpreting them through a servant leadership lens, I was able to create a tentative framework that may allow leaders to better integrate the ideas of servant leadership to promote a positive culture of assessment. Of course, the framework in this chapter is not definitive or exhaustive, and much work remains to be done regarding servant leadership and assessment, but this framework may be a start.

I employed a deductive coding scheme to reanalyze the themes from Fuller and colleagues' (2015) Delphi study. Following Coffey and Atkinson (1996), Allan (2008:60) argues that in deductive coding, which entails an a priori method, the researcher "approaches the data looking for segments of text that correspond with particular research questions, concepts or themes." For this framework, I utilized the literature on servant leadership as my a priori material, specifically the studies examined in chapter 1. I examined the first three ranked themes from the Delphi study for each question posited by the researchers to determine if any of the themes that emerged in the study aligned with ideas from servant leadership.

Trustworthiness

In an effort to ensure trustworthiness and validation (Creswell 2013; Terosky and Gonzales 2016a), I have provided a description and justification of the coding tool. I have also provided a description and explanation of how I assigned each code to each of Fuller and colleagues' (2015) data. Finally, I have asked an outside expert to review my coding scheme to ensure its transparency (Terosky and Gonzales 2016a).

Deductive coding entails the use of predetermined themes, which I codified into a coding tool. The studies below and the dimensions of servant leadership found in each study comprised the coding tool. The creation of this tool was iterative. As I read through the data, I began to reflect on which studies could best speak to and represent the data, but I also needed to have a boundary or limit of what studies I would use. In order to determine the studies that would form the tool, I surveyed the empirical literature on servant leadership beginning in 1999 (this is not an arbitrary date; as noted in the first chapter, 1999 largely saw the beginning of the empirical strand of servant leadership studies). I obviously could not use every study in this period. The studies I chose were a result of my selection of influential servant leadership pieces and pieces suggested by anonymous reviewers of the manuscript. My selection was also guided by existing reviews of servant leadership, mainly Pousa (2014) and van Dierendonck (2011). While I performed a number of informal readings, I performed four formal readings of the data. Each reading helped me to refine the coding process further. Fuller and colleagues posed four questions and ranked the answers to them. There were five responses to each question that were ranked from most to least important; I examined and coded the top three responses. I retained Fuller and colleagues' (2015) questions and top three responses to help structure my analysis and as a way to organize my findings and results.

As for the actual coding process, I examined and reflected on each of Fuller and colleagues' (2015) themes and responses in an effort to capture what the theme said with a dimension of servant leadership. The dimensions of servant leadership became the language to represent the themes and ideas elucidated in Fuller and colleagues' (2015) study. For instance, one of the responses in that study was that when data goes nowhere, this leads to a negative culture of assessment. One code assigned to data goes nowhere was transcendent spirituality (Sendjaya, Sarros, and Santora 2008), which deals with meaningful work. Sendjaya and colleagues (2008) argue that one tenet of servant leadership is making work meaningful for people, and data that goes nowhere obviously is *not* meaningful. Similarly, data that goes nowhere has no bearing on the future (thus the inclusion of the codes "keep one eye on the future" and "wisdom"). Finally, if data goes nowhere, it cannot be authentic, which was also included as a code.

Another way to help refine my coding process was to consider the contextual responses provided in Fuller and colleagues' (2015) study. The contextual responses were data supplied in Fuller and colleagues' study. So, for instance, for the first question, which asked participants about positive cultures of assessment, the contextual response mentioned that assessment leaders should provide professional development. As such, I coded this in part with the codes: conceptual skills (Liden et al. 2008), persuasive mapping (Barbuto and Wheeler 2006), provides direction (van Dierendonck 2011). All three of these codes deal with providing subordinates with the necessary skills to complete the tasks at hand, which is an essential function of servant leadership.

Another issue that I ran into was the overlap of terms. Many dimensions of servant leadership from the various studies overlap (Pousa 2014; van Dierendonck 2011). To account for this, I grouped similar terms together. Drawing on the above example again, the three terms conceptual skills (Liden et al. 2008), persuasive mapping (Barbuto and Wheeler 2006), provides direction (van Dierendonck 2011) all call for servant leadership providing the necessary skills for their subordinates to succeed; thus I grouped them together throughout the coding. I have provided a paragraph under each of my codes to demonstrate why I coded Fuller and colleagues' themes the way I did. There are other combinations possible; mine are just a starting point for future discussion. I have arranged the works chronologically to give some order. Some of the dimensions have been paraphrased, explained, or condensed.

Coding Tool

Russell and Stone (2002): nine functional attributes (vision, honesty, integrity, trust, service, modeling, pioneering, appreciation of others, and empowerment), and eleven accompanying attributes (communication, credibility, competence, stewardship, visibility, influence, persuasion, listening, encouragement, teaching, and delegation).

Patterson (2003, 2010): agapao love, humility, altruism, vision, trust, service, and empowerment.

Barbuto and Wheeler (2006): altruistic calling, emotional healing, persuasive mapping ("mapping issues and conceptualizing greater possibilities" [319]), wisdom (anticipation of possible future actions and an understanding of one's current environment and situation), and organizational stewardship (leave a beneficial legacy).

Liden and colleagues (2008): emotional healing, creating value for the community, conceptual skills (understanding what needs to be done and assisting others to do it), empowering (facilitating followers), helping subordinates grow and succeed, putting subordinates first, and behaving ethically.

Sendjaya and colleagues (2008): voluntary subordination, authentic self, covenantal relationship (equality), responsible morality, transcendental spirituality (meaningful work), and transforming influence.

van Dierendonck (2011): empowering people, humility, authenticity, interpersonal acceptance, providing direction, and being stewards.

van Dierendonck and Nuijten (2011): standing back, forgiveness, courage, empowerment, accountability, authenticity, humility, and stewardship.

Wheeler (2012): service to others is the highest priority, meeting needs of others, fostering problem solving and taking responsibility, emotional healing, recognition that the means are as important as the ends, keeping one eye on the present and one on the future, embracing paradoxes, leaving a legacy to society, modeling servant leadership, and developing more servant leaders.

Sipe and Frick (2015): person of character, puts people first, skilled communicator, compassionate collaborator, has foresight, systems thinker, and leads with moral authority.

Winston and Fields (2015): practice what he or she preaches; serves people without regard to nationality, race, or gender; sees serving as a mission of responsibility to others; genuinely interested in employees as people; understands that serving others is most important; willing to make sacrifices to help others; seeks to instill trust rather than fear; is always honest; is driven by a sense of higher calling; and transcends self-interest.

Wong and Page (2003): empowering others, power and pride (egotistical pride and authoritarian hierarchy), visionary leadership, servanthood, responsible leadership, integrity (honesty), integrity (authenticity), courageous leadership.

A number of respondents in Fuller and colleagues study mentioned servant leadership by name, thus the inclusion of Greenleaf (2002) and Spears (1995).

Analysis

Below I list paraphrased questions from Fuller and colleagues' (2015:340–342) study, the main themes that derived from their study, and how those themes may align with servant leadership.

What does a positive organizational culture of assessment look like?

1. *Commitment from administrators*: vision (Wong and Page 2003; Russell and Stone 2002), wisdom (Barbuto and Wheeler 2006), keep one eye on the present and one on the future (Wheeler 2012), conceptual skills (Liden et al. 2008), persuasive mapping (Barbuto and Wheeler 2006), provides direction (van Dierendonck 2011). Vision calls attention to the future, which is what assessment should be focused on; wisdom similarly focuses on anticipation of the future within the context

of the current situation, as does keeping one eye on the present. Vision, wisdom, one eye on the present, and future all require long-term commitment. In addition, professional development was specifically mentioned in Fuller and colleagues' study for this point, and direction, conceptual skills, and mapping call attention to training providing necessary skills.

2. *Focus on student learning*: helping subordinates grow and succeed (Liden et al. 2008), stewardship/leave legacy to society (Barbuto and Wheeler 2006; Dierendonck and Nuijten 2011; Wheeler 2012), creating value for the community (Liden et al. 2008), empowerment (van Dierendonck 2011). Helping subordinates succeed calls attention to development, as does empowerment, which is student learning; stewardship calls attention to the relationship between student learning and a better future, as does creating value for the community.
3. *A clear understanding of what assessing student learning means*: persuasive mapping (Barbuto and Wheeler 2006), conceptual skills (Liden et al. 2008), systems thinker (Sipe and Frick 2015), is driven by a sense of higher calling (Winston and Fields 2015), provides direction (van Dierendonck 2011), skilled communicator (Sipe and Frick 2015). Persuasive mapping, conceptual skills, and provides direction call attention to giving those participating in assessment the mental tools needed to do so; systems thinking and higher calling call attention to the fact that assessment is part of a larger systemic effort and has a larger purpose and is not simply a mandate. In addition, the ability to effectively communicate these data is paramount to ensure that all understand the larger purpose, which was directly mentioned in Fuller and colleagues' study under this point.

What does a negative organizational culture of assessment look like?

1. *Lacking administrative understanding*: vision (Wong and Page 2003; Russell and Stone 2002), persuasive mapping (Barbuto and Wheeler 2006), wisdom (Barbuto and Wheeler 2006), conceptual skills (Liden et al. 2008), skilled communicator (Sipe and Frick 2015), systems thinker (Sipe and Frick 2015). Assessment leaders must not only have technical skills and understanding and an appreciation for the importance of assessment, but a visionary understanding of assessment, of how it fits in with future activities (wisdom). Skilled communicator and provides direction call attention to assessment leaders being able to communicate the direction and overall purposes of assessment; systems thinker calls attention to assessment leaders and administrators

being able to situate their understanding of assessment in a systemic context. Future planning was specifically mentioned in the contextual responses.

2 *Externally motivated*: anti-authoritarian/hierarchical leadership (Wong and Page 2003), covenantal relationship (Sendjaya, Sarros, and Santora 2008), agapao love (Patterson 2003, 2010), humility (van Dierendonck 2011), seeks to instill trust rather than fear or insecurity (Winston and Fields 2015), authenticity (van Dierendonck and Nuijten 2011). Anti-authoritarian leadership/hierarchical leadership calls attention to imposing things in a top-down matter and how this is the antithesis of servant leadership; covenantal relationship, centered on equality, calls attention to equalizing status and authority in the assessment process to the best of the assessment leaders' ability; agapao love calls attention to social love, to ensuring that assessment leaders undertake their efforts not out of fear and authority; humility calls attention to minimizing hierarchy and authority in the assessment process, to assessment leaders not being arrogant or aggressive; seeking trust similarly calls attention to assessment leaders not leading from fear but from trust; and authenticity calls attention to ensuring that the assessment movement is not done solely for compliance purposes, but that it actually benefits the campus.

3 *Data that "go nowhere"*: transcendental spirituality or meaningful work (Sendjaya, Sarros, and Santora 2008), keep one eye on the present and one on the future (Wheeler 2012), wisdom (Barbuto and Wheeler 2012), authenticity (van Dierendonck and Nuijten 2011). Assessment should be meaningful; it should be future oriented (not simply box-checking), and it should have real uses and applications. Assessment should not just be done for the present; it should go somewhere, it should look toward the future. The term "meaningful data" was mentioned directly in the contextual responses.

What theories have assessment leaders used to guide assessment in their organization?

1 *Data-driven decision-making*: conceptual skills (Liden et al. 2008), persuasive mapping (Barbuto and Wheeler 2006), provides direction (van Dierendonck 2011). Conceptual skills, mapping, and provides direction all call attention to the fact that the assessment process should be driven by clear knowledge, and that all people involved should have the mental tools and outside resources and the knowledge to use these, to complete assessment and to understand the data.

Assessment should also be authentic (van Dierendonck and Nuijten 2011).

2 *Assessment should be systemic*: vision (Wong and Page 2003; Russell and Stone 2002), wisdom (Barbuto and Wheeler 2006), systems thinker (Sipe and Frick 2015). Vision, wisdom, and systems thinker all call attention to the findings of Fuller and colleagues (2015), namely, that assessment should be systematic. Vision and wisdom specifically call attention to the future aspect of assessment, how assessment is supposed to be make things better.
3 *Servant leadership*: servant leadership (Greenleaf 2002; Spears 1995).

In what ways do leaders of assessment help to facilitate a culture of assessment in their organization that is rooted in student learning?

1 *Alignment of institutional goals with assessment purpose*: vision (Wong and Page 2003; Russell and Stone 2002), systems thinker (Sipe and Frick 2015), stewardship/leave legacy to society (Barbuto and Wheeler 2006; Dierendonck and Nuijten 2011; Wheeler 2012). Vision again calls attention to the future, to the goals on which assessment should focus. Systems thinker calls attention to the situation of these goals and the assessment process in a larger systematic understanding. Stewardship calls attention to longer range understanding of the impact of student goals; these goals should center on societal betterment.
2 *Use of administrative support*: covenantal relationship (Sendjaya, Sarros, and Santora 2008); helping subordinates succeed (Liden et al. 2008), foster problem solving and taking responsibility at all levels (Wheeler 2012), provides direction (van Dierendonck 2011). Covenantal relationship calls attention to the fact that administrators and assessment leaders should try to minimize authority and power in the assessment process (as far as applicable). Helping subordinates succeed, fostering problem solving, and providing direction call attention to the support role. Relationships between leaders and subordinates were noted in the contextual responses.
3 *Administrators have refined an assessment process*: conceptual skills (Liden et al. 2008), persuasive mapping (Barbuto and Wheeler 2006), provides direction (van Dierendonck 2011), systems thinker (Sipe and Frick 2015). Conceptual skills, mapping, and direction call attention to the need for concrete skills to perform assessment and the process of assessment for all those involved; systems thinker also calls attention to the process of assessment.

The hope is that those who lead assessment can use this framework to create a more positive assessment culture. This study differs from the papers Letizia and Fuller presented as well as the study under consideration. In the AERA paper, we coded the data and created a frequency count. In the ASHE paper and the study under consideration, we then used the framework to interpret another data set. In this chapter, I used more studies in the a priori analysis, and thus the framework has slightly different dimensions. In addition, I did not create a frequency count; rather, I recast the framework as a constellation. Further, the framework was not used to interpret another data set, but a case study. A reviewer of one of the previous studies noted how the ranking of themes by frequency might be problematic because a ranking system may ignore interactions between different tenets of servant leadership. As such, it may be better to envision each tenet as part of a larger constellation of truth. As noted in an earlier chapter, Adorno (1966/1973) argued that words can never truly define what they intend to define. Concepts came together in clusters, which Adorno (1966/1973) referred to as constellations (Buck-Morss 1977). Adorno (1966/1973), however, did not see truth as a united thing, rather as contradictory (Buck-Morss 1977). Adorno (1966/1973) saw human thought driven by what it does not know (Buck-Morss 1977). If this is true, our constant reflection on assessment and its various characteristics can help lead us to new understandings.

Following this sentiment, the tenets of servant leadership that aligned with the themes from the Delphi study can be thought of as concepts, which, when brought together, form a constellation. Each concept (for example, persuasive mapping), aligned with the responses from the Delphi study, may represent part of the truth of what a beneficial culture of assessment may look like on a campus, but always with the understanding that there is still so much unknown and that contradictions and inconsistences will inevitably occur, and allow for movement. As such, similar ideas may play out differently on different campuses. Persuasive mapping on one campus culture with a certain mission and with certain students will most likely produce different results than persuasive mapping on a different campus with a different mission and with different students. In addition, there may be tensions between the different concepts. For example, different assessment leaders may have different visions or ideas of stewardship that can affect assessment, or there may be disagreement as to what skills are needed. Each tenet of servant leadership identified above should not be seen as a certainty, but rather as a method to discover and question more about the truth of assessment on campuses, and about what beneficial cultures of assessment may look like on particular campuses.

Following the ideas of persuasive mapping, conceptual skills, and providing direction, assessment leaders should work to ensure that those undertaking assessment truly have the skills to perform the task. Instead of assuming that people will figure it out, those who lead assessment must ensure that those partaking in assessment have the skills and knowledge needed to perform it. By providing the necessary skills, assessment leaders can work to empower their followers in the assessment process.

Assessment leaders must help to articulate the overarching purpose of assessment on their campuses and how assessment is linked to student outcomes such as growth and development, as well as how assessment can help to achieve the institution's mission and vision. If assessment is not linked to these things, it may not be seen as legitimate. The idea of systems thinker (Sipe and Frick 2015) can also help to position assessment as crucial to institutional goals, mission, and vision. Assessment must be seen in the wider organizational context. This is another way assessment leaders can serve those who must undertake assessment, by showing its value, its role in organizational processes, and how it promotes the growth of students and the institution. In the widest sense, following Barbuto and Wheeler (2006), Dierendonck and Nuijten (2011), and Wheeler (2012), this can also help to cast assessment as an act of stewardship and to leave a positive legacy.

An important part of building a positive culture of assessment is to ensure that employees do not see assessment as compliance (Fuller et al. 2016). Following Winston and Fields (2015), assessment leaders can also work from trust, not fear or insecurity. The notion of equality (Sendjaya, Sarros, and Santora 2008) can be of use here. Assessment leaders should treat those who must do assessment as equals and not subordinates. Essentially, administrators can work to reduce hierarchy. This also aligns with Wong and Page's (2003) call to reduce egoism and authoritarianism and hierarchy in organizations. Assessment leaders can see themselves not as hierarchical leaders, but as genuine servants who serve the campus by facilitating a beneficial assessment process and promoting a positive culture of assessment. Following Patterson (2010), this action can be cast as a type of social love. This can also be an act of humility.

Perhaps most important, assessment must be made meaningful. Giving meaning to work is an important notion of servant leadership (Sendjaya, Sarros, and Santora 2008). This also aligns with Winston and Fields's (2015:424) notion of being "driven by a sense of higher calling." Fairholm (1997:4) argues that "work is fast becoming the locus where most of us find our sense of full meaning." Following this sentiment, the tasks we do at work should be meaningful, and servant leaders can help to promote and facilitate this notion of meaningful work. This notion of making work meaningful is especially important with tasks such as assessment, which can be seen by many as mundane, useless, or an act of compliance. Lane and colleagues (2014) similarly argue that assessment leaders must work to create a vision for organizational members to help guide and legitimize the assessment process.

Assessment should not simply be the problem of administrators; all must take ownership of this process. Fostering problem solving and taking responsibility at all levels (Wheeler 2012:63) is a tenet of servant leadership that may be able to help promote ownership of assessment, as well as facilitate commitment and growth on the part of subordinates. As Wheeler (2012:64) notes, "The work of institutions is achieved by individuals, units and other groups." This is especially true of assessment, and a positive culture of assessment should promote this idea of ownership. Assessment leaders can serve their subordinates in the assessment process by promoting ownership at all levels.

Another tenet of servant leadership is keeping one eye on the present and one eye on the future (Wheeler 2012:102), and this tenet may be able to help to promote a positive culture of assessment. Assessment can be an ideal method to achieve dual action. If assessment is viewed as simultaneously looking at where you are and where you need to go instead of a mandate, it may be able to promote a positive culture of assessment. Assessment can have the ability to promote necessary improvement. In addition, following the notion of skilled communicator (Sipe and Frick 2015), all of these tenets should be undergirded with open lines of communication between leaders and followers.

All of the tenets of servant leadership identified as being able to promote a positive culture of assessment may form a larger, interconnected constellation that, while not being able to totally define what a positive culture of assessment is or looks like, can give some insight into it and provide avenues by which to grow and attain it. Each concept is part of "the truth," yet this truth is not unitary (Adorno 1966/1973; Buck-Morss 1977). This chapter has offered only one way to reframe a culture of assessment using servant leadership. The tenets of servant leadership were paired with results from Fuller and colleagues' (2015) Delphi study, and more work is needed to truly understand how servant leadership can help to reframe assessment. Nevertheless, the suggestions in this chapter can be a start to understand how to accomplish this task. The case study in the next section offers an example of how these ideas can be applied in real life. As noted earlier, the tenets of servant leadership that I have identified should not be the end, but the beginning. They are merely vehicles of movement, ways by which faculty, administrators, and those in charge of assessment can begin to truly probe what a positive culture of assessment looks like.

Another important factor that might affect assessment is the growing use of assessment platforms and companies that offer assessment services for a fee. Assessment has grown more onerous and time consuming for many campuses, especially smaller campuses with less resources. Contracting with companies to manage and handle assessment can be a huge boon and a way to save valuable time and labor. However, as I have written elsewhere (Letizia 2016b), universities should always approach partnerships with for-profit companies with some caution. While for-profit companies can provide tremendous support and products to higher education that are extremely useful, their primary motivation is profit, which sometimes may come at the expense of the institution.

Case Study

The events of this case study are part fictional, but are also drawn from conversations I have had and research. A new faculty member at a regional comprehensive university, Debbie, got her first taste of assessment, and it shocked her. Debbie was an assistant professor of nursing. She had been at her institution about a month. One day, her supervisor, Lisa, came frantically into Debbie's office and exclaimed, "We have to fill out this assessment report!" Debbie looked up from her computer screen and tried to process this. She had no idea what this entailed. Lisa had been at the institution for about ten years, so she had a good understanding of the institutional process and culture. Lisa anxiously spoke: "The assessment report is due in two weeks, but we might have some leeway when we get it in. In fact, I don't even know what they do with these damn reports!" Debbie was still trying to process this. She began asking questions. "What do we have to do?" Lisa spoke again: "First, we need to provide the data on our students' licensure exams for the last five years. Next, we need to provide our students' scores on the state assessment standards." Debbie had a vague understanding of these standards. "What exactly are these standards?" Lisa answered: "The state department of education has certain standards for many of the classes we teach. Professors have to grade each student in how well they meet these standards." "So," Debbie said "where is all this data located?" Lisa answered: "Judy [the administrative assistant] has all of this, but we need to arrange it, put it all together, and calculate averages." Debbie did not even know where to start, so she waited for guidance. "Okay, well what do we need to do?" she asked Lisa. Lisa thought a moment. "First," she said, "we need to get with Judy and have her email all this to us, then we need to create new Excel documents and arrange the information." Debbie then asked: "Where does this actually go?" Lisa, beginning to email Judy, answered: "It goes to George, the dean. George has been bugging us about it, I did not even hand it in last year! He never said anything to me, but I would like to get it in to him." Then Lisa looked up: "But really, I don't think it matters, I mean, two years ago I handed something in and I never heard back. No one does. These reports just go to him, and I think they are locked in a filing cabinet or something. It is so worthless!" Debbie tried to wrap her head around this. "That is pointless! What a waste of time!" Debbie began to bristle with resentment. Why did she have to waste her time working on useless assessment reports if they went nowhere? Judy emailed the required documents. "Check your email," Lisa directed Debbie. Debbie checked her email and opened the documents. Her eyes began scanning all the numbers. There were pages and pages of numbers! "Do you see what we have to do?" asked Lisa, exasperated. Debbie was still unsure, but she started putting it together. Lisa divvied up the tasks. Debbie started to have a vague understanding of what needed to be done, but she still harbored uncertainty.

The next week Debbie and Lisa put all else aside to complete these assessment reports. As the week ensued, Debbie's resentment grew. She had put *everything* aside to work on this, and she felt it was a giant waste of time if these reports simply sat in a filing cabinet. Debbie was tired of looking at numbers; she felt like an accountant not a nurse. She had looked at numbers all week and was tired of this. Finally, after countless mistakes, emails with Lisa, and revisions, they had just about finished the reports. Lisa told Debbie to send her the finished portions, and she would tidy them up and send them to George.

Weeks passed, and Debbie got back into her normal routines. She had forgotten about the assessment reports until one day weeks later when Lisa casually mentioned that she still had not handed in the reports to George. Debbie was shocked. They worked on these reports for a week, gave up everything for a week, and the reports were still not handed in. The reports seriously were a waste of time if they were not handed in. Eventually, Debbie did find out that some assessment data was posted on the universities webpage.

This is one anecdotal example of how assessment may be perceived as going nowhere. It is easy to see how assessment in this situation could be viewed as a bureaucratic hoop to jump through, an external mandate to be fulfilled only for the sake of checking boxes. Debbie was new and she did not know all the assessment procedures. She figured that assessment was important to the university, but at this stage, she simply was not made aware of its value.

So, how could servant leadership be used to reframe this situation? How could servant leadership be employed by various institutional members to promote a positive culture of assessment on campus? The real question is, would administrators and faculty actually utilize these tenets of servant leadership? This of course is hypothetical. In all reality, many leaders may scoff at this sentiment (as some reviewers did!). It should also be remembered that servant leadership is not applied or practiced, it must be *lived*. It must become a way of life, which may draw even more eye rolls from administrators and those who must lead assessment, especially when they are under pressure from state and federal policy makers. Nevertheless, the framework created from the Delphi study may still be useful.

First, the most obvious and glaring issue is that assessment in this case goes nowhere. As indicated by Fuller and colleagues' (2015) Delphi study, a negative culture of assessment usually exists when the data is perceived to go nowhere. Here, as argued above, Sendjaya and colleagues' (2008) notion of spiritual transcendence can be employed. George could communicate to faculty how and why assessment is meaningful toward the university's mission. Of course, George may be under the gun as well; he may be only demanding this data because higher-ups are demanding it of him. Moreover, the data may be very important, but this importance was not communicated clearly. In this case, George may have to have a hard conversation with his superiors about assessment (if that is even possible). How can George and the administration make assessment meaningful or at least communicate its importance more effectively? The notion of vision (Wong and Page 2003; Russell and Stone 2002), systems thinker (Sipe and Frick 2015), and skilled communicator (Sipe and Frick 2015) comes into play here as well. How does assessment fit into the larger picture, and can this sentiment be communicated effectively? These questions are crucial, because if the work is not meaningful, then why do it? We are so busy and overburdened, so why do more work that is pointless? If assessment is linked to the larger campus functioning, it can become more meaningful and worthwhile. In addition, the administration could look to the ideas of mapping, conceptual skills, and providing direction from the framework. Faculty may need more guidance in their ability to perform effective assessment that benefits the institution (Barbuto and Wheeler 2006; Liden et al. 2008; van Dierendonck 2011).

Taken together, the actions I call for above may be the concepts of a constellation. Each concept cannot fully describe a beneficial culture of assessment, but each may invite further questioning and growth on the part of administrators and faculty as to what should constitute good assessment practice and what type of culture is necessary to foster this view of assessment *on their campus*. Again, I do not argue that these questions should lead to some overarching conformity for a campus; rather, in the spirit of Adorno, these types of questions may lead to further contradictions, yet these contradictions may be necessary to uphold a truly beneficial culture of assessment.

Reflection Questions

1. In what other ways can servant leadership improve cultures of assessment?
2. How may servant leadership damage cultures of assessment?

7

Servant Leadership and Other Leadership Theories

Servant leadership shares characteristics with a number of other leadership types and theories. Winston and Fields (2015:419) argued that servant leadership, transformational leadership, ethical leadership, and authentic leadership share the dimensions of integrity, listening, empathy, goal setting, wisdom, influence, and behaving ethically. Most notably, servant leadership shares many similarities with the theory of transformational leadership (Prosser 2010b). Transformational leadership is largely concerned with the pursuit of a larger organizational vision in which employees take part; transformational leadership entails inspiring employees to achieve goals beyond their job description (Lynch 2012; Northouse 2016). Some points of congruence between servant leadership and transformational leadership are trust, respect, and vision, to a name a few (Lynch 2012:5). As pointed out by a number of authors in dozens of studies, however, one of the core differences between transformational leadership and servant leadership is that transformational leadership focuses largely on the goals of the organization, whereas the primary concern of servant leaders is on the growth of followers (Lynch 2012; Prosser 2010b). Nevertheless, it is obvious that there is overlap between the ideas of servant leadership and other leadership philosophies and theories. And while this can be a source of confusion in some respects, it may also open up new areas of exploration.

Understanding servant leadership in the context of other leadership theories may help to augment the understanding of servant leadership and leadership in general. In a sense, each leadership theory can contribute to a wider and fuller understanding of leadership, especially as leadership is practiced in such a volatile time as ours. Following the constellation analogy used earlier, each leadership theory is considered a concept that helps to define but does not fully represent what leadership actually is—all must be considered together and embraced in their contradictions. The purpose of this chapter is to add new concepts to the constellation of leadership.

This chapter is not meant to compare other theories with servant leadership. The purpose of this chapter is to augment our view of servant leadership with other leadership theories by looking for synergy, but always with the understanding of contradiction. It is highly unlikely that one leadership philosophy or theory has all the answers to leadership or can accurately describe best leadership practices in a world so fraught with change, in addition to leading educated followers. This of course is not say that the leadership philosophies and theories surveyed in this chapter are exhaustive of ideas that could be used to augment servant leadership. Rather, this chapter provides a beginning to think about how to find synergy with other theories. The two theories used in this chapter are distributed leadership and adaptive leadership.

Distributed Leadership

Prosser (2010b:37) argues that "servant leadership and concepts of distributed leadership are entirely compatible." Similarly, Gronn (2002) used Greenleaf's notion of *primus inter pares*, or leadership groups of equals, as an example of distributed leadership. The core of distributed leadership is that instead of viewing leadership as resting solely with individuals, distributed leadership sees leadership in the interplay between individuals, situations, artifacts, and their environment (Spillane, Halverson, and Diamond 2001, 2004). Following Fletcher (2004), Klar and colleagues (2016) argue that distributed leadership is part of the postheroic concept of leadership. Klar and colleagues (2016:112) argue, "Post-heroic forms of leadership emphasize the distributed, interdependent nature of leadership activities, leadership through social interactions and increased organizational learning outcomes." Distributed leadership views leadership as rooted in these interactions and spans from day-to-day tasks to the larger, more global concerns of the organization (Spillane, Halverson, and Diamond, 2001). Perhaps the most succinct articulation of distributed leadership is demonstrated in this passage from Spillane and colleagues (2001:26): "Leaders do not work directly on the world; their actions in and on the world are mediated by artifacts, tools, and structures of various sort." Spillane and colleagues (2001) further capture the notion of distributed leadership when they argue that leadership is "stretched" over individuals and their relations, artifacts, and organizational structures. This view of stretched leadership helps to envision leadership not as a solitary activity, but situated in interactions. Gronn (2002) also notes how distributed leadership is synergistic; the actions of various actors lead to a type of holism. Gronn (2002) explains that the division of labor also affects the distribution of leadership patterns. As new technology emerges, as new social norms emerge, different roles are created and consolidated, all of which affects how leadership is distributed (Gronn 2002).

Viewing leadership as stretched can add a new quality to servant leadership. How do leaders serve followers in this interconnected web or network? How is service mediated through people, structures, and resources? The focus on interactions between individuals, and not on individuals themselves, is especially pertinent for servant leadership. Service is not simply serving individuals, but service is in the interactions between individuals. For instance, how do the different types of interactions serve followers? Can different types of interactions serve followers? Of course, service is not a monolithic notion. As has been described in this book, there seem to be many different dimensions of service. So, the next question is, how do the different dimensions of service then play into the different types of interactions? Further, how do the different dimensions of servant leadership look when mediated through people, structures, and resources? For instance, can I empower my followers with new technology? Can I make work more meaningful for my followers by utilizing their job roles, their different positions (both formal and informal), organizational structures, and resources? These are some ways in which distributed leadership can begin to augment servant leadership.

Different authors have created frameworks to help understand how leadership may be distributed in organizations (Bolden 2011). Bolden (2011) gives a description of some these different frameworks, namely those of Spillane (2006), Leithwood et al. (2006), MacBeath Oduro, and Waterhouse (2004), and Gronn (2002). Spillane (2006) argued for three types of distribution: collaborative, collective, and coordinated (Bolden 2011). Collaborative distribution is when individuals work with each other to achieve leadership ideas. Collective distribution occurs when individuals do not work together, but they labor interdependently to achieve leadership tasks. Coordinated distribution is when individual actions are performed in progression to achieve leadership (Bolden 2011; Spillane 2006).

Leithwood and colleagues (2006) argued for planful alignment, when there is deliberate planning and allocation of resources toward certain goals; spontaneous alignment, when teams and partnerships are unplanned but beneficial; spontaneous misalignment, when these spontaneous partnerships do not work; and anarchist misalignment, when leaders pursue unit goals without regard to larger organizational goals (Bolden 2011; Leithwood et al. 2006).

MacBeath and colleagues (2004) argued for six types of networking. Formal distribution is when leadership is delegated by formal plan. Pragmatic distribution is "ad hoc" and is largely reactionary; people must assume different leadership roles as the needs arise (MacBeath, Oduro, and Waterhouse 2004:37). Strategic distribution is when new members with specific capabilities are introduced into the organization to take care of needs. Strategic distribution is focused on long-term aspirations (MacBeath, Oduro, and Waterhouse 2004). Incremental distribution is when people in the organization learn leadership by experience and gain confidence (Bolden 2011; MacBeath, Oduro, and Waterhouse 2004). Opportunistic distribution is when organizational members desire to take on more leadership roles and cultural distribution; where leadership is defined largely by the tasks, it is spontaneous and intuitive and largely embedded in organizational functioning (Bolden 2011; MacBeath, Oduro, and Waterhouse 2004). Gronn (2002) argued for spontaneous collaboration, where individuals with varying talents collaborate to undertake a task; intuitive working relations, where leadership emerges in the relations between individuals; and institutionalized practice, where organizational structures are created and enacted to promote partnership and collaboration, such as Greenleaf's notion of *prima inter pares* discussed earlier (Bolden 2011; Gronn 2002).

Gronn (2009), however, argues that many times in organizations, there are still powerful leaders who hold sway, but they do this alongside of distributed networks. Gronn (2009) argues for a new unit of study, that of configurations. Gronn (2009:384) goes on to argue that powerful individual leaders interacting with and working in the context of networks can be seen as a "hybrid." In this view, leadership is seen as comprising both individualistic and collective facets existing alongside each other and drawing on each other (Gronn 2009).

The different types of alignment and networking can further give servant leaders new ways to serve their followers. What is the best way to align people in the organization? Do different types of alignment create more opportunities for service? Does collaboration enhance the meaning of work? Does the collaborating of people with different skills create new groups with the ability to create more value for the organization and/or community? Specifically, following Gronn (2002), what type of organizational structures can be created that will promote collaboration between organizational members? This consideration of organizational structures adds a new dimension to fostering a synergy between distributed and servant leadership. Instead of service only occurring between individuals, a servant leader can be cognizant of how service is promoted by organizational structures and policies that allow organizational members to come together and collaborate, as well as informal and organic working relations within organizations. Following Gronn's (2009) notion of hybrid leadership, who are the influential individuals in an organization who hold power? What types of leadership configurations are they situated in, and how can a leader utilize these configurations for service?

There may also be contextual considerations to distributed leadership. Hall, Gunter, and Bragg (2013) found that that distributed leadership is impacted by organizational contexts. In one school in their study, distributed leadership reflected a more hierarchal system and was simply a way to delegate tasks, whereas in another school, distributed leadership was more associated with teacher freedom and agency (Hall, Gunter, and Bragg 2013). Yet, despite these differences, Hall and colleagues (2013) argue that the potential of distributed leadership to positively impact educational institutions is likely. While they only examined a few schools, this contextual element of distributed leadership is important. Distributed leadership is not a template to be applied to an organization, but rather shaped by particular organizational contexts. Further, if servant leadership is thrown into this mix, servant leaders must also contend with organizational complexities and nuances. Service in one organization may take on different meanings in another context. Servant leaders who wish to harness distributed leadership must be cognizant of this contextual feature.

Distributed leadership and other similar leadership theories may be well suited to the present age, due to the de-emphasis on autocratic and top-down forms of leadership (Eddy and Amey, 2015; Lynch 2012). Hartley (2007), following Biggart (1989), notes that it is increasingly difficult for organizations to control members via traditional hierarchical structures (Lynch 2012). Distributed leadership may align in some ways with this emerging trend (Eddy and Amey, 2015; Hartley 2007; Lynch 2012). As Leithwood, Mascall, and Strauss (2009) note, however, there is still debate regarding the effectiveness and impact of distributed leadership. On the one hand, Leithwood and colleagues (2009), citing a number of studies, argue that democratic and shared forms of distributed leadership in certain educational contexts were beneficial. Distributed leadership, when organizational members had some measure of authority and control, helped to promote ownership of organizational processes (Leithwood, Mascall, and Strauss 2009). On the other hand, Leithwood and colleagues (2009), after surveying the literature, note some possible negative features of distributed leadership. These included the idea that too much input from too many parties may create confusion; leadership and power are not necessarily distributed, but only responsibility; and distributed leadership can be used as a way to subtly dominate weaker members of the organizations (Leithwood, Mascall, and Strauss 2009). Some, such as Corrigan (2013), posit that distributed leadership may simply be a means for more powerful members in hierarchical organizations to gain support for their ideas.

Following these cautions, servant leaders can work to ensure that if distributed leadership does exist in organizations, that distributed leadership allows organizational members some measure of participatory action in guiding the organization, and that it is not simply a means to disguise traditional hierarchy. This action may be the most crucial for servant leaders in regard to distributed leadership. While distributed leadership may not actually empower organizational members, servant leaders can work to make it so. Servant leaders can first chart the actual distribution of power in their organization (by paying attention to different types of networking and collaboration schemes, and organizational structures that promote or hinder this). Once leaders understand how power is distributed, they can work to make the arrangement more service oriented.

Woods and Roberts (2016:139) argue that distributed leadership can help to foster social justice (defined as the cessation or at least the limiting of inequality due to socioeconomic means, encouraging participation and individual development, and respecting beliefs) and democracy. However, they also found that distributed leadership could also exist alongside more hierarchical structures. Woods and Roberts (2016:153) argue that "to develop DL [distributed leadership] that seeks to enhance social justice, it is necessary to recognize and address inequities and feeling of hurt and marginalization which we also found to be embedded in the day-to-day processes of dispersed leadership as perceived by participants." Recognition of injustice and pain in organizations aligns with the notions of empowerment and emotional healing, among others. A necessary action of servant leaders in a distributed leadership context is to work to rectify these feelings of marginalization and injustice through empowerment and healing.

As has been duly demonstrated by the research on servant leadership, one of the quintessential functions of a servant leader is that of empowerment. Moreover, in distributed leadership, many people are viewed as having some type of authority, expertise, or at least responsibility. This aligns with Bennis (2009), who argues that all people have leadership abilities. Combining these views, servant leaders can view all people in these different networks as potential leaders. As such, servant leaders can work to empower all these people or nodes in the networks (Landel and Ohana, 2006), in a variety of ways. If all are seen as potential leaders, and all are further seen as having some role to play in organizational success by utilizing their leadership capabilities (Dean, 2007), servant leaders can work to bring out and harness the useful and necessary talents of all in the organization, which would help to empower members and work to enhance the organization as a whole. Viewed in the context of distributed leadership, empowerment of followers has another facet. Empowering followers in a distributed leadership context calls attention to their specific authority and expertise in their role. It is not about simply "letting" them have more power, but truly allowing these people to exercise their occupational expertise and authority. This will obviously look different in different organizational contexts. Here, distributed servant leadership is a network of shared authority, where people are empowered and trusted to exercise their ability and talents as they see fit in the context of the organization. Another similar tenet of servant leadership is the creation of other servant leaders (Wheeler 2012). This vision of empowerment in the distributed leadership context can work not only to empower people but also to see them as potential servant leaders. While this vision of distributed servant leadership may just be an unachievable ideal, it nevertheless can call attention to a new way to view organizational reality.

Drawing on the above analysis of distributed servant leadership and its integration with the ideas of servant leadership, I propose a new concept to understand the synergy between both types of leadership, that of distribut*ing* servant leadership. Vaill (1998) calls attention to the importance of the phrasing in servant leadership literature. Following this sentiment, notice that I have highlighted the suffix "ing" above. At first, I had called it distributed servant leadership. However, after reflection, I believe that the grammatical change is of great importance. Distributed servant leadership implies a readymade concept, whereas distribut*ing* servant leadership calls attention to action; organizational members will most likely not find service already distributed in an organization. Rather, they will have to work at distributing service in a variety of ways.

Another important but perhaps less explicit consequence of the analysis above is that it can call attention to a new way of viewing servant leadership. Greenleaf argued that we must create servant institutions. Distributing servant leadership in an organization can help accomplish this task. Yet if viewed from the lens of distributed leadership, servant leadership is no longer simply vested in the actions of individuals. Rather, servant leadership, like distributed leadership, is "stretched." Service then occurs not just in actions but also in *interactions* between the organization's members, policies, structures, and artifacts (Spillane, Halverson, and Diamond 2001, 2004). The varying interactions and situations can give rise to service in a variety of forms. In the rest of this section, I highlight faculty roles as well as administrator roles in possibly distributing servant leadership. I present some minicases that, while fictional, are drawn from real events and should be relatable to a number of higher education faculty and administrators.

Jeremiah was a second-year faculty member in the arts and sciences department. He taught some classes in Roman history, as well as some medieval history courses. After reading about the synergy between servant leadership and distributed leadership, Jeremiah began to realize that he was connected to various other institutional members in a variety of ways (which seemed difficult to imagine when he was sitting for hours in his lonely office typing away on a manuscript that it seemed no one would ever read!). Jeremiah began to trace his linkages and to uncover the networks that he belonged to. First, he thought of his students. He was closely connected to his students, and while they were transient organizational members, they would become alumni and retain a permanent, if somewhat distant connection to the university. But

Jeremiah realized that he did not just teach them; his actions were mediated through the curriculum. The curriculum was largely created by him, but it also adhered to the rules and ultimately the mission of the university. Framed in terms of distributing servant leadership, the curriculum, however, was an organizational artifact that mediated and directed his relations to his students. Further, the curriculum, while it contained ideas of Roman or medieval history that he wished to convey to his students, also could be a vehicle for service. How could the course content promote service? What assignments could be created for this purpose? What disciplinary ideas could Jeremiah draw on to highlight the notion of service? Were there historical examples or philosophies that could be used to illustrate ideas of servant leadership? Here, Jeremiah sought to use the course content as a vehicle to inspire a vision of service based on autonomy and creativity for students.

Further, how could the assignments of the syllabus be situated in the mission of the university (which calls for positively influencing society)? The mission was important here and calls attention to how context affects the synergy between distributed and servant leadership. Jeremiah worked for a Catholic university, which obviously created a special type of organizational context to situate distributed leadership, and as Hall and colleagues (2013) point out, organizational context matters. As such, service was a key component of the university's mission. In this context, service was not simply a one-to-one endeavor between professor and student; rather, it was stretched over himself, the syllabus, the students, and the university's mission and policies. Further, this stretching aspect augmented how Jeremiah could promote service because there were more avenues to do it, and the university's mission and his reconceived assignments helped to augment and amplify how he served his students. Jeremiah considered his students as part of a type of network, connected to himself, the syllabus, and the university's mission. The ultimate goal was to see the students as potential servant leaders themselves, and by distributing leadership through the various organizational members and pieces, this could be accomplished, at least for a few students.

Jeremiah then looked at his relations with other faculty and staff members. For one, as part of his service to the university, Jeremiah had to sit on a number of committees. One particular committee he sat on was the Title IX and sexual violence committee. He was asked to join the Title IX committee by another faculty member who thought he would find the work interesting and because he had a minor in law and political science. This committee is a nonacademic committee and thus a little outside of Jeremiah's comfort zone, but once he learned the ropes, he found the work rewarding. In this role, Jeremiah deals mostly with university administrators, various deans, members of the HR department, and the Title IX coordinator. This was obviously a planned and deliberate committee and thus aligns with Leithwood and colleagues'

(2006) notion of planned alignment and MacBeath and colleagues' (2004) notion of formal distribution, both of which are centered on planned and deliberate leadership interactions. Jeremiah works well with his colleagues on the committee, and this committee performs a vital function for the university, investigating instances of sexual harassment, discrimination, assault, and violence as well as creating university policies that deal with these issues. In the spirit of distributed leadership, there is no one person who can do this work; all the people on the committee are important and necessary. So how can servant leadership be exercised here? Obviously, the entire committee centers around a federal policy, Title IX and its various regulations, which dictate how he and other committees act and lead. In a sense, the committee leads the university in the understanding and prosecution of sexual harassment and violence (obviously, their power is situated in the backdrop of the federal government and the local police department), and their authority is distributed among the different members of the committee, the federal policy and regulations, and the police department. This somewhat aligns with Gronn's (2009) notion of hybrid leadership, where certain individuals may hold power alongside of and situated in distributed networks and interactions.

In this role, Jeremiah will be dealing with potential victims and transgressors of some of the worst actions—sexual harassment up to sexual violence. Here, the notion of emotional healing, humility, empathy, and listening seem to be the most relevant. A victim will most likely need healing, and Jeremiah, not by himself, but through the policy and in conjunction with the committee and other people and departments on campus (such as counselors and student services), can help to provide this. Those who are accused (and even some who committed acts) may be misunderstood, and may at times need to be listened to and need empathy. Jeremiah, understanding his role in this network among various actors, some with more powers than others (Jeremiah as a new faculty has little power!), and not just those on the committee, can still begin to uphold these tenets of servant leadership in his dealings with victims, transgressors, and other committee members. The committee should not be a bureaucratic endeavor, or simply a structural endeavor, nor should it be primarily punitive (of course, punishments, and many times harsh punishments, will have to be meted out). Nevertheless, the committee should be an organ of love and understanding (always with an understanding of impartiality when called for), and this can only be accomplished in a distributed manner. Again, like the classroom example above, Jeremiah is not simply showing empathy or practicing emotional healing; rather, he does these things mediated through the policy and his role on the committee. This is the essence of distributed leadership (Spillane, Halverson, and Diamond 2001, 2004) and now distributing servant leadership—utilizing others, organizational artifacts, and policies to distribute various types of service in various ways.

Jeremiah also engages in many spontaneous partnerships that yield excellent results. One specific partnership is his relationship with the assistant librarian, Janet. Jeremiah began visiting with the librarian shortly after he was hired. She was able to secure a number of research articles and books that their small library did not have. But Jeremiah realized that Janet was not simply getting him books; she was inadvertently teaching him different aspects about the research process, aspects of which he only had a rudimentary knowledge—search engine mechanics, copyright laws, embargos, and journal subscription policies, to name a few. Jeremiah then began to utilize Janet's skills not just for his own research but also for his students. The library offered services to faculty to help build online research portals for their students, tailored to specific courses. Jeremiah utilized this service and saw it as just that, a service to his students. Jeremiah was able to guide them toward their goals, similar to persuasive mapping, and build their skills through a network that was spread over himself, the librarian, the online portal, and the students. Jeremiah also utilized Janet's expertise in his published work and cited her. This instance aligns with Leithwood and colleagues' (2006) notion of spontaneous alignment, where leadership activities are not planned but nonetheless are beneficial.

What the above case study highlights is how faculty members, and really anyone in a higher education institution, can begin to distribute servant leadership through various organizational networks and channels.

Adaptive Leadership

Adaptive leadership, like distributed leadership, may have tremendous synergy with servant leadership. As noted earlier, Heifetz, Grashow, and Linsky (2009) note that there exist two different types of issues in leadership, technical issues and adaptive issues. The answers to technical problems are already known. Technical problems are by no means simple, but the answers to these problems require the "application of authoritative expertise and through the organization's current structures" (Heifetz, Grashow, and Linsky 2009:19). On the other hand, the answers to adaptive problems require more than the application of preexisting structures and knowledge; they require people to learn new ideas and to act (Heifetz, Grashow, and Linsky 2009). In addition, most problems are not totally adaptive or technical. Most of the time, problems share elements of both types (Heifetz, Grashow, and Linsky 2009). Heifetz and colleagues (2009:6) argue that leadership is comprised of two facets: "diagnosis first and then action." Diagnosis is crucial to truly understand what the hell is happening!

In order to diagnose the situation, Heifetz and colleagues (2009) argue that leaders must examine formal organizational structures, such as policies.

Leaders must then analyze institutional culture. Leaders should also examine what Heifetz and colleagues (2009:63) call "defaults." Essentially, a default is a solution for a problem that used to work and that organizational members have grown accustomed to using. However, due to changing conditions, defaults may no longer work and may simply restrict the range of options and the ability for organizational members to consider new solutions to problems (Heifetz, Grashow, and Linsky 2009).

Leaders can ask what elements of the problem can be fixed with existing knowledge and what elements of the problem require new ways of thinking and understanding (Heifetz, Grashow, and Linsky 2009; O'Malley and Cebula 2015). Of course, as Heifetz and colleagues (2009) point out, this is no simple task. Next, leaders must examine the political context of the organization. Crucial at this point is an understanding of loss. People will inevitably lose something during change; as Heifetz and colleagues (2009:96) note: "Resistance to change stems from a fear of losing something important." Some examples of loss that Heifetz and colleagues (2009:96) give are identity, competence, comfort, security, power, control, and independence. Heifetz and colleagues (2009:28) state that "to practice adaptive leadership, you will have to help people navigate through a period of disturbance as they sift through what is essential and what is expendable." This also can be a prime opportunity for servant leadership. True leaders will have to come to understand the loss that people will experience from change and work to understand and mitigate this loss the best they can. One of the core tenets of servant leadership is emotional healing. Emotional healing is not medical or physical; rather, it entails helping others to mend their broken psyches and to assuage their broken dreams (Barbuto and Wheeler 2006; Wheeler 2012). Following Heifetz and colleagues (2009), leadership and change will create loss, and the healing aspect of servant leadership may be able to help remedy this loss in some ways.

Next, Heifetz and colleagues (2009) call for leaders to identify hidden alliances that exist in an organization that may affect or derail change. Heifetz and colleagues (2009:102) also call for leaders to "name the elephants in the room," which entails unearthing sensitive and uncomfortable issues. In addition, leaders should also call for the contribution of various organizational members no matter their role in the organization (Heifetz, Grashow, and Linsky 2009).

Diagnostic actions shape and set the ground for leadership and action. Leaders must understand the parameters of action by understanding organizational norms, cultures, defaults, and political configurations (Heifetz, Grashow, and Linsky 2009). Adaptive leaders cannot jump to action (Heifetz, Grashow, and Linsky 2009), and neither should servant leaders. In fact, these diagnostic actions can be reframed as a type of service. Northouse (2016), while not employing the term "servant leadership" for this purpose, does note a connection between adaptive leadership and service. Northouse

(2016:260) writes, "Similar to a physician, an adaptive leader uses his or her expertise or authority *to serve* the people by diagnosing their problems and prescribing possible solutions." Leaders can serve people by helping to diagnose situations, by enabling people to understand situations and problems so thoughtful and sustainable remedies can be enacted, not quick fixes. These remedies must include the expertise of many people in the organization as well. Diagnostic actions can help organizations slow down and truly evaluate the problems surrounding them.

Many of the various dimensions of servant leadership in this book align with these diagnostic ideas from adaptive leadership. The diagnostic actions called for by adaptive leadership align with the notions of systems thinking in a number of ways, as well as listening and humility. Heifetz and colleagues (2009:7) argue for leaders to get "on the balcony." From the metaphorical balcony, leaders can distance themselves from the situation and see the problem and issues from a different light. Systems thinking can be of use here, because only when you get some distance and see the forest and not just the trees can you appreciate the entire system in all its complexity. In addition, listening and humility align with the practice of seeing the elephants in the room and calling for contributions of many organizational members. As they diagnose the situation, leaders must listen to all viewpoints and perspectives, especially the ideas of their followers, which are difficult to hear and which may cause discomfort. This calls for humility and a recognition that "servant leaders acknowledge their limitations and therefore actively seek the contributions of others in order to overcome those limitations" (van Dierendonck and Nuijten 2011:252).

The next step in the adaptive leadership process is what Heifetz and colleagues (2009) call mobilizing the system. This step entails the move from diagnosis to action. As noted earlier, many times organizational members will revert to default interpretations. After defaults are recognized, then leaders can help members to create a number of new interpretations. Multiple interpretations (as opposed to one interpretation) open the door for action (Heifetz, Grashow, and Linsky 2009). Mobilizing the system then entails leaders making interventions to get people to take action to remedy adaptive issues (Heifetz, Grashow, and Linsky 2009), although interventions can also ensue during the diagnose stage as well. Some examples of interventions are "questions, process ideas, frameworks, single change initiatives," to name a few (Heifetz, Grashow, and Linsky 2009:109).

The notion of mobilization is a type of empowerment using the ideas of servant leadership. For one, the action of creating new and multiple interpretations is the epitome of empowerment; the servant leader can see followers as capable and worthy of these challenges, and see herself or himself as a facilitator, not an authoritarian with all the answers. As a servant leader who empowers, she or he can see these interpretations as valuable, crucial, and necessary. The facilitation of new interpretations also aligns with van Dierendonck and Rook's (2010) call for servant leaders to foster creativity among their followers. Having organizational members generate new interpretations of problems and issues will require creativity on the part of all organizational members.

Another consideration of mobilization is to act politically. Perhaps one of the most daunting challenges of this phase is fostering a sense of cooperation with your opponents (Heifetz, Grashow, and Linsky 2009). Heifetz and colleagues (2009) call for empathy and compassion. Empathy is also at the heart of servant leadership. Relating to opponents will also require listening. We must empathize and listen to people who disagree with us and, in the extreme sense, who may hate us. This may be one of the most difficult challenges for servant leaders, but it is crucial if leaders are to understand what will hinder change. Leaders must also own up to the necessary damages they inflict that are due to their actions and the changes they seek to make (Heifetz, Grashow, and Linsky 2009). This will be explored in detail shortly. Acting politically aligns with Sipe and Frick's (2015) pillar of skilled communicator, specifically the demonstration of empathy.

Creating conflict is an important part of mobilizing people. Creating and successfully managing conflict can help leaders to tease "out the *unacknowledged* differences in perspectives on work issues" that prevent change (Heifetz, Grashow, and Linsky 2009:150). Conflict should not be stopped or ignored, because it can allow for people to realize and acknowledge different values, ideas, and visions, and work through them to create some sort of compromise (Heifetz, Grashow, and Linsky 2009). Conflict will open up wounds and create uneasiness and feelings for hurt. Emotional healing will be crucial here as well.

After orchestrating conflict, the next step is more long term. The next step requires the creation of an adaptive culture. An adaptive culture in an organization "will enable your organization or community to meet an ongoing series of adaptive challenges into the future" (Heifetz, Grashow, and Linsky 2009:165). Some ways to do this are to allow and encourage organizational members to bring up and air difficult issues, create a feeling of ownership in employees for organizational goals and achievements, promote leadership abilities in organizational members, and allow for members to experiment (and encourage learning from failed experiments), to name a few (Heifetz, Grashow, and Linsky 2009). Building an adaptive culture, like servant leadership, is centered on follower growth and creativity, and one way to ensure that followers grow is to ensure that they have the necessary mental capabilities, tools, direction, and confidence to tackle problems. This is a form of empowerment, a new way to view empowerment in the lens of adaptive leadership. This also aligns with the promotion of conceptual skills and mapping, as well as with the call for servant leaders to create more servant leaders.

The lens of adaptive leadership highlights some of the main tenets of servant leadership—systems thinking, humility, listening, empowerment, mapping, and the creation of servant leaders, to name a few. However, perhaps the greatest synergy between the two theories of leadership is emotional healing. Progress and change usually entail loss, and Heifetz and colleagues (2009) argue that leaders must be cognizant of this loss, and help to mitigate it. Emotional healing is a facet of servant leadership; however, the actual act of healing may be beyond research in some ways. What does it mean to heal someone? What does healing actually look like and feel like? As noted earlier, Heifetz and colleagues (2009) identified some things that people may lose in times of change. Some of the more obvious things are money, control, or jobs. How does one comfort another when one is facing the loss of money (especially in times of growing inequality) or their job? How does one heal someone who must relinquish control? Moreover, some of the other things that people may lose in a transition may be even harder to grapple with and help people recover from, such as reputation, status, or independence. How can a leader serve her or his followers and at least work to heal them when they face the loss of these things? What does one say when one is facing the loss of one's reputation or identity? These are not easy tasks and can be emotionally draining for the servant leader as well as for those who are facing loss. There is probably no preset way to handle these situations, no guidebook. Leaders will have to struggle through these questions and draw on their experiences (as they accrue). Loss and healing should not be tangential or ancillary to leadership, but following adaptive leadership should be a central concern of leaders. Moreover, servant leaders, by acting as servants, may be better able to help those facing loss.

Managing loss is not simply about being a shoulder to cry on. As Heifetz and colleagues (2009) note, leaders who are pursuing change will many times *create* loss and pain in the process of the change they are pursuing. As Heifetz and colleagues (2009:144–145) note: "If you are trying to exercise adaptive leadership, you will need to shoulder responsibility for these inevitable casualties." How do you as a leader practice emotional healing when you are the one causing pain? As a servant leader, you must begin to probe the depths of loss, and especially the loss and hurt that you cause. Van Dierendonck and Nuijten (2011) note that a tenet of servant leadership is accountability; this can extend to oneself. A leader must be accountable to her or his followers for the losses and pain that she or he causes in the process of change.

Adaptive leadership especially resonates with the notions of empowerment. As Northouse (2016:258) notes, adaptive leadership "is actually more follower centered. It focuses primarily on how leaders help others do the work they need to do." This is the purpose of adaptive leadership; mobilizing people to work on problems (Heifetz, Grashow, and Linsky 2009; Northouse 2016). The leader does not do the work for them, but facilitates people doing the hard work themselves. This is empowerment; it is getting people to act. The priority of servant leadership, like adaptive leadership, is followers. Cast in terms of servant leadership, leaders must empower their followers to accomplish the work.

Adaptive leadership is meant for all people in all positions (Heifetz, Grashow, and Linsky 2009). The ideas of adaptive leadership, especially reframed through servant leadership, can be practiced by college presidents with faculty and administrators, faculty members with students, athletic coaches with players, and support staff with followers. This book has stressed that servant leadership can and should be employed at all levels of higher education. In addition, I have not done full justice to the theories of adaptive leadership. Rather, I have simply pointed out some of the synergy between certain tenets of adaptive leadership and servant leadership in an effort to illustrate how servant leadership can be applied in different ways or with different leadership theories.

Case Study

This section presents two case studies, one dealing with accountability and one dealing with research norms. Chapter 5 dealt with the topic of accountability. This case study casts the reframing of accountability as an adaptive challenge. There is no easy answer, no plan to follow in order to achieve accountability. Further, different types of accountability will most likely cause some groups and individuals to feel a sense of loss. For instance, institutions and policy makers may lose the certainty of having easy quantifiable measures and be left with fuzzy and uncertain measurements. If colleges shift to a model of accountability outlined in chapter 5, it could generate more uncertainty that is unnerving because, as Giroux (2016) points out, many in higher education are preoccupied with data and measurement. Notwithstanding this uncertainty, how could this new vision of accountability and servant leadership emerge? There is no one set way, but individuals and institutions could follow the tenets of adaptive leadership and cast this as an adaptive challenge.

First, some people will have to take up the cause. These could be administrators and/or faculty members. They might be at a single university or across universities. In addition, policy makers or those outside the university could work for this cause as well. Those wishing to cast accountability as an adaptive challenge must first diagnose the situation; they could examine the structural implications and cultural norms that underpin accountability, both in their organization and in wider contexts. Structural implications are policies and rules in place. What cultural attitudes prevail regarding higher education accountability in different circles? Next, they must look at default interpretations. What default interpretations are they (higher education members) utilizing? Which members hold these default norms? What is comforting about the current state of accountability, and to which groups? These are crucial questions. Those wishing to challenge accountability may need to ask different stakeholders in higher education.

As noted earlier, there are usually technical and adaptive aspects to each challenge, and those tackling challenges should work to ferret these out and understand the differences. What are the adaptive aspects to changing accountability? What are the technical aspects? Specifically, for technical aspects, actual ways to measure these far-reaching forms of accountability might be necessary. The adaptive aspects are discussed throughout this case study.

Working from the premise of loss, who loses what as things change? In order to answer this, hostile parties should be engaged, such as politicians who are known to be hostile of education. What are their grievances? Concerns? These groups cannot be written off as ignorant; they must be engaged (which may be increasingly difficult in our current political climate, both on the federal and state levels). The most important question is, what do these groups stand to lose if accountability can be reframed as service—service to students, society, and posterity? In order to embrace this view, leaders can ask who loses by it, both inside and outside the academy. Why is this loss felt, and how can it be mitigated?

What new interpretations of accountability can be created? In chapter 5, I detailed a number of ways that service aligns with accountability. These could be a starting point. Organizational members can think about their organizations, their communities, and their profession in the long term to create new interpretations relating to accountability. What interventions can be pursued? Could politicians be lobbied and educated as to different types of accountability? Could those wishing to change accountability engage politicians in more formal ways such as lobbying, or in more grassroots ways?

Next, those wishing to reframe accountability could work to seek out allies and build political alliances. Who, inside and outside of higher education, would support a new vision of accountability built on servant leadership? Perhaps before this action, who will first spearhead this cause? Are there players even interested in this? Are there similar movements going on already? Is this the job of faculty, administrators, staff, or a combination? (I believe it would be a combination.) Where can alliances be built and with whom? Conflict between hostile parties should also not be avoided, but unearthed and managed in healthy ways.

The above may sound like a fairy tale, and it most likely is. The point of the exercise is not to implement the ideas as I have written them; rather, the point is to get organizational members thinking in different ways about how adaptive leadership and servant leadership can be used to reframe the daily operations of higher education as well as its relation to the community.

Another issue that I have touched upon in this book, which can be cast as an adaptive issue, is the understanding and evaluation of academic research by academic researchers themselves. In chapter 3, I outlined four strands of research. Currently, the strand of research for prestige and promotion is one that is prevalent. I specifically want to focus on the notion of loss. If framed as an adaptive issue, the research for prestige and promotion strand can entail loss. However, who loses? Of course, we are not assessing a singular organization, but rather a much more nebulous phenomenon, a collection of scholars and researchers who adhere to certain norms. These norms are self-enforced, and enforced by research institutions, journals, and funding agencies. Heifetz and colleagues (2009) note that there is usually a belief that systems and organizations are broken, and this is the reason for negative results. However, Heifetz and colleagues (2009) note that this is a myth because someone or groups of people benefit from the way the system currently runs. Following this line of reasoning, we must assess who stands to lose something and what stands to be lost. Who would not want to see this system changed?

The most obvious answer to who loses something if the current system of research were to be changed are the top-level researchers, the ones who consistently publish in the top journals. As Bok (2015) notes, in the sciences, there is a small group of researchers who are responsible for the majority of publications and who are cited the most (Cole and Cole 1972). If this sentiment holds true for a number of disciplines and if the norms of research were changed, this might disempower the current top researchers in these disciplines. Specifically, following Heifetz and colleagues (2009), some things that these researchers may lose are status and reputation. Large research universities and high-ranking journals may also stand to lose status and reputation if the norms of research are changed. Assessing loss from an adaptive leadership lens can help to add a new facet of understanding to the research debate for those like myself who wish to inculcate norms of service. What threats do the visions of service, mainly the intellectual service, pose? Who would stand to lose from this?

I have given a truncated view of adapted leadership, and I have tailored it to accountability and research in higher education that is not the concern of one organization, but many. This case study is meant as a guide to accomplish change for those concerned about higher education accountability and research.

Reflection Questions

1. What other leadership theories can servant leadership align with or augment?
2. How may servant leadership detract from distributive and adaptive leadership?

8

Opportunities and Barriers to Servant Leadership

Different institutional types, such as research universities, comprehensive universities, and community colleges, may also offer different opportunities for integrating servant leadership. Further, institutional structures and norms, such as athletic teams and service to the university, may also offer opportunities. There are also a number of potential barriers to integrating servant leadership, including the accreditation process, organizational culture and structure, as well as the existence of bigoted ideology, to name a few. These opportunities and barriers are by no means exhaustive.

Institutional Type

It is no secret that large research universities garner the most attention and prestige (Bok 2015; Boyer 2015). Yet different institutional types may be able to utilize servant leadership in different ways and accomplish different goals. Moreover, those in different institutional types may be able to use the ideas of servant leadership to accentuate the strengths of their lesser-known institutions. Of course, servant leadership will not dismantle hierarchies in higher education, but it might help less prestigious institutions define themselves in a new and progressive way.

It does, however, make sense to acknowledge different types of institutions, not to put them in a pecking order, but to highlight their strengths and look for opportunities to promote servant leadership. The list below partially follows Bok's (2015) typology. Further, another important consideration is that classifications of universities should not be seen as rigid and immutable, but a fluid conceptual tool. For instance, a great deal of teaching takes place at research universities, while a great deal of research takes place at what are termed primarily teaching institutions. So all labels are fluid.

Public Universities

As noted earlier, Hutner and Mohamed (2016) have called for public universities to play a new role in society, which is marked by rising inequality, by helping to promote democracy. I extended this call to all universities, but there is a reason for seeing this as an initiative of public universities. Newfield (2016) defines the public university as centered on access, quality, and inclusion. Regarding access, you did not have to be rich to attend college (Newfield 2016). As for quality, Newfield (2016) argues that public universities were dedicated to quality in research and teaching, in many cases surpassing private institutions. In particular, for teaching, Newfield (2016) argues that public universities worked to improve and develop students (they did not simply take the cream of the crop as private universities did). Finally, public universities (at least ideally and not without a fight) were inclusive of many types of students (Newfield 2016).

Newfield (2016) argues this vision of the public is faltering. Public funding has all but dried up (replaced by unsustainable tuition hikes). Further, public universities are now most interested in "supporting industry and spreading quantitative skills" (Newfield 2016:168). Newfield (2016:170) boldly calls for higher education "to make itself chief architect on a national project whose mainstream branch could be called 'rebuilding a middle-class society' on an egalitarian model."

Public universities serve non-elite students, or at least have in the past. This is why they are so important and why they are so suited to servant leadership. They served the masses; they sought to admit and develop those with non-elite backgrounds, even and including nonwhites; they were committed to growth.

Of course, public research universities, comprehensive universities, and community colleges (dealt with next) have different students and goals. Comprehensive universities, most of which are public, serve a wide variety of students and are less selective than public research universities (Bok 2015). These universities sometimes have a difficult time actually articulating their mission because they try to do so much and serve many students (Bok 2015). The research undertaken at comprehensive universities is more practical, and they usually collaborate with public schools and small businesses (Bok 2015).

The point is that public universities, all of them, serve their students, communities, and society in unique ways. Public research universities and public comprehensive universities undertake teaching and research (and obviously assessment and planning). Following Newfield (2016), the notion of developing students from non-elite and nonwealthy backgrounds is extremely relevant for servant leaders. These universities may need to reinvigorate some of the ideas that Newfield has put forth to be servant universities. Following Newfield's assertions, there is a dormant or latent notion of service in public universities, in the actual meaning of the term "public" that can be reinvigorated by servant leadership in some ways.

The Community College

One of the driving reasons for the creation of the community college was centered on the American ideal of equality; community colleges became means for individuals to attain a higher education who may not normally have a chance to achieve one (Bok 2015; Brint and Karabel 1989; Kisker and Ronan 2016; Mullin, Baime, and Honeyman 2015). However, the community college was also created as a way to sort and filter people into more subordinate roles and dull their educational and occupational aspirations (Brint and Karabel 1989). As Brint and Karabel (1989) note, there are only a limited number of spots at the top, and not everyone can make it. Brint and Karabel (1989) argue that the community college serves two functions: democratic advancement and sorting. As such, the community college represents a complicated arrangement, but one that nonetheless serves a large proportion of American students (Bok 2015; Mullin, Baime, and Honeyman 2015). Moreover, the number enrolled at community colleges will most likely keep increasing (Mullin, Baime, and Honeyman 2015).

Perhaps more than any other institution, community colleges serve an extremely wide variety of students, ranging from large numbers of minorities, many part-time students, older students, vocational students, and dual enrollment students (Bok 2015; Mullin, Baime, and Honeyman 2015). As Bok (2015) notes, community college students many times enter deficient in necessary academic skills and are in need of remedial instruction. In addition, community colleges are the main access point for nonwhite students (Mullin, Baime, and Honeyman 2015). This variety of students, and their sometimes precarious situations, may make servant leadership more necessary at community colleges. Another subset of students that community colleges are dealing with are dual enrollment students (Mullin, Baime, and Honeyman 2015). Dual enrollment students are students who are enrolled simultaneously in high school and college classes (Hofmann 2012). Some dual enrollment students receive instruction on a college campus, while many are taught in high schools by instructors certified by a community college (Hofmann 2012). Dual enrollment students, especially if they are high school students, are a unique type of community college student even though they may not actually be on a community college campus.

Perhaps the variety of students invites community colleges to embrace the ideas of servant leadership. Community colleges, and those that lead and teach in them, must be sensitive to the different types of students, more so than their counterparts at traditional four-year schools, simply because the students entering community colleges are more complex and demand more attention for a variety of reasons. Different types of students will necessitate different types of service and different ideas from servant leadership. As an example, service to a nonwhite working mother may look different than service to a rural eighteen-year-old or a dual enrollment student. If community colleges are the access point for the majority of nonwhite students, how does this fact affect service to these students? It is no secret that racial and ethnic tensions in the United States are high. Wealth inequality is also rising. As such, faculty and administrators should account for this in their dealings with students, both white and nonwhite, as well as those who come from low socioecomonic status backgrounds. The point is not to coddle these students, or give them more chances, but to truly *engage* them. If the community college is a place of opportunity, how can these types of students be served? How do they grow in an atmosphere of hate and limited opportunity? What can the community college offer, at the structural level and classroom level, for these students to grow and become contributing members of society? Dual enrollment students offer yet another facet to servant leadership and community colleges. How can community colleges serve dual enrollment students, especially those in high school?

Community colleges enroll many diverse students. As such, perhaps the notion of servant leadership as constellation is nowhere more evident than in the community college. Yet faculty members at community colleges may also need support. As Bok (2015) notes, many community college instructors do not have PhDs; many are part-time and work other jobs. Administrators and full-time faculty could reach out to contingent faculty and simply listen to their concerns and treat them like real faculty.

Of course, colleges have to deal with fiscal realities, especially during times of economic downturns (Mullin, Baime, and Honeyman 2015). As such, the service I am advocating may not seem feasible at times. However, I believe that, upon reflection, service can be pursued, especially by faculty members. There do not have to be university-wide programs dedicated to service; rather, individual faculty members—those on campus, those in high schools, and those teaching online—could simply understand that their students, and many of their fellow faculty members are unique and, in some cases, vulnerable.

Shugart (1997), following Greenleaf, warns community colleges not to be duped by their own morality. Following this, community colleges should not assume that they are automatically serving their students simply by their students attending. Service must be conscious and deliberate, even in and despite tough economic conditions. Simply put, those in community colleges, especially faculty members, must find a way to serve. Community colleges can keep in mind the wide variety of students they serve as they promote servant leadership through pedagogy, research, planning, assessment, and accountability.

Religious Institutions of Higher Education

Greenleaf (2002) argued that "the thing to be done with religious concern is to rebind humankind to the cosmos, to heal the pervasive alienation." Moreover, to some extent, churches did take up an ameliorative role throughout the 1970s. Schulman (2002), drawing on Gallup polls conducted in the 1970s, argued that religion provided direction for people in the tumultuous times in which they found themselves. And not just mainstream religion, but New Age religious ideas as well (Schulman, 2001). Religion also became political, with the rise of the Moral Majority (Schulman, 2001). By the 1980s, religious organizations had emerged as powerful political players (Phillips 2006). By the early 2000s, Christianity played a dominant role in politics in America (Phillips 2006). Phillips (2006:x), however, argues that this is a "simplistic Christianity." Military might and the denial of science are some of the foundational planks that buttress this type of Christianity. Hill (2006) similarly argues that a number of churches have forsaken the missions of healing and binding humanity in favor of pursuing initiatives that run counter to the words of Jesus and servant leadership. Phillips (2006) does note that secularism is strong in the United States. However, he argues that the politics of the George W. Bush administration represented a serious development in the emergence of religion as a political force. Phillips (2006) went so far as to call it an "American Theocracy." (It is the title of his 2006 book.) Further, there are certain rules that churches must abide by when entering politics. Yet Phillips (2006) argued that in the mid-2000s, while stopping short of violating the separation of church and state, many advocates and churches exerted a strong political influence on the Republican Party. In 2017, this struggle only intensified.

A true examination of the role of religion, especially Christianity, in American politics warrants another book. All I argue here is that the religious intervention into politics can transform Jesus's words and ideas. Racism, bigotry, and decadence for many, but by no means all, religious adherents have usurped Jesus's simple words and ideas, mainly of loving each other and living a simple life. Religion has been usurped by politics in a number of ways, while Jesus's message is disfigured and transformed into something unrecognizable. Again, I do not mean to stereotype all religious institutions. There are many good churches and religious adherents in all religions in the United States. I personally believe that Pope Francis's words and actions are a step in the right direction, and can serve as an exemplar for religion in the twenty-first century. Fundamentalism and violence should not only be associated with religion, however. As Ferch (2011) notes, many atheistic and nonreligious doctrines have fallen prey to cruelty and violence; he gives Stalin and Pol Pot as examples.

Beaver (2014) notes that Greenleaf sought to fight against religious fundamentalism. Following Hill (2006), Beaver notes that Greenleaf believed fundamentalism restricted creativity and action. Hill (2006:12) bluntly notes, "Witnessing fundamentalist religions on the rise and gaining a particular stronghold of power gives us a vivid, firsthand, opportunity for noting that a fundamentalist agenda is, by its very nature, incongruent with the principles and outcomes of servant leadership." Hill (2006) also notes how many times fundamentalists will evoke the term "servant leadership" as a cover for prejudice and bigotry. As Hill (2006) notes, however, fundamentalism does provide a sort of comfort for people and societies that are experiencing threats and anxiety. This is a strong appeal of fundamentalism (Hill 2006) and one that must be contended with. Fundamentalism will not be easily stopped precisely because it does provide comfort.

Religious institutions of higher education, when promoting servant leadership, must follow Greenleaf in this respect; they must resist the picture of Christianity sketched by Phillips and Hill, which is based on fundamentalism, dogmatism, intolerance, and denial of science, to name a few. Dogmatism and fundamentalism are pitfalls of religion and can destroy the good and true power of religious doctrines. Religious institutions of higher education in the United States can promote servant leadership through pedagogy, research, planning, accountability, and assessment in different and more overtly religious ways than their secular counterparts by using their religious denomination and its doctrines as a vehicle to do this, but not falling victim to fundamentalism. Further, by not falling victim to fundamentalism, religious institutions can be exemplars in a world rife with religious division and polarization. This fundamentalism is not limited to one religion; there is more than enough fundamentalism in Christianity as well, and religious institutions of higher education could combat this through servant leadership.

Religious institutions of higher education can heed Greenleaf's call from over forty years ago and become a truly binding force by utilizing the tenets of servant leadership in nonfundamentalist and nondogmatic ways. Many religious institutions do integrate ideas that align with servant leadership. Alverno College and Viterbo College, to cite two examples, have employed ideas that align with servant leadership (Farnsworth 2007; Sipe and Frick 2015). Gonzaga University also has dedicated programs to servant leadership. Not surprisingly, Christian religious institutions of higher education may be able to utilize the tenets of servant leadership in unique ways by specifically drawing on the ideas of Jesus. As Wong and Page (2003) note, Jesus is an example of servant leadership. Beaver (2014) also notes that Jesus is considered a servant leader and that he placed the notion of service to one's fellows above the self. In addition, Greenleaf was impacted heavily by Quaker thought (Beaver 2014). Religious institutions of higher education, specifically Christian institutions, can truly work to bind society by adhering to the true tenets of Christianity that also align with servant leadership.

Sendjaya (2010) grapples with the oft-repeated criticism that servant leadership is only for the religious. He argues that both the religious and the secular can utilize servant leadership. However, many times servant leadership is connected with religious ideas. Sendjaya (2010:45) argues that "for those of some religious persuasion, it emerges from an internal conviction that the servant-leader is a servant of a higher being." The point is that religious institutions, while they do not have a monopoly on servant leadership, can make a strong claim to it.

Private Liberal Arts Colleges

Sendjaya (2010) point outs that servant leadership has a number of secular influences. Beaver (2014) specifically notes that the ideas of servant leadership embody a deep spirituality that can go beyond one specific religion. As Sendjaya (2010:45) argues: "For those with spiritual orientation but no religious attachment, the motivation to practice servant leadership comes from not a higher being, but from a set of core values, ideals or causes." Servant leadership can be completely secular, and one subset of institutions that may embody this nonreligious spirituality is liberal arts institutions. Bok (2015) notes how these types of institutions do not serve many students. Many small, private, four-year institutions are geared toward the liberal arts; of course, many have also had to broaden their offerings to stay competitive (Bok 2015). Nevertheless, in the widest sense, the liberal arts focus is similar to religion. In some sense, the religious institution is a sort of foil to the liberal arts institutions. Small private colleges can draw on the many and varied ideas of the liberal arts to promote a type of nonreligious spirituality centered in wholeness and interconnectedness. These schools can help to foster connection between their students and between their students and the wider society.

There is, however, an important distinction to make. Hutner and Mohamed (2016) argue that public universities must continue to make a strong claim for why teaching liberal arts and the humanities is necessary at public universities and necessary for democracy. They argue that liberal arts education cannot simply be undertaken at elite private universities. Liberal arts education is vital to all students and our democracy (Hutner and Mohamed 2016). (This argument is close to my heart. I majored in history at a regional comprehensive university. While I am probably biased, I believe that the liberal arts instruction I received was incredible. My professors taught me how to challenge ideas and truly think differently about the world in which I lived.) Therefore, in no way do I argue that private liberal arts colleges should be the *only* places teaching liberal arts with an eye to spirituality and wholeness as described by servant leadership. This should also, and needs to, take place at public institutions as well. I simply call attention to the fact that one of the primary purposes of these colleges is the liberal arts, and that this purpose can be reframed with servant leadership.

Opportunities for Servant Leadership

Astute administrators and faculty could find and create new ways to integrate servant leadership on their campuses. As has been stressed throughout the book, no two campuses are the same. As such, administrators and faculty may need to assess their campuses and look for ways to integrate servant leadership that will work best on their campuses. Service to the profession and athletics may be two more ways to accomplish this task.

Service to University and Profession

Research, teaching, and service are the main tasks of university faculty. Yet equal weight is not given to each of these tasks. At most universities, service is not valued as highly for tenure and promotion (Mamiseishvili, Miller, and Lee 2016; Toews and Yazedjian 2007). "Service" is a wide-ranging term and usually encompasses service to the university, service to the profession, and service to the community (Mamiseishvili, Miller, and Lee 2016). This section focuses on service to the university. As Towes and Yazedjian (2007) note, service obligations can limit the time that faculty members can dedicate to teaching and research. Service to the university, while perhaps the least valued in regard to tenure, is integral to the university in a number of ways (Mamiseishvili, Miller, and Lee 2016; Toews and Yazedjian 2007).

As such, faculty members can utilize their service obligations to integrate servant leadership. Service to the university usually entails committee work. So, the question is, how can faculty use their committee work to implement servant leadership? In the case study on distributed leadership, I pointed out how a faculty member could bring the ideas of servant leadership to a specific committee, the Title IX committee. The Title IX committee is a serious committee, whereas other committees may not hold the same gravity. Nevertheless, faculty members could begin to reconceptualize their committee work and look for ways to utilize servant leadership. For instance, committees that deal with professional development or diversity concerns on campus may offer opportunities for servant leadership. The very purpose of certain committees is faculty or student development, promoting a positive campus climate, or promoting social justice, and these concerns align with servant leadership.

Newer faculty, however, may not have the influence on committees that their tenured counterparts may have. Nevertheless, committee work can also serve as an excellent means for new faculty to understand their institution's structures and procedures (Adams 2002; Toews and Yazedjian 2007). Young faculty can learn to navigate their institution and learn where opportunities may exist in their institution to integrate and practice the ideas of servant leadership.

Athletic Coaching

Another opportunity to integrate servant leadership may be an unlikely one: athletic coaching. Coaches of team sports have long been seen as leaders, and rightfully so; they lead a team and by doing so create something more than the sum of its parts. Sports can help to promote a number of important characteristics in participants, such as character and morality (Constantinou 2014). Rieke, Hammermeister, and Chase (2008) argue that servant leadership can be a new way to frame athletic coaching. Rieke and colleagues (2008), who also cited an earlier study done by Hammermeister and colleagues, found that servant leadership on the part of coaches helps to promote healthy development in athletes. Again, following Greenleaf's idea and the bedrock of servant leadership, when coaches exercise servant leadership, they can help their athletes grow in a number of ways. My argument specifically centers on Division II (DII) and especially Division III (DIII) National Collegiate Athletic Association (NCAA) sports.

As Watt and Moore (2001) argue, participation in DII and DIII programs differs from participation in Division I (DI) programs. One difference is the heightened demand to win as well as increased scrutiny from the media in DI sports (Watt and Moore 2001). The starkest contrast between DII and DIII sports and DI sports, however, is the motivation of the athletes. DII and DIII athletes play because they love the game, and they do not seek extrinsic rewards and praise (Watt and Moore 2001). This fact is perhaps the most important to understand the heart of a DIII athlete. It is this fact that servant leaders can emphasize. No scholarships are offered at the DIII level (Watt and Moore 2001). Therefore, in a sense, DIII athletes truly play for the love of the game. While all collegiate sports and coaches can benefit from the ideas of servant leadership, as Rieke and colleagues (2008) suggest, it is DII and specially DIII that may offer a special opportunity for this.

Citing a number of research studies, Watt and Moore (2001) note that some of the benefits of participating in collegiate sports are increased well-being, better health, higher self-esteem, the promotion of leadership capacities, increased discipline, teamwork, as well higher motivation. There are a number of drawbacks to participating in college sports as well. Again, citing a number of research studies, Watt and Moore (2001) note that some of the drawbacks are an overemphasis on winning, increased sexual aggressiveness, homophobia, as well as distorted body image (Watt and Moore 2001). Servant leadership may be able to shed new light on these benefits and drawbacks and help coaches be better able to understand and promote or deter them. The drawbacks to participating in college sports can be especially devastating. Unfortunately, many times college athletes who have committed rape and other instances of sexual violence are not held accountable due to their status as athletes. This is one extreme example, but it does show how coaches, if cognizant of some of the negative aspects of participation, can work to mitigate them. If coaches do overemphasize winning at all costs, coaches may neglect the fact that they are dealing with human beings, and not just human beings, but impressionable individuals. Player growth and development is the cornerstone of coaching. Yet coaches must be responsible not just for the players' growth on the field, but off it as well. This is a type of service.

Coaches can show their players the much larger picture and how DIII sports fit into this picture, how the lessons of their playing days are more than just sports lessons. Coaches can emphasize the notions of humility and covenantal relationships (Sendjaya, Sarros, and Santora 2008). Players of team sports must be humble and realize that winning is a team effort. Unfortunately, this message sometimes is lost in the media that lauds certain high-profile individuals at the expense of other less-skilled but no less-important players. Further, the media many times neglect the team aspect. This team aspect also points to covenantal relationships. All players, no matter the level of talent, should be treated equally. This of course is not the reality on many teams, and I do not argue that excellent players should not be recognized. Nevertheless, coaches can promote the idea that all team members are valuable because everyone has a role to play and that one member should not be glorified so much over the others. While not getting into specifics, coaches can emphasize the notion of systems thinker here as well (Sipe and Frick 2015). Teams are systems, and even the most talented athletes are components of the larger system. Star athletes cannot simply will a win; winning is largely the result of a system. While the system could not function effectively without star athletes, star athletes must also realize that they could not function as effectively without the system in place.

DI football, following the professional game, is largely a business. Star players are lauded and become fodder for the pro game. DI football is essentially a training ground for the National Football League (NFL). This is not to bash DI or the NFL. However, there are many negative aspects to the commercialized games today. DII and especially DIII sports can separate themselves from this commercialization and become a ground for truly meaningful work. In the widest sense, whatever the sport, DIII coaches can truly emphasize the fact the DIII players play for something greater than themselves; they play for the love of the game, which is something supremely meaningful. This goes beyond money and commercialization. This may be a powerful lesson in today's commercialized society.

I must give full disclosure here. I played DIII football, so this account is biased. Nevertheless, having played as a DIII athlete, I fully understand the notion of playing for the love of the game. Moreover, my wife had a stellar DIII career as a field hockey player. She started for four years on defense and anchored a national championship team her junior year as captain. I, on the other hand, only made varsity as a junior and senior. My senior year I started two games, and we were awarded a small regional bowl game, which we won. Nevertheless, while our playing experiences differed, they both had a tremendous impact on us. The point is, coaches at the DII and DIII levels can see their programs as a vehicle of service. While these coaches want to win just the same as DI coaches, they also have more responsibility and opportunity to influence their players in ways that DI coaches cannot. DI sports, especially football and basketball, are largely centered on businesses and profit. The experiences of DII and DIII athletes are usually different (Watt and Moore 2001). I knew I would never go to the NFL, and my wife knew she would never go to the Olympics, but we both loved our sports and gave them everything we had. Even today, the lessons I learned from my coaches and the game itself stick with me. I also should point out that, at least for football, servant leadership may seem at odds with the typical yelling and screaming coach. I do not argue for coaches to change their demeanor or become soft. Rather, tenets of servant leadership may simply help coaches see a much larger picture of DIII sports, as a vehicle to serve players and not just to win.

Barriers to Implementation

There are a number of potential barriers to integrating and practicing servant leadership in higher education. The barriers I have listed are by no means exhaustive. Further application of servant leadership will most likely uncover more barriers. However, while these barriers do pose serious threats, they are not fatal. They simply may require more reflection on the part of committed servant leaders.

Superficiality

As has been stressed throughout this book, the practice and integration of ideas of servant leadership cannot be a superficial endeavor. Rather, this endeavor must be lived; it must be believed by leaders and followers. Kezar

(2005) pointed to the notion of fads. Kezar (2005:7) describes fads as such: "fads come and go, with limited to no effectiveness or enhancement of campus operations." Following Birnbaum (2000), Kezar (2005) also notes that fads are usually greeted by administrators and top officials in higher education with much anticipation, but this excitement does not extend to other members in the organization. The fad is also spoken about with exuberant language, but the ideas usually do not take hold (Kezar 2005). Birnbaum (2000) does argue, however, that fads many times can have positive impacts, but fads also can be costly. While recognizing that not all fads are bad, those wishing to implement servant leadership should strive for something more than a fad. Servant leadership should not be a superficial endeavor; those implementing servant leadership should look to the long term.

Kezar (2001), in an earlier study, examined a community college in the mid-1990s that sought to promote a more inclusive environment on campus using the ideas of servant leadership. Kezar (2001) ultimately concluded that servant leadership failed to achieve this objective on this campus. Kezar (2001) criticized the notion of servant leadership and argued that it may not actually be able to accommodate diverse views and ideas. However, Kezar did not examine servant leadership in any detail, and left out crucial components to what servant leadership actually is, and thus I do not think her claim holds up. Nevertheless, Kezar (2001) noted that the ideas of servant leadership did not transform this community college because they could not promote an inclusive environment. Rather, servant leadership (at least the way it was practiced at this community college, which was missing many key elements of servant leadership) actually worked to alienate many faculty at the community college. Many faculty did not feel like they fit in to this new model, and the community college remained hierarchical. Again, in a wider sense, whatever the merit of Kezar's (2001) criticism, it does point to the fact that servant leadership must be inclusive; it must not simply be something pushed by the administration or a top-down mandate. Those who are served must truly feel like they are served; they must feel empowered. Service must become part of an organization's way of operating.

One way to correct this is for faculty to embrace servant leadership, see themselves as servant leaders, and truly believe in the ideas of servant leadership if they so choose. Throughout this book, I have argued that servant leadership should not simply be for administrators but for faculty as well. While faculty may not have the reach and power that administrators do, faculty may be able to exercise true and genuine servant leadership in their small corner of the universe, which is infinitely better than a superficial fad that only breeds resentment. Yet even faculty could run the risk of servant leadership becoming a fad. For instance, faculty may say they are servant leaders in their classroom, but only give this lip service. In their dealings with students, despite their exhortations of servant leadership, they could still deal with them in an authoritarian matter, or they may only implement ideas of servant leadership that suit their own needs. Thus, at all levels, servant leadership cannot simply be a fad or a superficial endeavor. People must believe in it.

Authoritarian Hierarchies

Wong and Page (2003) argue that authoritarian hierarchies are obstacles to servant leadership. For one, an authoritarian hierarchy "serves to ensure the longevity of incompetent, unethical and unpopular leaders" (Wong and Page 2003:6). Authoritarian hierarchies also stymie creativity in organizational members and deter creative people from coming into an organization (Wong and Page 2003).

As noted earlier, Corrigan (2013) criticized distributed leadership as a method for more powerful members in an organization to gain acceptance for their ideas in a hierarchical organization. While Corrigan aimed his arguments at distributed leadership, the argument may also shed light on servant leadership as well. Corrigan (2013) argues that schools are hierarchical, and because of this, distributed leadership cannot be truly effective. Simply put, can servant leadership survive in highly hierarchal organizations? Can servant leadership, with its emphasis on follower development and humility, really be practiced in an organization that is built on power?

While difficult, it is not impossible. Wong and Page (2003:6) argue that "you can have a servant leader in a highly hierarchical organization." Wheeler (2012:169) notes something similar: "The bottom line is you can operate as a servant leader as long as you are meeting the outcomes expected." Wheeler (2012) goes on to note that the administration may not totally understand what you are doing, but as long as you perform your duties, you should be okay. Therefore, authoritarian and hierarchical organizations may inhibit and stymie servant leadership in some ways, but servant leadership can still be practiced in these types of organizations.

Accreditation

One potential barrier to integrating servant leadership ideas in higher education may be the accreditation process. While a potential barrier, however, accreditation may also provide some opportunities. As Farnsworth (2007:48) notes, a number of public universities have attempted to pursue learning outcomes that are similar with the ideals of servant leadership, yet "often shy away from aspirations that are too subjective or might be construed as advocating certain values." Obviously, private and especially religious universities would have more leeway here. Farnsworth (2007) further notes regional accreditation bodies require universities to show quantifiable measures of meeting university goals, and servant leadership ideas are obviously difficult to quantify.

Despite these challenges, Farnsworth (2007) still calls for leaders of universities to promote a dialogue centered on values regarding the institutional mission. He argues that if accrediting bodies demand quantifiable measures, then universities must create ways to demonstrate these types of values. Farnsworth's (2007) observation is important because it points to the difficulties that campuses may face in trying to articulate, pursue, and demonstrate learning outcomes that embody servant leadership, especially in regard to the accreditation process.

Schneider (2015) has noted that there exists a "dangerous public vacuum" in regional accreditation. There are a number of respected regionally accrediting bodies, but they all have different outcomes and standards for assessing and accrediting (Schneider 2015). As Schneider (2015) explains, while there is some evidence of and consensus around beneficial learning outcomes, regional accrediting bodies largely leave it to the institution to create and measure their own learning outcomes in the name of institutional autonomy. Schneider (2015) calls for accreditors to provide leadership by agreeing on beneficial learning outcomes, and promoting these outcomes. At the same time that learning outcomes are kept vague, Schneider (2015) notes that there is a growing impetus in both the Democratic and Republican Parties to measure universities on economic data, such as how many students find employment and starting salaries. In time, Schneider (2015) argues that economic data could replace learning outcomes. Schneider (2015) argues that if economic indicators are used, this would threaten the use of outcomes such as ethical and critical thinking and other outcomes associated with the liberal arts.

If this were to occur, how could institutions pursue the servant leadership initiatives I have proposed in this book? How could servant leadership gain a foothold if economic data are the only data that are measured? This has not happened, but even if it never happens, it still requires us to ask how servant leadership initiatives can be pursued in a climate where colleges are seen primarily as vocational centers. However, institutional autonomy may allow certain higher education institutions to have leeway to create learning outcomes that align with servant leadership, but even if there were some articulated agreement on learning outcomes, presumably many ideas of servant leadership would align with those outcomes. Nevertheless, the prospect of relying on economic indicators and outcomes could seriously impede the implementation of servant leadership on campuses because the ideas of servant leadership may not be viewed as economically viable or useful.

Listening to Nonsense

Another barrier for servant leaders is the presence of unethical political and social ideologies that are widely held and are seen as unproblematic and desirable. A core facet of servant leadership is the notion of listening (Fitzgerald

2015; Spears 1995). Yet, as a servant leader, how can I listen to and entertain racist, bigoted, homophobic, misogynistic, and other derogatory ideologies that others may hold? Do I have to give people who hold these ideals an opportunity to speak? If I give them this opportunity, do I somehow legitimize their claims? As an extreme example, if a servant leader lived in Nazi Germany, would he or she have to entertain and seriously listen to Nazi ideology?

Again, this is an extreme example. In contemporary America, as noted in the preface, the election of Donald Trump nonetheless has given rise to many racist and bigoted ideas. How do we listen to people who hold them? In addition, I am no way calling for cessation of debates that involve race or other touchy subjects. People critical of affirmative action, for instance, should not be silenced because they are taking a stance against a perceived social justice policy. Informed positions, even if these positions may be critical of social justice or other perceived emancipatory policies, must be given credence and are crucial to a functioning democracy. What I am arguing is that racist or bigoted arguments, such as blacks are lazy or women should be in the kitchen, for instance, should never be given credence.

However, if I deny these claims, could I maybe be shutting out people with real but misguided and misplaced grievances? It might be easy to dismiss these people, but these derogatory ideologies may be a symptom of deeper issues in our society. People who are fearful and anxious over social change, for example, and thus easier to mislead, may direct their anger at scapegoats (Green, 2017). This does not justify derogatory attitudes. The question is then, how do we listen to these types of people and engage with ideas that are unethical and downright repulsive and dangerous?

Organizational Culture

Organizational culture can seriously impede organizational change (Kezar and Eckel 2002). This cannot be overstated. Those wishing to implement servant leadership cannot neglect a serious consideration of their organizational culture (Wheeler 2012). In chapter 4 on strategic planning, I argued that servant leadership could help to change institutional culture. In this section, I follow Kezar and Eckel (2002) and argue that a neglect of institutional culture can stymie institutional change. Kezar and Eckel (2002) created a framework to help higher education leaders consider organizational culture in their change efforts. The framework utilized Bergquist's (1992) cultural archetypes, as well as Tierney's (1991) cultural work. The four cultural types identified by Bergquist (1992) were the *collegial culture*, marked by the values of the faculty and faculty input into the governance of the university; the *managerial culture*, marked by fiscal responsibility, evaluation, and supervision; the *developmental culture*, marked by growth and development of organizational members; and the *negotiating culture*, marked by maneuvering between different groups on campus (Kezar and Eckel 2002). Kezar and Eckel (2002) note, however, that frameworks may not be able to capture the nuances of specific organizational cultures. Kezar and Eckel (2002) also note that culture is made up of many facets, from the institution to the subgroup, to name a few. Bess and Dee (2012) also point out the role of subcultures within a larger organization.

In addition, Bess and Dee (2012) demonstrate that other scholars have proposed other frameworks, such as Smart and Hamm (1993), who proposed a market culture, which is marked by competition. In order to capture the nuances of individual cultures, Kezar and Eckel (2002) then turned to Tierney's (1991:130) cultural framework, which is divided into six categories: environment, mission, socialization, information, strategy, and leadership (Kezar and Eckel 2002). Kezar and Eckel (2002) explain that each category helps to understand organizational culture. Bess and Dee (2012) also note that many scholars do not see culture as a unified thing to study; rather, many scholars in the postmodern tradition see the idea of culture as too confused and always in transition to understand as a unified whole.

The above theories of organizational culture leave much open to debate, but the ideas above can at least begin to point to the importance of paying attention to culture. Servant leaders must begin to start asking themselves what servant leadership will look like in different cultures. Can servant leadership be practiced in a managerial culture? What will it look like in a market culture? The simplest questions to ask are what is the actual culture of this organization, and what is compatible with servant leadership and what is not? Are there things in this culture that could prevent or accelerate ideas from servant leadership taking hold? However, as has been stressed throughout this book, servant leadership is a multifaceted idea, a constellation. As such, those wishing to integrate servant leadership may need to look more closely at the different facets of servant leadership. Different facets of servant leadership may be compatible with organizational culture, while others may not. Further, if organizational culture is a transitory thing, then the question of what facets of servant leadership are compatible may become even more complex. The point is that organizational culture can be a barrier to servant leadership. It need not be a fatal barrier, but it can be a barrier, and leaders must consider it. Different cultural configurations can affect how servant leadership is undertaken.

Reflection Questions

1. What other opportunities and obstacles may exist for practicing servant leadership in higher education?
2. What are some ways servant leadership can subvert or deceive members inside and outside the academy? How can those in power exploit servant leadership?

9

Conclusion

At the risk of sounding too idealistic and as van Dierendonck (2011) notes, idealism is prevalent in servant leadership research, and following the notion of constellation thinking (Adorno 1966/1973; Buck-Morss 1977) put forward throughout this book, there may always be an unknown element in our understanding of servant leadership, and this uncertainty perpetually drives our thinking forward. I urge future researchers to test ideas put forth in this study. Researchers more skilled than I will need to undertake studies that can measure the effectiveness of servant leadership interventions, such as teaching interventions. However, some of the ideas put forth in this book may prove difficult to empirically measure. How can we say if a research project can serve humanity and posterity? How do we truly know what type of impact our teaching will have on individuals and society? Surveys and interviews may be able to scratch the surface, but how can we truly measure meaning? Writing about spirituality in the workplace and leadership, Fairholm (1997:x) writes, "Spirituality is not easily susceptible to theory building using standard methods of search and research." Servant leadership may be similar in this respect. The questions of servant leadership may not be able to be answered with standard methods, but this is no reason not to pursue them. In fact, this may be even more reason to pursue them because, as Patterson (2010:76) bluntly states, "a plausible hope for the future of humanity, and leadership, lies in the very idea of servant leadership."

Product-based research can be a complement to standard research methods and also help to bring servant leadership down to a more day-to-day level. For instance, if I am a faculty member wishing to be a servant leader in my classroom, I now have a plethora of measurement instruments and conceptual models at my disposal. However, how do I actually become a servant leader? How do I truly serve another human being? Moreover, how can I know if I served that human being? This may be a raw primal question and one that is highly particularistic. Epstein (2014:4) argues that teaching is particularistic and contextual for different teachers and different students; she calls attention to "the different ways that teachers and students pursue excellence." This sentiment may be true for many of the functions of individual universities. Further, as noted earlier, Smith (1995) argues that there are no ready-made plans or models for promoting ownership in servant-led organizations. If I am a professor, I can teach my students in such a way, informed by the ideas of servant leadership, and then "measure" my effectiveness by speaking with my students, by informed observations, and by looking at the things they create. These products can be particular to class discussions and assignments or current happenings. This type of research may add a new dimension to servant leadership on more particularistic and personal levels.

The above sentiments call attention to the act of creation. Specifically, each chapter entails the creation of something, of some product. The creation of products can be a rough measurement of servant growth and creativity. This follows Greenleaf's original and oft-quoted maxim of servant leadership, where Greenleaf prioritized follower development and growth. Again, we do not want to fall into the trap of measurement, where we only value what is measured. Rather, the form of measurement must be ongoing and dynamic and a complement to more traditional methods of research. This is the main purpose of this book, to reframe servant leadership and add a new way to think about servant leadership research. I briefly revisit selected chapters and highlight how the ideas in those chapters can help servant leaders facilitate this creative process among their followers.

Chapter 2

Despite the major push for and prestige of research in higher education, teaching is central to the functioning and purpose of higher education institutions. Framed through the notion of servant leadership, pedagogy can take on a new meaning. Higher education institutions serve their students by teaching them, and thus teaching is framed in terms of servant leadership. Teaching, however, should not simply be a way to impart knowledge in a dogmatic fashion. Paulo Freire (2000:73) argued against what he termed the "banking" model of education, where knowledge is simply given to students. Rather, Freire argued that students and teachers could come to new and higher understandings in dialogue together. Freire (2000:88) argues that "if it is in speaking their word that people, by naming the world, transform it, dialogue imposes itself as the way by which they achieve significance as human beings. Dialogue is thus an existential necessity." Following Freire, teachers and students come together to create new ideas to affect the world. I follow this idea and cast it as a type of service. Servant leadership can help professors and students create new things together, such as sound papers containing new ideas. Creation through pedagogy, however, is not just an individual act. It has implications for society. Professors will care and cultivate the individual development of each student. In a wider sense, however, each student can plausibly become a better member of society, with more creative ideas to help society grow. Therefore, the individual student becomes a conduit to society; the professor serves the student, who then may serve society.

So what can professors and students actually create? Chapter 2 focused specifically on scholarly papers. Professors can highlight that paper writing is not simply to satisfy a grade; rather, professors should prod students to take ownership of their work, to see their work as a contribution to human knowledge and ultimately as a way to create meaning for themselves and humanity. Papers are vehicles of meaning vetted by a professional (the professor). Pedagogy is a type of service to the student (and humanity in general).

Professors can evaluate these products in a number of ways. Professors can look at the actual ideas that students are producing. They can further look at how those ideas can help humanity. The preceding ideas can spark a class discussion that the professor can facilitate. The professor can first look at each piece of writing and add comments, point out good ideas that students wrote, and offer constructive criticism as well. Then the professor can distribute the papers to the class (with the names taken off!) and ask students to reflect on the ideas in their peers' papers. How do these ideas guide humanity? In what specific ways? This could lead to fruitful discussions of class material. The professor or appointed class members could record ideas that emerge from the discussion, or categorize all the ideas that students create. When students leave a course, they can leave having produced something of value to themselves and to humanity, and the professor can take the time and effort to cultivate these products and point out this significance to the students. As Fairholm (1997:12) argues, "Unfortunately, many of us can no longer take satisfaction in our work. We don't make anything anymore; our contribution is often only a small part of the final product." Allowing students to create and highlighting these creations and how they can be of use to society may be the greatest act of service that faculty can perform. In its most primal form, professors can serve their students by facilitating the creation of ideas, and these ideas can materialize in student products.

Researchers can also examine student products and look at how ideas of service have materialized in the product. Researchers could use deductive and inductive coding (Allan 2008; Coffey an Atkinson 1996; Creswell 2014) methods to assess these products. Deductively, researchers could compare products to existing ideas. Inductively, researchers can look toward the products and see what ideas emerge. However, the products should never be seen just as a means to study servant leadership, but rather, also and more important, as the unique ends of servant leadership. As an end, the products become important in their own right.

Chapter 3

Many faculty members are producing high-quality research. Moreover, many faculty members must produce research as part of their tenure process. Therefore, in regard to research, products are produced already. As I argued in chapter 3, however, faculty and administrators who want to promote and practice servant leadership can begin to look at these products in a different light. Similar to how faculty can look at the products of their students as outlined in the last section, faculty and administers can look at research. How does the research contribute to society? How does research shed light on an issue or problem in education or society in general? How does this research serve people and society? What insights does this research leave for humanity and posterity?

The research process of course is fraught with uncertainty, dead ends, difficulties, and mistakes. As such, the products of research share the same qualities. In some ways, research is a snapshot of knowledge production, albeit always an incomplete picture of knowledge at any given point in time. Nevertheless, the negative qualities of research, the potential for mistakes and dead ends, must always be kept in mind when assessing the products of research.

This ideal of service to humanity (and it most likely will remain only an ideal) can be something to aspire to, even if it is never reached. Academic research has irrevocably changed humanity for the better, and faculty and administrators should not lose sight of this awesome capability. This is how research can serve people.

For me personally, I have struggled with what constitutes meaningful research. As a young assistant professor in the field of education, I know that journal articles in the top-tier research journals are usually what is valued most. Yet, as pointed out by the participants in Terosky and Gonzales's (2016a) study, which I examined in chapter 3, publication requirements can dampen researcher freedom and passion and force researchers to only publish ideas that are popular and well accepted. Should I labor to write the perfect article and hope to be accepted into a top-tier journal? What if I must sacrifice my creativity? What if I cannot really say what I want to say in that article because I must write a certain way and in a certain expected format to gain entry in the journal? Would I be better served writing for other quality venues that would allow me to say what I want to say? Should I concentrate on writing books? Here I weigh quality with creativity. I can be as creative as I want if I self-publish a book or write for a low-quality venue, but I do not want to sacrifice creativity for quality. The point is that I seek to balance my own ability to be creative and say something profound and meaningful, while still having my work vetted by experts and professionals and going through a rigorous peer-review process. Do I sacrifice some prestige for the ability to say something meaningful? Researchers may have to grapple with these questions if they want to produce meaningful research. I do not mean to deride the top-tier journals or imply that all the research that is accepted by them is meaningless, far from it. I draw on this research to create my own ideas. I struggle with this question, and I am sure other researchers struggle with it as well. Further, what does it mean if I (or any other aspiring researcher) never lands an article in a top journal? Does that mean my research is not any good, is subpar? The point is that there is no immutable standard for what is good and bad; there are guidelines and endless variations. In the end, I want my research to have meaning; I want it to outlive me, not simply fulfill a tenure requirement. I want my research to leave a positive legacy. This can be an excellent measurement of servant leadership and leaders: how well do they facilitate this view of research? How do they view research as a means to serve people and humanity in general?

Again, similar to student products, other researchers can look at research and ask this question: how does this research impact society? Of course, this question might be highly subjective. Nevertheless, multiple scholars who study servant leadership could begin to establish certain guidelines as to what constitutes service in research; of course, these guidelines should not be rigid. This question may be the most important of this book. How can research be a type of service to researchers and to society and posterity? If research norms begin to change, or if at least some people in academia begin to see research differently, researchers may be able to grow in new ways and not just write for promotion. Researchers may also be able to serve society in new and more meaningful ways. The most basic questions for service are: How can research give meaning to society? What can I create that will embody meaning and be meaningful? Again, traditional research methods may not be able to answer these questions, but they are of the utmost importance.

Chapters 4 and 6

I have combined chapters 4 and 6 out of order because their products are similar. Strategic planning and assessment reports can produce written and online documents. Strategic plans are available on websites for public viewing, and assessment reports may be internally circulated. These documents, framed with servant leadership, can take on new significance. They can become snapshots of how members in an organization serve employees and the public. A well-crafted strategic plan can highlight service in a number of ways. Strategic plans can be evidence of how organizations have served people and provide a foundation for future service. Strategic planning can force questions such as: Whom have we served in the past? What types of service have we provided? How do we conceptualize service? Has our mission transformed by integrating service over the past strategic planning cycles? Has our vision become more inclusive of service? Organizational members can measure organizational progress with their strategic plans. Organizational members can ask themselves, how have we realized our mission? Our vision? Have we served people we said we would serve?

Assessment reports can serve as a similar function. Essentially, what I envision as an assessment report is a summary of specific assessment processes on campus to highlight the power and meaning of assessment in various ways. Assessment reports will obviously vary by institution, department, and unit. As argued in chapter 6, if the assessment process is imbued with servant leadership, it may yield more valuable results than if assessments sit in a filing cabinet or are done solely for compliance. Institutions could make the results of their assessment process transparent. Assessment reports, as products, can help faculty and administrators see assessment as an evolutionary thing in their institution. If assessment reports are noteworthy products that institutions produce, they can act as progress markers and indicators of growth. They can indicate not only the growth of students, but, in a wider sense, the growth of the faculty and the institution that serves the students. Again, this is in line with Greenleaf's (2002) assertion that followers should grow as a result of servant leadership. Institutions can take pride in assessment reports and strategic plans as measures of this growth, and they can become powerful organizational symbols of growth.

Assessment reports can force questions such as: How have we fared in assessing our students? What do the results of assessments tell us about our students and our institution? How can this information help us serve students, faculty, and the public? Assessment reports and strategic plans can be viewed as reference items of the institution that have the ability to guide future planning and assessment in the direction of service. Following Wheeler (2012), there may not be extrinsic rewards for this. Again, as with most of this book, these are lofty aims. But even if they cannot be achieved in full, they can give institutional members something to aspire to and work toward.

As noted with student products, deductive and inductive research methods can be applied to strategic plans and assessment reports by researchers. Again, the plans and assessment reports cannot just be means to ends, but ends themselves. Well-crafted strategic plans and assessment reports built on the notion of service can also serve as examples to other institutions. For instance, while not a strategic plan, Farnsworth (2007) uses Alverno College's catalog as an exemplar of how to integrate servant leadership. Looking at strategic plans and assessment reports can serve a similar purpose. Institutions that seek to promote servant leadership need examples. Researchers can help examine and promote plans and assessment reports, and make them intelligible and presentable to wider audiences.

Chapter 5

Creating products for accountability may pose a special challenge. One such approach can be to charge the task force with creating written reports documenting evidence of how the university is being accountable to different stakeholders. Organizational members should be awarded points for their service to the university or some such professional recognition. These reports (which could also be the basis for future research) could serve as evidence of accountability. Has the university increased diversity? Access to education? Educational outcomes? These actions could also align with the institution's strategic planning. The most basic questions here are: How is the institution affecting society for the better? How does the institution, and its members, serve its students and wider society?

Of course, as noted in the chapter, many times accountability may simply be an individual phenomenon. As such, how can a single professor or administrator promote localized accountability? One way could be to view these accountability efforts as organizational stories (Bolman and Deal 1991). Simply put, stories can provide meaning in the chaos and volatility in which organizations must operate (Bolman and Deal 1991). However, stories can also be ways to obfuscate and sully the truth (Bolman and Deal 1991), and deep accountability should never be used in this manner. Stories of accountability should simply be a way to convey to members of the organization the powerful effects of thinking beyond simplistic numerical benchmarks, and the necessity of this action as well. Deep accountability, showing how institutions and individuals in those intuitions can give back, can be a powerful and much needed source of meaning. Again, any products relating to this type of accountability will most likely not lead to extrinsic rewards, but true servant leaders do not pursue extrinsic rewards (Wheeler 2012). Accountability actions can simply be evidence of service.

Concluding Thoughts

This book has called for new ways to implement servant leadership. Yet servant leadership is a complex concept, which is a constellation composed of differing and sometimes contradictory concepts. This book has also called for a new type of research on servant leadership to complement the traditional qualitative and quantitative approaches. Specifically, this book has argued for an approach that uses the creations of a number of stakeholders. Researchers can use these products in various ways to study servant leadership. Researchers can study the products and use inductive and deductive research methods to analyze them. In addition, Winston (2010) has called for exemplar case studies to understand servant leadership further. Following this idea, all of the products in this book can form part of case study research as well. Of course, many times, traditional research methods may prove inadequate, and methods that are more creative are necessary.

Servant leadership is exemplified in a number of unique ways. Chapter 9 specifically argued for use of student writing assignments, faculty research, strategic plans, assessment reports, and accountability documents as products that may be able to accomplish this task. Universities could further collect a number of these products and create some type of institutional portfolio. This does not have to be at the university level; it could be at the department level as well. Yet this book is only a beginning; the ideas for products to display follower growth are literally endless.

Reflection Questions

1. What other products can be used to illustrate follower growth?
2. How might the product approach hinder our understanding of servant leadership, or at least what pitfalls may exist in using this product approach?

Acknowledgments

Writing the acknowledgments may be the most difficult task for me, simply because there are so many people who had an impact on the writing of this book. For one, I would like to acknowledge Matthew Fuller. Our continued research partnerships and our work on servant leadership and assessment have been a tremendous boon to my career. This book would not be possible without him. I would like to thank my dissertation adviser and mentor, Pamela Eddy, who is a true servant leader, even if she will never admit it. I am indebted to a number of my graduate school professors for their guidance, especially to Michael DiPaola, who first introduced me to the ideas of servant leadership; to Brenda Williams, who introduced me to the ideas of strategic planning; to James Barber, who introduced me to the ideas of self-authorship; and to Dot Finnegan, who introduced me to the important ideas and literature on the history of higher education. I would also like to acknowledge my current colleagues, especially Gina Marx, particularly our conversations regarding the diagnostic process of adaptive leadership as well as our conversations of good communication, Max Frazier, who always is willing to listen to me; and Justin Hawpe, for his suggestion on the importance of students using a variety of sources. I am particularly indebted to the staff at the Newman University Library, Steve Hamersky and Jeanette Parker, who never fail to obtain the research I need and are always willing to work with me. In addition, a grant by the Milton Center at Newman University helped to sustain me as I completed this work. I would like to thank Arturo Rodriguez for our conversations on a number of matters in higher education, particularly research. In addition, I would like to acknowledge Samuel Stringfield, a truly great researcher who mentored me and who left this life too early.

Throughout my undergraduate and graduate career as a student, I was privileged to make the acquaintance of many fellow students who, through class discussions, group work, and informal conversations, have helped refine my own understanding of many topics. I cannot possibly thank them all here. As a professor myself, I have taught many talented students, and my conversations with them have helped to refine my understanding of many topics; they influenced my writing of this book. I have also benefited tremendously from many excellent teachers and undergraduate instructors. Their influence is present in this work. Similarly, throughout my professional career as a K–12 teacher, adjunct instructor, and assistant professor, as well as my role in professional organizations, conferences, as well as committees and even sports teams, I was also able to meet many colleagues and friends who helped deepen my understanding of a number of topics and issues. Recently, I read a book in which the author referred his readers to the sources in his past book. I would extend this idea. All the sources I have used in my previous books, while maybe not cited directly in this book, helped in some way to influence my thought process. In addition, I would also like to acknowledge the two anonymous reviewers of this book, as well as the reviewers of some of my other servant leadership projects. I have listened to their critical feedback and incorporated many of their suggestions, which has made the book that much stronger, such as adding case studies and reflections questions. I would also like to acknowledge the editors at the Purdue OWL, which has been a tremendous resource for me. For chapter 5, I am thankful to my colleagues at the Association of Study of Higher Education conference for our discussion of white men and their role in exposing privilege. For chapter 6, I owe a great deal of thanks to a great number of people. First, I owe a huge debt of thanks to Matthew Fuller. I have worked with Matthew on a number of research projects that involve assessment and servant leadership. Matthew is truly an expert on assessment, and my understanding of assessment on college campuses has grown tremendously due to my work with him. He provided guidance in the writing of chapter 6. I am grateful to a colleague who attended my roundtable session at the American Education Research Association conference and who suggested some ideas to ensure the trustworthiness of my qualitative findings in chapter 6. I am especially grateful to Ruth Slotnick, an assessment director of a large public university, who provided invaluable assistance in preparing this chapter and served as the outside expert who reviewed and validated my coding procedure. In addition, for chapter 6, I am also indebted to a number of anonymous reviewers from mine and Fuller's many projects on servant leadership and assessment, whose invaluable feedback has helped to shape the content of the chapter. I attended a Civil Rights/Title IX training put on by ATIXA, and the ideas I learned from this training helped to inform the case study in chapter 7, specifically the ideas of impartiality. For chapter 8, I am indebted to a colleague who I met at a national conference for suggesting to look at community colleges, which helped me to refine the whole section dealing with different institutions in that chapter.

Finally, I would like to acknowledge the role of various editors and those on hiring committees who rejected me, because even though it was painful, I learned a great deal from their feedback and critiques.

This project would not have been possible without the vision and direction of Kim Guinta, who recognized my work and gave me chance. I would like to thank the staff at Rutgers University Press for their patience and diligence. Inevitably, there are some people that I missed.

References

Ackermann, F., and C. Eden. 2011. *Making strategy: Mapping out strategic success*. 2nd ed. Los Angeles: Sage.

Adams, K. A. 2002. Preparing future faculty. *Occasional Paper Series*. Washington, DC: Association of American Colleges and Universities.

Addison, C., and E. Meyers. 2013. Perspectives on information literacy: A framework for conceptual understanding. *Information Research* 18(3). Paper 27.

Adorno, T. W. 1966/1973. *Negative dialectics*. Trans. E. B. Ashton. New York: Continuum.

Alexander, F. K. 2000. The changing face of accountability: Monitoring and assessing institutional performance in higher education. *Journal of Higher Education* 71(4): 411–431.

Allan, E. J. 2008. *Policy discourses, gender and education: Constructing women's status*. New York: Routledge.

Amibile, T. M. 1996. *Creativity in context: Update to the social psychology of creativity*. Boulder, CO: Westview Press.

Association of College and Research Libraries. 1989. *Presidential committee on information literacy: Final report*. Chicago: Association of College and Research Libraries.

Barber, J. P. 2012. Integration of learning: A grounded theory analysis of college students' learning. *American Education Research Journal* 49(3): 590–617.

Barbuto, J. E., and D. W. Wheeler. 2006. Scale development and construct clarification of servant leadership. *Group and Organizational Management* 31(3): 300–326.

Basken, P. 2016, January 24. Is university research missing what matters? *Chronicle of Higher Education*, 1–18.

Baudrillard, J. 1981/1994. *Simulacra and simulation*. Trans. S. F. Glaser. Ann Arbor: University of Michigan Press.

Baumann, P., M. Millard, and L. Hamdorf. 2014. *State civic education policy framework*. Denver: Education Commission of the States.

Baxter Magolda, M. B. 2009. *Authoring your life: Developing an internal voice to meet life's challenges*. Sterling, VA: Stylus.

———. 2004a. Preface. In *Learning partnerships: Theory and models of practice to educate for self-authorship*, ed. M. B. Baxter Magolda and P. M. King, xvii–xxvi. Sterling, VA: Stylus.

———. 2004b. Self-authorship as the common goal of 21st-century education. In *Learning partnerships: Theory and models of practice to educate for self-authorship*, ed. M. B. Baxter Magolda and P. M. King, 1–36. Sterling, VA: Stylus.

Beach, A. L. 2015. Boyer's impact on faculty development. In D. Moser, T. C. Ream, J. M. Braxton, and Associates, *Scholarship reconsidered: Priorities of the professoriate*, 13–18. San Francisco: Jossey-Bass.

Beall, J. 2013. Scholarly publishing free for all. *College Quarterly* 16(2).

Beaver, T. L. 2014. Historical derivative of servant leadership and the untold story of the influence of Quakerism on Greenleaf's teachings. In R. Selladurai and S. Carraher, *Servant leadership: Research and practice*, 244–261. Hershey, PA: Business Science Reference.

Beckman, M. 2013. The option for the poor in community-based education. In *The preferential option for the poor beyond theology*, ed. D. Groody and G. Gutierrez, 183–198. Notre Dame, IN: University of Notre Dame Press.

Bennis, W. 2009. *Becoming a leader*. Revised and updated. New York: Basic Books.

———. 2004. Foreword: Why servant leadership matters. In *Practicing servant leadership: Succeeding through trust, bravery, and forgiveness*, ed. L. C. Spears and M. Lawrence, xi–xvi. San Francisco: Jossey-Bass.

Bergquist, W. H. 1992. *The four cultures of the academy: Insights and strategies for improving leadership in collegiate organizations*. San Francisco: Jossey-Bass.

Bess, J. L., and J. R. Dee. 2012. *Understanding college and university organization: Theories for effective policy and practice*. Vol. 1, *State of the system*. 2nd ed. Sterling, VA: Stylus.

Biggart, N.W. 1989. *Charismatic capitalism: Direct selling organizations in America*. Chicago, IL: University of Chicago Press.

Birnbaum, R. 2000. *Management fads in higher education: Where they come from, what they do and why they fail*. San Francisco: Jossey-Bass.

Black, G. L. 2010. Correlational analysis of servant leadership and school climate. *Catholic Education: A Journal of Inquiry and Practice* 13(4): 437–460.

Bloom, B. S. 1956. *Taxonomy of educational objectives: The classification of educational goals. Handbook I: Cognitive domain*. New York: David McKay.

Bloom, B. S., J. T. Hastings, and G. F. Madaus. 1971. *Handbook on formative and summative evaluation of student learning*. New York: McGraw-Hill.

Bok, D. C. 2015. *Higher education in America*. 2nd ed. Princeton, NJ: Princeton University Press.

Bolden, R. 2011. Distributed leadership in organizations: A review of theory and research. *International Journal of Management Reviews* 13:251–269.

Bolman, L. G., and T. E. Deal. 1991. *Reframing organizations: Artistry, choice, and leadership*. San Francisco: Jossey-Bass.

Booth, W. C., G. G. Colomb, and J. M. Williams. 2003. *The craft of research*. 2nd ed. Chicago: University of Chicago Press.

Boyer, E. L. 2015. *Scholarship reconsidered: Priorities of the professoriate*. In D. Moser, T. C. Ream, J. M. Braxton, and Associates, *Scholarship reconsidered: Priorities of the professoriate*, 53–160. San Francisco: Jossey-Bass.

———. 1996. The scholarship of engagement. *Journal of Public Service and Outreach* 1(1): 11–20.

Bransford, J. D., A. L. Brown, and R. R. Cocking, eds. 2000. *How people learn: Brain, mind, experience, and school*. Washington, DC: National Academy Press.

Brint, S., and J. Karabel. 1989. *The diverted dream: Community colleges and the promise of educational opportunity in America, 1900–1985*. New York: Oxford Press.

Brookhart, S. M. 2013. *How to create and use rubrics for formative assessment and grading*. Alexandria, VA: ASCD.

———. 2008. *How to give effective feedback to your students*. Alexandria, VA: ASCD.

Brown, K. 2008. Writing what I want in a publish-or-perish world. *Academe* 94(4): 62–63.

Bryson, J. M. 2011. *Strategic planning for public and nonprofit organizations: A guide to strengthening and sustaining organizational achievement*. 4th ed. San Francisco: Jossey-Bass.

Buchen, I. H. 1998. Servant leadership: A model for future faculty and future institutions. *Journal of Leadership and Organizational Studies* 5(1): 125–134.

Buck-Morss, S. 1977. *The origin of negative dialectics: Theodor W. Adorno, Walter Benjamin and the Frankfurt Institute*. New York: Free Press.

Burke, J. C. 2005. The many *faces* of accountability. In *Achieving accountability in higher education: Balancing public, academic and market demands*, ed. J. C. Burke, 1–24. San Francisco: Jossey-Bass.

Calhoun, C. 1998. The public good as a social and cultural project. In *Private action and the public good*, ed. W. W. Powell and E. S. Clemens, 20–35. New Haven, CT: Yale University Press.

Cheney, L. V. 1991, July 17. Foolish and insignificant research in the humanities. *Chronicle of Higher Education*, B2.

Coffey, A., and P. Atkinson. 1996. *Making sense of qualitative data*. Thousand Oaks, CA: Sage.

Cole, J. R., and S. Cole. 1972. The Ortega hypothesis. *Science* 178(4059): 368–375.

Conger, J. A. 1989. *The charismatic leader: Behind the mystique of exceptional leadership*. San Francisco: Jossey-Bass.

Constantinou, P. 2014. Promoting healthy competition using modified rules and sports from other cultures. *Strategies: A Journal for Physical and Sports Educators* 27(4): 29–33.

Corrigan, J. 2013. Distributed leadership: Rhetoric or reality? *Journal of Higher Education Policy and Management* 35(1): 66–71.

Covey, S. R. 2002. Foreword. In R. K. Greenleaf, *Servant leadership: A journey into the nature of legitimate power and greatness*. 25th anniversary ed. Mahwah, NJ: Paulist Press. Kindle edition.

Creswell, J. W. 2014. *Research design: Qualitative, quantitative and mixed methods approaches*. 4th ed. Los Angeles: Sage.

———. 2013. *Qualitative inquiry and research design: Choosing among five approaches*. 3rd ed. Los Angeles: Sage.

Daft, R. L., and R. H. Lengel. 2000. *Fusion leadership: Unlocking the subtle forces that change people and organizations*. San Francisco: Berrett-Koehler.

Darder, A. 2016. Critical leadership for social justice: Unveiling the dirty little secret of power and privilege. *Radical Imagine-Nation* 1(1): 41–76.

Dayton, J. 2012. *Education law: Principles, policies, and practice*. Sunnyvale, CA: Wisdom Builders Press.

Dean, D. 2007. Thinking globally: The national college of school leadership—a case study in distributed leadership development. *Journal of Research on Leadership Education*. 2(1): 1-62.

Dean, D. R. 2014. Review of *Servant leadership for higher education: Principles and practices* by D. Wheeler. *Review of Higher Education* 37(2): 274–277.

Dee, J. 2006. Institutional autonomy and state-level accountability: Loosely coupled governance and the public good. In *Governance and the Public Good*, ed. W. G. Tierney. Kindle edition.

DeGraaf, D., C. Tilley, and L. Neal. 2004. Servant-leadership characteristics in organizational life. In *Practicing servant leadership: Succeeding through trust, bravery, and forgiveness*, ed. L. C. Spears and M. Lawrence, 133–166. San Francisco: Jossey-Bass.

Dennis, R. S., and M. Bocarnea. 2005. Development of the servant leadership assessment instrument. *Leadership and Organization Development Journal* 26(8): 600–615.

Denzin, N. K., and M. G. Giardina. 2009. Introduction. In *Qualitative inquiry and social justice: Toward a politics of hope*, ed. N. Denzin and M. Giardina, 11–52. Walnut Creek, CA: Left Coast Press.

DePree, M. 2002. Servant leadership: Three things necessary. In *Focus on leadership: Servant-leadership for the twenty-first century*, ed. L. C. Spears and M. Lawrence, 89–100. New York: John Wiley and Sons.

Dewey, J. 1988. *John Dewey: The later works, 1925–1953*. Vol. 14. Ed. J. A. Boydston and A. Sharpe. Carbondale: Southern Illinois University Press.

———. 1916. The nature of subject matter. In *On Education*, 359–372. Ed. R. D. Archambault. Chicago: University of Chicago Press.

———. 1902. The child and the curriculum. In *On Education*, 339–358. Ed. R. D. Archambault. Chicago: University of Chicago Press.

Dickeson, R. C. 2010. *Prioritizing academic programs and services: Reallocating resources to achieve strategic balance*. 2nd ed. San Francisco: Jossey-Bass.

Drew, J., W. Lyons, and L. Svehla. 2010. *Sound bite saboteurs: Public discourse, education and the state of democratic deliberation*. Albany, NY: SUNY Press.

Eddy, P. L., and M. J. Amey. 2015. *Creating strategic partnerships: A guide for educational institutions and their partners*. Sterling, VA: Stylus.

Eddy, P. L., and J. Hart. 2012. Faculty in the hinterlands: Cultural anticipation and cultural reality. *Higher Education* 63(6): 751–769.

Eden, C., and F. Ackermann. 2011. Strategy as competitive advantage. In *Making strategy: Mapping out strategic success*, ed. F. Ackermann and C. Eden, 177–206. Los Angeles: Sage.

Eden, C., F. Ackermann, and K. Gallimore. 2011. Strategy as purpose: Agreeing goals and aspirations for the organization. In *Making strategy: Mapping out strategic success*, ed. F. Ackermann and C. Eden, 109–146. Los Angeles: Sage.

Eden, C., F. Ackermann, and K. Page. 2011. Strategic management is a social process. In *Making strategy: Mapping out strategic success*, ed. F. Ackermann and C. Eden, 14–38. Los Angeles: Sage.

Eliot, T. S. 1964. *Selected poems*. San Diego, CA: A Harvest Book.

Epstein, S. E. 2014. *Teaching civic literacy projects: Student engagement with social problems*. New York: Teachers College Press.

Evans, B., and H. A. Giroux. 2014. Intellectual violence in the age of gated intellectuals: Critical pedagogy and a return to the political. In H. A. Giroux, *Neoliberalism's war on higher education*, 103–130. Chicago: Haymarket Books.

Evans, N. J., D. S. Forney, F. M. Guido, L. D. Patton, and K. A. Renn. 2010. *Student development in college: Theory, research and practice*. 2nd ed. San Francisco: Jossey-Bass.

Ewell, P. T. 2002. An emerging scholarship: A brief history of assessment. In *Building a scholarship of assessment*, ed. T. Banta, 3–25. San Francisco: Jossey-Bass.

Fairholm, G. W. 1997. *Capturing the heart of leadership: Spirituality and community in the new American workplace*. Westport, CT: Praeger.

Farling, M. L., A. G. Stone, and B. E. Winston. 1999. Servant leadership: Setting the stage for empirical research. *Journal of Leadership and Organizational Studies* 6(1/2): 49–72.

Farnsworth, K. A. 2007. *Leadership as service: A new model for higher education in a new century*. Westport, CT: ACE/Praeger Series on Education.

Ferch, S. R. 2011. Servant-leadership: Healing the person, healing the world. In *The spirit of servant leadership*, ed. S. R. Ferch and L. C. Spears, xxvii–xxxvi. Mahwah, NJ: Paulist Press.

Fitzgerald, R. J. 2015. Becoming Leo: Servant leadership as a pedagogical philosophy. *Critical Questions in Education* 6(2): 75–85.

Fletcher, J. K. 2004. The paradox of postheroic leadership: An essay on gender, power, and transformational change. *Leadership Quarterly* 15:647–661.

Foster, P. J. 1989. *Celebration of discipline: The path to spiritual growth*. London: Hodder and Stoughton.

Freire, P. 2000. *Pedagogy of the oppressed*. New York: Continuum.

Fritz, R. 1989. *The path of least resistance: Learning to become the creative force in your own life*. New York: A Fawcett Book.

Fullan, M. 2001. *Leading in a culture of change*. New York: John Wiley and Sons.

Fuller, M. B., and S. T. Skidmore. 2014. An exploration of factors influencing institutional cultures of assessment. *International Journal of Educational Research* 65:9–21.

Fuller, M. B., S. Henderson, and R. M. Bustamante. 2015. Assessment leaders' perspectives of institutional cultures of assessment: A Delphi study. *Assessment and Evaluation in Higher Education* 40(3): 331–351.

Fuller, M. B., S. T. Skidmore, R. Bustamante, and P. C. Holzweiss. 2016. Empirically exploring higher education cultures of assessment. *Review of Higher Education* 39(3): 395–429.

Geiger, R. L. 2000. Introduction: New themes in the history of nineteenth-century colleges. In *The American college in the nineteenth century*, ed. R. L. Geiger, 1-36. Nashville, TN: Vanderbilt University Press.

———. 2016. From the land-grant tradition to the current crisis in the humanities. In *A new deal for the humanities: Liberal arts and the future of public higher education*, ed. G. Hutner and F. G. Mohamed, 18–30. New Brunswick, NJ: Rutgers University Press.

Giroux, H. A. 2016. Towards a politics of revolt and disruption: Higher education in dangerous times. *Radical Imagine-Nation* 1(1): 19–40.

———. 2014a. *Neoliberalism's war on higher education*. Chicago: Haymarket Books.

———. 2014b, July 14. Thinking dangerously in an age of political betrayal. *Truthout*. http://www.truth-out.org/opinion/item/24869-henry-a-giroux-thinking-dangerously-in-an-age-of-political-betrayal.

———. 2011. *On critical pedagogy*. New York: Continuum.

Giroux, H. A., and M. A. Peters. 2014. Democracy unsettled: From critical pedagogy to the war on youth, an interview with Henry A. Giroux. In H. A. Giroux, *Neoliberalism's war on higher education*, 181–206. New York: Bloomsbury.

Glassick, C. E., M. T. Huber, and G. I. Maeroff. 1997. *Scholarship assessed: Evaluation of the professoriate*. San Francisco: Jossey-Bass.

Gonzales, L. D., and A. L. Terosky. 2016. From the faculty perspective: Defining, earning, and maintaining legitimacy across academia. *Teachers College Record* 118(7): 1–44.

Grayling, A. C. 1998. Editor's introduction. In *Philosophy 1: A guide through the subject*, ed. A. C. Grayling, 1–6. Oxford: Oxford University Press.

Green, E. May 9 2017. It was cultural anxiety that drove white working class votes to Trump. *The Atlantic*.

Greene, K. 2013. Critical democracy audits. A response to "teacher, researcher, and accountability discourses: Creating space for democratic science teaching practices in middle schools". *Democracy and Education*, 21(2): Article 6. Retrieved from http://democracyeducationjournal.org/home/vol21/iss2/6

Greenleaf, R. K. 2003. Teacher as servant. In *The servant-leader within: A transformative path*, ed. H. Beazley, J. Beggs, and L. C. Spears, 75–240. Mahwah, NJ: Paulist Press.

———. 2002. *Servant leadership: A journey into the nature of legitimate power and greatness*. 25th anniversary ed. Mahwah, NJ: Paulist Press. Kindle edition.

———. 1998. Education and maturity. In *The power of servant leadership*, ed. L. C. Spears, 61–76. San Francisco: Berrett-Koehler.

Gronn, P. 2009. Leadership configurations. *Leadership* 5(3): 381–394.

———. 2002. Distributed leadership as a unit of analysis. *Leadership Quarterly* 13(4): 423–451.

Hall, D. J., H. Gunter, and J. Bragg. 2013. The strange case of the emergence of distributed leadership in schools in England. *Educational Review* 65(4): 467–487.

Hamilton, D. P. 1991. Research papers: Who's uncited now? *Science* 251(4989): 25.

Hartley, D. 2007. The emergence of distributed leadership in education: Why now? *British Journal of Educational Studies* 55(2): 202–214.

Harvey, D. 2005. *A brief history of neoliberalism*. Oxford: Oxford University Press. Kindle edition.

Hatch, M. J., and A. L. Cunliffe 2013. *Organization theory: Modern, symbolic and postmodern perspectives*. 3rd ed. New York: Oxford University Press.

Haynes, C. 2004. Promoting self-authorship through an interdisciplinary writing curriculum. In *Learning partnerships: Theory and models of practice to educate for self-authorship*, ed. M. B. Baxter Magolda and P. M. King, 63–90. Sterling, VA: Stylus.

Heifetz, R., A. Grashow, and M. Linsky. 2009. *The practice of adaptive leadership: Tools and tactics for changing your organization and the world*. Boston: Harvard Business Press.

Hernandez, M., M. B. Eberly, B. J. Avolio, and M. D. Johnson. 2011. The loci and mechanisms of leadership: Exploring a more comprehensive view of leadership theory. *Leadership Quarterly* 22(6): 1165–1185.

Hill, T. 2006. *Common strength: Building leaders, transforming recovery*. Booklet 12. Westfield, IN: Greenleaf Center for Servant Leadership.

Hodge, D. C., M. B. Baxter Magolda, and C. A. Haynes. 2009. Engaged learning: Enabling self-authorship and effective practice. *Liberal Education* 95(4).

Hofmann, E. 2012. Why dual enrollment? *New Directions for Higher Education*, 1–8.

Huber, M. T. 2015. Foreword: *Scholarship reconsidered*'s influence in later Carnegie foundation work. In D. Moser, T. Ream, J. Braxton, and Associates, *Scholarship reconsidered: Priorities of the professoriate*, xxi–xxv. San Francisco: Jossey-Bass.

Hunter, E. M., M. J. Neubert, S. J. Perry, L. A. Witt, L. M. Penney, and E. Weinberger. 2013. Servant leaders inspire servant followers: Antecedents and outcomes for employees and the organization. *Leadership Quarterly* 24:316–331.

Hutner, G., and F. G. Mohamed. 2016. Introduction. In *A new deal for the humanities: Liberal arts and the future of public higher education*, ed. G. Hutner and F. G. Mohamed, 1–17. New Brunswick, NJ: Rutgers University Press.

Jay, M. 1996. *The dialectical imagination: A history of the Frankfurt school and the Institute of Social Research, 1923–1950*. 2nd ed. Berkeley: University of California Press.

Jay, P., and G. Graff. 2012, January 5. Fear of being useful. *Inside Higher Ed*. https://www.insidehighered.com/views/2012/01/05/essay-new-approach-defend-value-humanities.

Kegan, R. 1994. *In over our heads: The mental demands of modern life*. Cambridge, MA: Harvard University Press.

Keith, K. M. 2012. Foreword. In D. Wheeler, *Servant leadership for higher education: Principles and practices*, ix–x. San Francisco: Jossey-Bass.

Keller, G. 1997. Examining what works in strategic planning. In *Planning and management for a changing environment: A handbook on redesigning postsecondary institutions*, ed. M. W. Peterson, D. D. Dill, L. A. Mets, and Associates, 158–170. San Francisco: Jossey-Bass.

Kellner, D. 2015. Jean Baudrillard. In *The Stanford encyclopedia of philosophy*, ed. E. N. Zalta.

Kezar, A. J. 2005. What campuses need to know about organizational learning and the learning organization. *New Directions for Higher Education*, 7–22.

———. 2001. Investigating organizational fit in a participatory leadership environment. *Journal of Higher Education Policy and Management* 23(1): 85–101.

Kezar, A. J., and P. D. Eckel. 2002. The effect of institutional culture on change strategies in higher education: Universal principles or cultural responsive concepts? *Journal of Higher Education* 73(4): 435–460.

Kim, D. H. 2004. Foresight as the central ethic of leadership. In *Practicing servant leadership: Succeeding through trust, bravery, and forgiveness* ed. L. C. Spears and M. Lawrence, 201–224. San Francisco: Jossey-Bass.

Kisker, C. B., and B. Ronan. 2016. Introduction. *New Directions for Community Colleges*, 7–11.

Klar, H. W., K. S. Huggins, H. L. Hammonds, and F. Buskey. 2016. Fostering the capacity for distributed leadership: A post-heroic approach to leading school improvement. *International Journal of Leadership in Education* 19(2): 111–137.

Kleinman, D. L. 2016. Sticking up for liberal arts and humanities education: Governance, leadership, and fiscal crisis. In *A new deal for the humanities: Liberal arts and the future of public higher education*, ed. G. Hutner and F. G. Mohamed, 86–100. New Brunswick, NJ: Rutgers University Press.

Kouzes, J. M., and B. Z. Posner. 1995. *The leadership challenge: How to keep getting extraordinary things done in organizations*. San Francisco: Jossey-Bass.

Ladson-Billings, G. 1995. Toward a theory of culturally relevant pedagogy. *American Educational Research Journal* 32(3): 465–491.

Landel, C. and C. Ohana. Emerging Conceptions of Effective K-12-Higher Education Partnerships (draft paper). *North Cascades and Olympic Science Partnership MSP Evaluation Summit*.

Lane, M. R., P. L. Lane, J. Rich, and B. Wheeling. 2014. Improving assessment: Creating a culture of assessment with a change management approach. *Journal of Case Studies in Accreditation and Assessment* 4.

Laub, J. 2017. Organizational health. *OLA Group*. http://www.olagroup.com/Display.asp?Page=organizational_health.

———. 2010. The servant organization. In *Servant leadership: Developments in theory and research*, ed. K. Patterson and D. van Dierendonck, 105–117. New York: Palgrave MacMillan.

Leary, M. R., and R. H. Hoyle, eds. 2009. *Handbook of individual differences in social behavior*. New York: Guilford Press.

Leithwood, K., C. Day, P. Sammons, A. Harris, and D. Hopkins. 2006. *Successful school leadership: What it is and how it influences pupil learning*. Nottingham, UK: Department of Education and Skills.

Leithwood, K., B. Mascall, and T. Strauss. 2009. New perspectives on an old idea: A short history of the old idea. In *Distributed leadership according to the evidence*, ed. K. Leithwood, B. Mascall, and T. Strauss, 1–14. New York: Routledge.

Letizia, A. J. 2017a. *Teaching democracy and social justice in the information age*. New York: Palgrave-MacMillan.

———. 2017b. Turning neoliberalism on its head: A historical and pedagogical analysis. In *Imagining education beyond the logic of global neoliberal capitalism*, ed. A. Rodriguez and K. Magill, 53–72. Charlotte, NC: Information Age Press.

———. 2016a. Student writing for self-authorship and democracy. *Journal of College Student Development* 57(2): 219–223.

———. 2016b. The hollow university: Disaster capitalism befalls American higher education. *Policy Futures in Education* 14(3): 360–376.

———. 2016c. Writing about the past is essential for the future: Fostering student writing for citizenship in K–12 and community college classrooms. *History Teacher* 49(2): 1–22.

———. 2015. *Performance-based funding: The state of truth in the information age*. Lanham, MD: Lexington Press.

———. 2014. Radical servant leadership: A new practice of public education leadership in the post-industrial age. *Journal of Critical Education Policy Studies* 12(2): 175–199.

———. 2013. Strategic blunder? Strategic planning for changing demographics in higher education. *Educational Planning* 21(2): 18–31.

Letizia, A. J., and M. B. Fuller. 2017. *Using servant leadership to reframe cultures of assessment*. Paper presented at the 101st Annual Conference of the American Education Research Association, San Antonio, TX.

———. 2015. *Examining inequalities in faculty and administrators' perceptions about assessment as servant leadership*. Paper presented at the Forty-First Annual Conference of the Association for the Study of Higher Education, Denver.

Levin, J. S., and A. Aliyeva. 2015. Embedded neoliberalism within faculty behaviors. *Review of Higher Education* 38(4): 537–564.

Lickona, T., and M. Davidson. 2005. *Smart and good schools: Integrating excellence and ethics for success in school, work and beyond*. Cortland, NY: Center for the 4th and 5th Rs (Respect and Responsibility) State University of New York College at Cortland.

Liden, R. C., S. J. Wayne, J. D. Meuser, J. Hu, J. Wu, and C. Liao. 2015. Servant leadership: Validation of a short form of the SL-28. *Leadership Quarterly* 26(2): 254–269.

Liden, R. C., S. J. Wayne, H. Zhao, and D. Henderson. 2008. Servant leadership: Development of a multidimensional measure and multi-level assessment. *Leadership Quarterly* 19(2): 161–177.

Lynch, M. 2012. *A guide to effective school leadership theories*. New York: Routledge.

Lynton, E. A. 1996. Ensuring the quality of outreach: The critical role of evaluating individual and collective initiatives and performance. *Journal of Public Service and Outreach* 1(2): 16–22.

———. 1994. Knowledge and scholarship. *Metropolitan Universities: An International Forum* 5(1): 9–17.

MacBeath, J., G. K. T. Oduro, and J. Waterhouse. 2004. *Distributed leadership in action: A study of current practice in schools*. Nottingham, UK: National College for School Leadership.

MacTaggart, T. J. 1998. Why the time is ripe for restructuring. In T. MacTaggart and Associates, *Seeking excellence through independence: Liberating colleges and universities from excessive regulation*, 3–20. San Francisco: Jossey-Bass.

Maki, P. L. 2010. *Assessing for learning: Building a sustainable commitment across the institution*. 2nd ed. Sterling, VA: Stylus.

Mamiseishvili, K., M. T. Miller, and D. Lee. 2016. Beyond teaching and research: Faculty perceptions of service roles at research universities. *Innovative Higher Education* 41(4): 273–286.

Mansbridge, J. 1998. On the contested nature of the public good. In *Private action and the public good*, ed. W. W. Powell and E. S. Clemens, 3–19. New Haven, CT: Yale University Press.

Marginson, S. 2010. Introduction: The protean and the global. In S. Marginson, P. Murphy, and M. A. Peters, *Global creation: Space, mobility and synchrony in the age of the knowledge economy*, 1–17. New York: Peter Lang.

Marshall, T. 1991. *Understanding leadership: Fresh perspectives on the essentials of New Testament leadership*. Chichester, UK: Sovereign World.

McGee-Cooper, A. and D. Trammell. Servant-leadership: Is there really time for it? In *Reflections on leadership: How Robert K. Greenleaf's theory of servant leadership influenced today's top management thinkers*, ed. L. C. Spears, 113-120. New York: John Wiley and Sons.

McGee-Cooper, A., and G. Looper. 2001. The essentials of servant-leadership: Principles in practice. Innovations in Management Working Paper. Waltham, MA.

McLaren, P. 2007. The future of the past: Reflections on the present state of empire and pedagogy. In *Critical pedagogy: Where are we now?*, ed. P. McLaren and J. L. Kincheloe, 289–314. New York: Peter Lang.

McMahon, W. W. 2009. *Higher learning, greater good: The private and social benefits of higher education*. Baltimore: Johns Hopkins University Press.

Merriam, S. B. 1998. *Qualitative research and case study application in education*. 2nd ed. New York: John Wiley and Sons.

Miller, A. N., T. G. Shannon, and A. G. Bedeian. 2011. Publish or perish: Academic life as management faculty live it. *Career Development International* 16(5): 422–445.

Mitroff, I. I., and E. A. Denton. 1999. A study of spirituality in the workplace. *Sloan Management Review* 40(4): 83–92.

Moser, D., and T. C. Ream. 2015. The origins of scholarship reconsidered. In D. Moser, T. Ream, J. Braxton, and Associates, *Scholarship reconsidered: Priorities of the professoriate*, 3–12. San Francisco: Jossey-Bass.

Mueller, R. A. 2015. Do values drive the plan? Investigating the nature and role of organizational values in university strategic planning. *Tertiary Education and Management* 21(1): 41–55.

Mullin, C. M., D. S. Baime, and D. S. Honeyman. 2015. *Community college finance: A guide for individual leaders*. San Francisco: Jossey-Bass.

Nash, R. J., and J. J. Jang. 2015. *Preparing students for life beyond college: A meaning-centered vision for holistic teaching and learning*. New York: Routledge.

———. 2013, September–October. The time has come to create meaning-making centers on college campuses. *About Campus*, 2–9.

Nash, R. J., and M. C. Murray. 2010. *Helping college students find purpose: The campus guide to meaning-making*. San Francisco: Jossey-Bass.

Nelson, I. A., R. A. London, and K. R. Strobel. 2015. Reinventing the role of the university researcher. *Educational Researcher* 44(1): 17–26.

Neubert, M. J., K. M. Kacmar, D. S. Carlson, L. B. Chonko, and J. A. Roberts. 2008. Regulatory focus as a mediator of the influence of initiating structure and servant leadership on employee behavior. *Journal of Applied Psychology* 93(6): 1220–1233.

Neumann, A. 2014. Staking a claim on learning: What we should know about learning in higher education and why. *Review of Higher Education* 37(2): 249–267.

Newfield, C. 2016. What are the humanities for? Rebuilding the public university. In *A new deal for the humanities: Liberal arts and the future of public higher education*, ed. G. Hutner and F. G. Mohamed, 160–178. New Brunswick, NJ: Rutgers University Press.

———. 2008. *Unmaking the public university: The forty-year assault on the middle class*. Cambridge, MA: Harvard University Press.

Newman. F. 1987. Changing quality: Reducing conflict between the state and university. Denver, CO: Education Commission of the States.

Nichols, J. D. 2011. *Teachers as servant leaders*. Lanham, MD: Rowman Littlefield.

Nietzsche, F. 1889/1954. *Twilight of the idols*. In *The portable Nietzsche*, trans. and ed. W. Kauffman, 463–564. New York: Viking.

Noland, A., and K. Richards. 2015. Servant teaching: An exploration of teacher servant leadership on student outcomes. *Journal of Scholarship of Teaching and Learning* 15(6): 16–38.

Northouse, P.G. 2016. *Leadership: Theory and practice*. 7th ed. Los Angeles: Sage.

Nutt, P. C. 2001. Strategic decision making. In *The Blackwell handbook of strategic management*, ed. M. A. Hitt, R. E. Freeman, and J. S. Harrison, 35–69. Oxford: Blackwell.

O'Connor, B. 2013. *Adorno*. New York: Routledge.

Office of Community Engagement and Partnerships Homepage 2017. University of South Florida. http://www.usf.edu/engagement/events-programming/research-that-matters.aspx.

Olsen, J. B., and D. C. Eadie. 1982. *The game plan: Governance with foresight*. Washington, DC: Council of State Planning Agencies.

O'Meara, K., and A. L. Terosky. 2010. Engendering faculty professional growth. *Change: The Magazine of Higher Learning* 42(6): 44–51.

Parker, W. C. 1996. Curriculum and democracy. In *Democracy, education and the schools*, ed. R. Soder, 182–243. San Francisco: Jossey-Bass.

Parris, D. L., and J. W. Peachey. 2013. A systematic literature review of servant leadership theory in organizational contexts. *Journal of Business Ethics* 113(3): 377–393.

Patterson, K. 2010. Servant leadership and love. In *Servant leadership: Developments in theory and research*, ed. K. Patterson and D. van Dierendonck, 67–76. New York: Palgrave Macmillan.

———. 2003. Servant leadership: A theoretical model. PhD diss., Regent University.

Perna, L. W. 2016. Throwing down the gauntlet: Ten ways to ensure that higher education research continues to matter. *Review of Higher Education* 39(3): 319–338.

Peterson, M. W. 1997. Using contextual planning to transform institutions. In *Planning and management for a changing environment: A handbook on redesigning postsecondary institutions*, ed. M. W. Peterson, D. D. Dill, L. A. Mets, and Associates, 127–157. San Francisco: Jossey-Bass.

Peterson, M. W., and D. S. Vaughan. 2002. Promoting academic improvement: Organizational and administrative dynamics that support student assessment. In *Building a scholarship of assessment*, ed. T. Banta, 26–46. San Francisco: Jossey-Bass.

Phillips, K. 2006. *American theocracy: The peril and politics of radical religion, oil, and borrowed money in the 21st century*. New York: Viking Press.

Pink, D. H. 2005. *A whole new mind: Why right-brainers will rule the future*. New York: Riverhead Books.

Poster, M., ed. 2001. *Jean Baudrillard: Selected writings*. 2nd ed. Stanford, CA: Stanford University Press.

Pousa, C. 2014. Measuring servant leadership. In R. Selladurai and S. Carraher, *Servant leadership: Research and practice*, 211–243. Hershey, PA: Business Science Reference.

Priess, R. April 1, 2014. Conceptualizing and measuring servant leadership: Wheeler & Barbuto. *Viterbo University Servant Leadership Blog*.

Prosser, S. 2010a. Opportunities and tensions of servant leadership. In *Servant leadership: Developments in theory and research*, ed. K. Patterson and D. van Dierendonck, 25–38. New York: Palgrave Macmillan.

———. 2010b. *Servant leadership: More philosophy, less theory*. Westfield, IN: Greenleaf Center for Servant Leadership.

Pusser, B., and S. Marginson. 2013. University rankings in critical perspective. *Journal of Higher Education* 84(4): 544–568.

Ramaley, J. A. 2006. Governance in a time of transition. In *Governance and the Public Good*, ed. W. Tierney. Albany, NY: SUNY Press. Kindle edition.

Rasmussen, T. 1995. Creating a culture of servant-leadership: A real life story. In *Reflections on leadership: How Robert K. Greenleaf's theory of servant leadership influenced today's top management thinkers*, ed. L. C. Spears, 282–297. New York: John Wiley and Sons.

Rieke, M., J. Hammermeister, and M. Chase. 2008. Servant leadership in sport: A new paradigm for effective coach behavior. *International Journal of Sports Science and Coaching* 3(2): 227–239.

Russell, R. F., and A. G. Stone. 2002. A review of servant leadership attributes: Developing a practical model. *Leadership and Organization Development Journal* 23(3): 145–157.

Saarinen, T. 2008. Position of text and discourse analysis in higher education policy research. *Studies in Higher Education* 33(6): 719–728.

Salter, B., and T. Tapper. 1994. *The state and higher education*. Ilford, UK: Woburn Press.

Saltmarsh, J. 2016. Ernest Lynton and the tyranny of research. *Journal of Higher Education Outreach and Engagement* 20(1): 45–51.

Sandel, M. J. 2009. *Justice: What's the right thing to do?* New York: Farrar, Straus and Giroux.

SanFacon, G., and L. C. Spears. 2011. Holistic servant-leadership: A multidimensional approach. In *The spirit of servant-leadership*, ed. S. R. Ferch and L. C. Spears, 113–123. Mahwah, NJ: Paulist Press.

Schedler, A. 1999. Conceptualizing accountability. In *The self-restraining state: Power and accountability in new democracies*, ed. A. Schedler, L. Diamond, and M. F. Plattner, 13–28. Boulder, CO: Lynne Rienner.

Schein, E. H. 1998. *Organizational culture and leadership*. 2nd ed. San Francisco: Jossey-Bass.

Schneider, C. G. 2015, December 2. Policy priorities for accreditation put quality college learning at risk: A message from AAC&U president Carol Geary Schneider. *Association of American Colleges and Universities*. https://www.aacu.org/about/statements/2015/accreditation.

Schulman, B. J. 2001. *The seventies: The great shift in American culture, society, and politics*. Cambridge, MA: Da Capo Press.

Schulman, L. S. 2004a. *Teaching as community property: Essays on higher education*. Ed. P. Hutchings. San Francisco: Jossey-Bass.

———. 2004b. *The wisdom of practice: Essays on learning, teaching, and learning to teach*. Ed. S. M. Wilson. San Francisco: Jossey-Bass.

Schwab, J. 1978. Education and the structure of disciplines. In *Science, curriculum, and liberal education*, ed. I. Westbury and N. J. Wilkof, 229–274. Chicago: University of Chicago Press.

Sendjaya, S. 2010. Demystifying servant leadership. In *Servant leadership: Developments in theory and research*, ed. K. Patterson and D. van Dierendonck, 39–54. New York: Palgrave Macmillan.

Sendjaya, S., J. C. Sarros, and J. C. Santora. 2008. Defining and measuring servant leadership behaviour in organizations. *Journal of Management Studies* 45(2): 402–424.

Shafer, J. G. 2013. Higher level thinking, writing, and democracy among community college students. *Community College Journal of Research and Practice* 37(5): 382–387.

Shaker, G. G. 2015. Seeing philanthropy in faculty work: An introduction. In *Faculty work and the public good: Philanthropy, engagement, and academic professionalism*, ed. G. G. Shaker, 3–18. New York: Teacher's College Press.

Shalley, C. E., J. Zhou, and G. R. Oldham. 2004. The effects of personal and contextual characteristics on creativity: Where should we go from here? *Journal of Management* 30(6): 933–958.

Sharratt, L., and M. Fullan. 2012. *Putting faces on the data: What great leaders do!* Thousand Oaks, CA: Corwin/Ontario Principals Council.

Shugart, S. 1997. *Servant leadership: Robert K. Greenleaf's legacy and the community college.* Paper presented at the Sixth Annual Conference of the International Conference of the Cahir Academy, Reno, NV.

Simons, R. 1995. *Levers of control: How managers use innovative control systems to drive strategic renewal.* Boston: Harvard Business Press.

Sipe, J. W., and D. M. Frick. 2015. *Seven pillars of servant leaders: Practicing the wisdom of leading by serving.* 2nd ed. Mahwah, NJ: Paulist Press.

Slaughter, S., and G. Rhoades 2004. *Academic capitalism and the new economy: Markets, state, and higher education.* Baltimore: Johns Hopkins University Press.

Smart, J. C., and R. E. Hamm. 1993. Organizational culture and effectiveness in two-year colleges. *Research in Higher Education* 34(1): 95–106.

Smith, R. W. 1995. Servant-leadership: A pathway to the emerging territory. In *Reflections on leadership: How Robert K. Greenleaf's theory of servant leadership influenced today's top management thinkers*, ed. L. C. Spears, 198–216. New York: John Wiley and Sons.

Spears, L. C. 1995. Introduction: Servant-leadership and the Greenleaf legacy. In *Reflections on leadership: How Robert K. Greenleaf's theory of servant leadership influenced today's top management thinkers*, ed. L. C. Spears, 1–16. New York: John Wiley and Sons.

Spillane, J. P. 2006. *Distributed leadership.* San Francisco: Jossey-Bass.

Spillane, J. P., R. Halverson, and J. B. Diamond. 2004. Towards a theory of leadership practice: A distributed perspective. *Journal of Curriculum Studies* 36(1): 3–34.

———. 2001. Investigating school leadership practice: A distributed perspective. *Educational Researcher* 30(3): 23–28.

St. John, E. P. 2013. *Research, actionable knowledge and social change: Reclaiming social responsibility through research partnerships.* Sterling, VA: Stylus.

Stoddard, J. 2014. The need for media education in democratic education. *Democracy and Education* 22(1): Article 4.

Sullivan, T. M., and E. C. Richardson. 2011. Living the plan: Strategic planning aligned with practice and assessment. *Journal of Continuing Higher Education* 59(1): 2–9.

Swindoll, C. R. 1981. *Improving your serve.* Nashville, TN: W. Publishing Group.

Terosky, A. L., and L. D. Gonzales. 2016a. Re-envisioned contributions: Experiences of faculty employed at institutional types that differ from their original aspirations. *Review of Higher Education* 39(2): 241–268.

———. 2016b. Scholarly learning as vocation: A study of community and broad access liberal arts college faculty. *Innovative Higher Education* 41(2): 105–120.

Tierney, W. 1991. Organizational culture in higher education: Defining essentials. In *ASHE reader on organization and governance*, ed. M. Peterson, 126–139. Needham Heights, MA: Ginn Press.

Toews, M. L., and A. Yazedjian. 2007. The three-ring circus of academia: How to become the ringmaster. *Innovative Higher Education* 32(2): 113–122.

Truth, F. 2013. Pay big to publish fast: Academic journal rackets. *Journal for Critical Education Policy Studies* 10(2): 54–105.

Turner, J., and P. Bernard. 2000. The German model and the graduate school: The university of Michigan and the origin myth of the American university. In *The American college in the nineteenth century*, ed. R. L. Geiger, 221–241. Nashville, TN: Vanderbilt University Press.

Vaill, P.B. 1998. Forward. In *The Power of Servant-Leadership*, ed. L.C Spears, ix-xvii. San Francisco, CA: Berrett-Koehler Publishers.

Van de Ven, A. H., and M. S. Poole. 1995. Explaining development and change in organizations. *Academy of Management Review* 20(3): 510–540.

van Dierendonck, D. 2011. Servant leadership: A review and synthesis. *Journal of Management* 37(4): 1228–1261.

van Dierendonck, D., and I. J. Nuijten. 2011. The servant leadership survey: Development and validation of a multidimensional measure. *Journal of Business Psychology* 26(3): 249–267.

van Dierendonck, D., and L. Rook. 2010. Enhancing innovation and creativity through servant leadership. In *Servant leadership: Developments in theory and research*, ed. K. Patterson and D. van Dierendonck, 155–165. New York: Palgrave Macmillan.

Veysey, L. R. 1965. *The emergence of the American university*. Chicago: University of Chicago Press.

Walumbwa, F. O., C. A. Hartnell, and A. Oke. 2010. Servant leadership, procedural justice climate, service climate, employee attitudes, and organizational citizenship behavior: A cross-level investigation. *Journal of Applied Psychology* 95(3): 517–529.

Ward, S. C. 2012. *Neoliberalism and the global restructuring of knowledge and education*. New York: Routledge.

Washburn, J. 2006. *University, Inc.: The corporate corruption of higher education*. Cambridge, MA: Basic Books.

Watt, S. K., and J. L. Moore. 2001. Who are student athletes? *New Directions for Student Services* 93:7–18.

Weerts, D. J., C. J. Rasmussen, and V. Singh. 2015. Using design thinking to drive collective impact in higher education. In *Higher education reconsidered: Executing change to drive collective impact*, ed. J. Lane, 119–138. Albany, NY: SUNY Press.

Weerts, D. J., V. Singh, A. Horn, and L. Taylor, L. 2015. *Design thinking for higher education policy innovation*. Paper presented at the Forty-First Annual Conference of the Association for the Study of Higher Education, Denver.

Weiner, E. J. 2007. Critical pedagogy and the crisis of the imagination. In *Critical pedagogy: Where are we now?*, ed. P. McLaren and J. L. Kincheloe, 57–78. New York: Peter Lang.

Wheeler, D. 2012. *Servant leadership for higher education: Principles and practices*. San Francisco: Jossey-Bass.

Wink, J. 2011. *Critical pedagogy: Notes from the real world*. 4th ed. New York: Pearson.

Winston, B. E. 2010. The place for qualitative research methods in the study of servant leadership. In *Servant leadership: Developments in theory and research*, ed. K. Patterson and D. van Dierendonck, 180–191. New York: Palgrave Macmillan.

———. 2002. *Be a leader for God's sake*. Virginia Beach, VA: Regent University-School of Leadership Studies.

Winston, B. E., and D. Fields. 2015. Seeking and measuring the essential behaviors of servant leadership. *Leadership and Organization Development Journal* 36(4): 413–434.

Woods, P. A., and A. Roberts. 2016. Distributed leadership and social justice: Images and meanings from across the school landscape. *International Journal of Leadership in Education* 19(2): 138–156.

Wong, P. T. P., and P. Page. 2003. *Servant leadership: An opponent-process model and the revised servant leadership profile*. Paper presented at the Servant Leadership Roundtable, Virginia Beach, VA.

Zizek, S. 2009. *First as tragedy, then as farce*. London: Verso.

Zohar, D., and I. Marshall, I. 2000. *Spiritual intelligence: The ultimate intelligence*. New York: Bloomsbury.

Zumeta, W. M. 2011. What does it mean to be accountable? Dimensions and implications of higher education's public accountability. *Review of Higher Education* 35(1): 131–148.

Zumeta, W. M., and A. Kinne. 2013. Accountability policies: Directions old and new. In *The states and public higher education policy: Affordability, access and accountability*, ed. D. E. Heller, 173–199. 2nd ed. Baltimore: Johns Hopkins University Press.

Index

About the Author

ANGELO J. LETIZIA is currently an assistant professor of graduate education at Newman University in Wichita, Kansas. His current research interests include servant leadership and citizenship in the information age. His other books include *Teaching Democracy and Social Justice Education in the Information Age* (2017) and *Performance-Based Funding in Higher Education: The State of Truth in the Information Age* (2015).